And He Spake Unto Me

Structural Revelations and Prophetic Pattern in 1 Nephi

Marcus M. Ladd

Tafiat Publishing

Copyright 2012 by Tafiat Publishing

Fifth Printing

ISBN 978-0-615-57977-1

Tafiat Publishing

Please send E-mail correspondence to tafiat@yahoo.com

Contents

"The last word has not been spoken on any subject. Streams of living water shall yet flow from the Eternal Spring who is the source of all truth. There are more things we do not know about the doctrines of salvation than there are things we do know"[1]

Bruce R. McConkie

Introduction

A difficult hurdle for many who read the Book of Mormon is found in the fourth chapter where Nephi is constrained by the Spirit to slay Laban. Most of us consider for a moment this challenging scene and then move on to the next chapter without having resolved the conflict within us that the story creates. Surely, we tell ourselves, there was another way to accomplish the recovery of the plates without such extreme measures. We are left wondering if we would have the resolve to obey as Nephi, usually until the next time (months later) we return to this chapter and again deliberate our personal willingness to wholly follow the Lord's consuming will.

Typical of this dilemma, in the September 1976 Ensign, submitted to the "I Have a Question" section, is the following inquiry: "How can I explain Nephi's killing Laban to my nonmember friends? Some really reject it as scriptural." Jeffrey R. Holland gives an insightful answer: "Nephi intentionally records this experience in elaborate detail, even though his small plates were limited in both size and subject matter. Why did he take such pains to preserve for future readers an action which was so difficult for him to perform and which has been so widely misunderstood? Why not simply leave it out? Why, indeed, when the small plates were to be restricted to "things which are pleasing unto God" and "of worth unto the children of men"? (1 Ne 6:5-6) Maybe there's a clue in all of that."[2]

We have all seen the routine where someone is embarrassed to ask for himself, so he pretends that a friend needs help with a problem. I feel like this is the case with the question above. Who is the "non-member" friend? It seems likely that the person asking also questions the story's scriptural value. I appreciate Brother Holland forceful tact that in fact the opposite is true, that the story of Nephi slaying Laban is "pleasing unto God" and "of worth" to us. If that is the case, then perhaps there are aspects of this story that deserve closer inspection.

The story of Nephi and Laban has been approached from a variety of angles. A popular scholarly approach tells us that according to Middle Eastern legal codes of Nephi's day, Nephi was well within his rights to execute judgment on Laban[3]. However, ultimately such exploration, even if it legally clears Nephi (and God who gives the command) can be unsatisfying. For many, the question persists – how is this compatible with the new commandment (John 13:34) that we love one another? In a book that speaks so beautifully of the Atonement of Christ, the Book of Mormon must surely have an answer for this dilemma. Again, Jeffrey Holland in contemplation writes:

> "'I will go and do the things which the Lord hath commanded.' (1 Nephi 3:7.) I confess that I wince a little when I hear that promise quoted so casually among us. Jesus knew what that kind of commitment would entail and so now does Nephi. And so will a host of others before it is over. That vow took Christ to the cross on Calvary and it remains at the heart of every Christian covenant. 'I will go and do the things which the Lord hath commanded'? Well, we shall see." [4]

Though acted out in the streets of Jerusalem, I believe that the story of Nephi and Laban, as Brother Holland suggests, is centered in Gethsmane and on the cross, and is at the "heart of every Christian covenant." Using the light of ancient scriptural pattern, one of the many questions that this book will examine is the extent to which Nephi's story is a similitude of that great atoning act. My hope is to not distract from, but build upon our understanding and appreciation of that greatest sacrifice. Consider for a moment the words of Nephi from 2 Nephi 11:4,

> 4 Behold, my soul delighteth in **proving** unto my people the truth of the coming of Christ; for, for this end hath the law of Moses been given; and **all things** which have been given of God from the beginning of the world, unto man, **are the typifying of him**.

Writing circa 600 BC, Nephi is referring to all scripture up until his time, which is roughly our present Old Testament up through much of Jeremiah. There are a couple of noteworthy observations in this verse; 1. That all things (scripture) given from God up to that time typified of

2

Christ, and 2; That Nephi delighted in identifying these types in order to prove the truth of Christ's coming. Implicit in the meaning of the word "type" is symbolism (one thing representing another). Also, the fact that Nephi needs to "prove" anything indicates that something is not readily apparent or needs explaining.

Yet, Nephi also speaks many other times of "plainness", and will later tell us in 2 Nephi 31:3 that his "soul delighteth in **plainness**; for after this manner doth the Lord God work among the children of men. For the Lord God **giveth light unto the understanding**; for he speaketh unto men according to their language, unto their understanding." Nephi makes it clear that it is only with God's involvement that scripture is made "plain" to men; equating or paralleling plainness to "light unto the understanding". Likewise, in 2 Nephi 25:4, regarding Isaiah's difficult writings, Nephi reiterates how Isaiah words are also "plain":

> 4 Wherefore, hearken, O my people, which are of the house of Israel, and give ear unto my words; for because the words of Isaiah are not plain unto you, nevertheless they are **plain unto all** those that are **filled with the spirit of prophecy**.

"Plainness" is not so much a matter of simplicity, for even the most uncomplicated communications can be misinterpreted, but rather it has to do with revelation or light given from God to the one reading the word. In 1 Nephi 17, Nephi speaks of the Israelites in the wilderness:

> 41 And he did straiten them in the wilderness with his rod; for they hardened their hearts, even as ye have; and the Lord straitened them because of their iniquity. He sent fiery flying serpents among them; and after they were bitten he prepared a way that they might be healed; and the labor which they had to perform was to look; and because of the **simpleness** of the way, or **the easiness of it**, there were many who perished.

The instructions given to the Israelites were plain and simple, yet many fail to look. In the same chapter (1 Nephi 17), Nephi insightfully compares (parallels) the events of the brass serpent to the building of the ship, only now the reason for his brothers' disobedience was because it was "so great a work." Whether easy, as in the story of the brass serpent, or difficult, as in building a ship (1 Nephi 17), the common denominator determining success was not the complexity of the task, but an abiding love for the Lord and a willingness to faithfully obey his instruction. Indeed, the Spirit cannot penetrate hardened hearts, and without spiritual light even the "plain" is perplexing.

And so it is with us as we read the scriptures, without the guidance of the Spirit we might also miss that which is plain. Granted, some scripture is decidedly more complicated without additional historical, cultural, or language background. However, many would like the scriptures to be so "plain" so as to be entirely void of secondary meaning, typology, or symbolism. But plainness without symbolism would be scripture that Nephi was not familiar with, and also irrelevant with regard to what he meant by "plainness". We have all had the experience of reading a verse of scripture dozens of times and gleaning the same understanding each time, yet on another occasion suddenly discovering new and significant meaning within the same verse. What changed? Typically this happens when we are searching for answers in the scriptures with real intent. It becomes "plain" because we are experiencing what Nephi called "the Spirit of prophecy", or "light unto the understanding", when the heart is soft and receptive to the planting of the word (Mat 13).

Consider for a moment the word "mystery." For instance, what does it mean in the context of 1 Nephi 10:19.

> 19 For he that diligently seeketh shall find; and the **mysteries** of God shall be
> unfolded unto them, **by the power of the Holy Ghost**, as well in these times as in
> times of old, and as well in times of old as in times to come; wherefore, the course
> of the Lord is one eternal round.

Mysteries, as well as things that are plain, are revealed in the same way, unfolded through the power of the Holy Ghost. Like Nephi, the Holy Ghost delights to prove or testify that Jesus is the Christ, and that all things (scripture) given by God to man are a type of his coming. The Holy Ghost, therefore, helps us to better understand how and where Christ, though perhaps initially hidden, is typified in scripture, which is everywhere (see 2 Ne 11:4). Though the word mystery is not found in the Old Testament, we know that Paul in the New Testament used it frequently. If we

4

look in a Bible Greek Lexicon under mystery (*mysterion)* we find that it is elementally from the verb *muo* which means "to be mute."[5] Thus, a mystery is something that is muted or unspoken, suggesting that words spoken by men cannot reveal to your heart and mind the truth of God, but only the Holy Ghost. Indeed, truth is confirmed inaudibly, as Nephi tells us, by the gentle stirrings of the Spirit. This is revelation, which activates and brings God's word to life within us.

Delighting in the seemingly improbable scriptural partners - plainness and symbolism, Nephi maintains a record of his people, trusting that through the attendance of the Holy Ghost we, his readers, will discern the truth of his words which testify of Christ (Moroni 10:4). However, there are other surprising witnesses which emerge as we carefully search Nephi's writing which also attest to the truth of his record. The recognition of ancient Hebraic literary forms and patterns contained in Nephi's first book is such a witness. Not surprising, the more one plumbs the depths of the Book of Mormon, the more these kinds of evidences become a joyful consideration. Preserved by the inspiration of God, they are also an important part of the sacred things "kept for the knowledge of my people" (1 Ne 19:6).

Along these lines, Dallin H. Oaks tells us that, "on the subject of the historicity of the Book of Mormon, there are many subsidiary issues that could each be the subject of a book." Regarding these "subsidiary issues" which are precious to our faith's state of health, Elder Neal A. Maxwell shares:

> Though argument does not create conviction, lack of it destroys belief. What seems
> to be proved may not be embraced; but what no one shows the ability to defend is
> quickly abandoned. Rational argument does not create belief, but it maintains a
> climate in which belief may flourish. (Austin Farrer on C. S. Lewis.)[6]

We might contemplate that the strength and vitality of our testimony is a product of the many spiritual and intellectual strands that it is composed of, bound and twisted together for maximum load bearing. Line upon line shouldn't mean one or two, but many. Taking a bit of interpretive license, when Nephi spoke of the fragile nature of a "compound in one", he was comparing it to the weakness of a single point of view or experience ("one body'), so much so that all creation would cease to exist if it were dependent on such a weakly engineered concept (2 Ne 2:11). Most of us are taught as children that there is strength in numbers, and in a similar way our faith's spiritual fiber is favorably influenced by the range of nourishing ideas\arguments that we allow into our minds and hearts. As we seek truth, each "line" can be measured and validated or rejected by the influence of the Holy Ghost which abides within us (Alma 32:28-42); each argument's impurities refined by its fire; spiritually purchased (Rev 3:18) a fragment at a time, over a lifetime.

- **What is a parable? How does this relate to Nephi and Laban?**

As an example of multiple witnesses, consider Jesus' words to his disciples who had difficulty identifying the elements in Christ's parables which testified of him. In Mathew 13 we read:

> 10 And the disciples came, and said unto him, Why speakest thou unto them **in parables**?
> 11 He answered and said unto them, Because it is given unto you to know the **mysteries** of the kingdom of heaven, but to them it is not given.
> 12 For whosoever hath, to him shall be given, and he shall have more abundance: but whosoever hath not, from him shall be taken away even that he hath.
> 13 Therefore speak I to them **in parables**: because they seeing see not; and hearing they hear not, neither do they understand.

Since parables evidently contain the mysteries of the kingdom of heaven, if we want to gage how we're doing with these mysteries, then assessing our understanding of Christ's parables is a good barometer. In fact, if you want to know the mysteries abundantly (as Christ recommends) then the study of parables is a great source for such growth. This being the case, we might do well to examine the meaning of the word "parable." From the Greek Lexicon we read:

παραβολή, -ῆς, ἡ, (παραβάλλω, q. v.), Sept. for מָשָׁל;
1. *a placing* of one thing *by the side of* another, *juxta-position*, as of ships in battle, Polyb. 15, 2, 13; Diod. 14, 60. 2. metaph. *a comparing, comparison of one thing with another, likeness, similitude*, (Plat., Isocr., Polyb., Plut.): univ., Mt. xxiv. 32; Mk. xiii. 28; an example by which a doctrine or precept is illustrated, Mk. iii. 23; Lk. xiv. 7; a thing serving as a figure of something else, Heb. ix. 9;   7

Notice that a parable is a metaphor, a likeness, a similitude, or "a thing serving as a figure of something else." In other words, a parable is the very thing that Nephi talks about in 2 Nephi 11:4, that "all things which have been given of God from the beginning of the world, unto man, are the typifying of him", related in metaphor, likeness, or similitude. In the same way, there are many stories in scripture (not just official parables) which use these same devises to testify of Christ's messiahship, his kingdom, and true doctrine. By this measure, the story of Nephi and Laban, though historic, is also a parable, "an example by which a doctrine or precept is illustrated." Just as the early disciples needed to widen the scope of their spiritual vision in order to see Christ in his parables (he is the sower they failed to recognize), as modern day disciples we perhaps need to do the same in order to better visualize Christ in the stories of the Book of Mormon.

In this regard, the apostle Paul also spoke of "plainness" and how the Lord can liberate one's mind from the veil which sometimes shrouds scripture meaning:

2 Cr. 3:12 Seeing then that we have such hope, we use great **plainness of speech**:

13 And not as Moses, which put a vail over his face, that the children of Israel could not stedfastly look to the end of that which is abolished:

14 But their minds were blinded: for until this day remaineth the same vail untaken away in the reading of the old testament; which **vail** is done away in Christ.

15 But even unto this day, when Moses is read, the **vail is upon their heart.**

16 **Nevertheless when it shall turn to the Lord, the vail shall be taken away**.

17 Now **the Lord is that Spirit**: and where the Spirit of the Lord is, there *is* liberty.

To fully benefit from Paul's words, we need to consider how his insight does, and does not, apply to our situation. For whereas the Jews of Paul's day apparently lacked the Spirit in order to "see" Christ in the books of Moses in Old Testament, our dilemma tends to be that we lack their Jewish background. Unfortunately, even with an open heart, because we are not ancient Jews, our ability to "see" Christ also often remains shrouded when we read scripture of ancient origin like the Old Testament. We should contemplate that the Book of Mormon, which we also esteem as ancient Jewish scripture, presents similar language, literary, and cultural problems. This suggests that there are likely stories of Christ within its pages to which our minds are also unavoidably clouded. However, by adding a few well known concepts to our scriptural arsenal, there awaits the prospect of deeper understanding and abiding spiritual strength to be unlocked through its stories, even stories we think we know well already.

Brief Primer - Introduction to a Few Literary Ideas

In order to follow the ideas of this book, which explores the Book of Mormon by means of limited literary analysis, let's quickly consider a few important Hebraic writing devices; chiasmi, parallelism, and allusion.

- Chiasmus – "from the center outward and from the extremities towards the center"[8]

One ancient writing device is indispensable. Part of Nephi's literary pallet and ancient perspective is his use of the chiasmus. A chiasmus is comprised of statements that are parallel in thought. When you put several lines of these parallel thoughts together, you have a chiasmus. A simple example comes from Mark 10:31,

> first
> > shall be last;
> > and the last
> first.

Notice how the parallel thoughts move from the outside to the center and then return in inverse order to the outside. For this reason a chiasmus is also called an inverse parallel. A little longer example comes from 1 Jn 3:9.

> Whosoever is born of God
> > doth not commit sin;
> > > for his **seed** remaineth in him:
> > and he cannot sin,
> because he is born of God.

Perhaps still reluctant you might ask, must we bother with these parallel structures, or of what value are they? Encouragement comes from the Savior himself. As he prepares the remnant of Lehi's seed for his ascension, we read in 3 Nephi 23:14 that Christ had "expounded all the scriptures", and not only that, he has "expounded all the scriptures in one". We are then given a glimpse of how the Savior accomplishes this, using a word that is used just once in all of scripture! In verses 4-6 of chapter 3 Ne 26 we find:

> 3 And he did **expound all things**, even from the beginning until the time that he should come in his glory -- yea, even all things which should come upon the face of the earth, even until the elements should melt with fervent heat, and the earth should be wrapt together as a scroll, and the heavens and the earth should pass away;
>
> 4 And even unto the great and last day, when all people, and all kindreds, and all nations and tongues shall stand before God, to be judged of their works, whether they be good or whether they be evil --
>
> 5 If they be good, to the resurrection of everlasting life; and if they be evil, to the resurrection of damnation; **being on a parallel**, the one on the one hand and the other on the other hand, according to the mercy, and the justice, and the holiness which is in Christ, who was before the world began.
>
> 6 And now there cannot be written in this book even a hundredth part of the things which Jesus did truly teach unto the people;

Christ teaches the people using the "parallels" that exist in scripture, "the one on the one hand," parallel to the "other on the other hand." (For the chiastic version see pg 199.) Referring back to the lexicon explanation for "parable" (pg 6), the primary meaning is "placing one thing by the side of another" for "comparison of one thing with another." Each parallel statement works in conjunction with the other to reveal or enhance the understanding of the other statement. In such a way the "literate of ancient time were long time trained for this sacramental task to grasp the hidden vision. They were taught not properly to read, but to "see" the text; they were taught how to look at it in a chiastic manner, by approaching it 'from the center outward and from the extremities towards the center.' Vision of the text was thus structured around a center."[9] This "encompassing" thought is one of the driving forces of this book, which is the examination of these parallels in their varied and wonderful forms, preserved for us and revealed by the Spirit. I would recommend that you don't pass over them quickly, but rather spend some time with each one as you would a parable of the New Testament. You may also want to highlight them in your personal scriptures; for many ideas which Nephi develops are most clearly revealed by his chiasmi.

- **Allusion**

One of the reasons for the footnotes found in our scriptures is to alert us to other verses that are being alluded to or directly referenced by the scripture writer. However, as you can imagine, there is not always room for all of the possible references or allusions. In most regards, an allusion is also a parallel, intentionally placed by the writer so as to draw attention to a similar or related event, person, place, or idea. Below is a definition of allusion:

> An **allusion** is a literary device that stimulates ideas, associations, and extra information in the reader's mind *with only a word or two*. Allusion means 'reference'. It relies on the reader being able to understand the allusion and being familiar with all of the meaning hidden behind the words. Allusions in writing help the reader to visualize what's happening by evoking a mental picture. But the reader *must be aware of the allusion* and *must be familiar with what it alludes to*. In general, the use of allusions by an author shows an expectation that the reader is familiar with the references made, otherwise the effect is lost. A piece of writing with many allusions (some of which may be very obscure) will be very rich with evoked images, but will do nothing for a reader who is not well-read. [10]

Remember, the Book of Mormon is a direct result of the brass plates, which is the seedbed of its literary allusion. Consequently, we would expect its writers, especially those in tune, to often allude to its inspired pages. As mentioned in the definition above, if we are not "well-read" in the Old Testament (brass plates) then "the effect is lost", "the meaning behind the words" is unrevealed, and a holy text "very rich with evoked images" remains to a degree unappreciated or unrewarding. For instance, in 1 Ne chapter 18 Nephi mentions that his father's "grey hairs were brought down to the grave". To what might that allude in the brass plates? Chapter 12 in this book will discuss the passage in Genesis that Nephi likely wants us to contemplate. By locating the scriptural allusion (where else these words are used in scripture) our comprehension of his suffering on the ocean voyage is amplified.

- **The book of 1 Nephi is a chiasmus, with chiasmi paralleling chiasmi**

In 1 Ne 16, Nephi is led by the Liahona to the top of the mountain. At that time he records that he beheld on the pointers of the ball "a new writing", which did give understanding concerning the ways of the Lord, and that what was written, "changed from time to time, according to the faith and diligence that we gave it." Our scriptures are today's Liahona, and the "small means" by which the Lord can bring about great things in our lives. With some "faith and diligence" perhaps we will also see unexpected and marvelous "new writing" in the words of Nephi, preserved in his many wonderful chiasmi.

In this spirit of "new writing", the entire book of 1 Nephi is constructed as a chiasmus. Below is this structure as it was presented in the 1972, Feb, New Era:

A) Lehi's dream leads him to prophesy warnings to the Jews (Ch. 1)

  B) The departure from Jerusalem (2)

    C) Nephi accomplishes a great feat in obtaining the Brass Plates and the brothers are confounded (3-5)

        D) The Brass Plates, a source of spiritual guidance as they travel through the wilderness of this life towards the spiritual promised land: Heaven

          E) Ishmael joins the group with his daughters (7)

            F) The Tree of Life (8)

              G) Lehi prophesies about the Old World and the Coming of the Lamb 10)

                H) Nephi and the Spirit of the Lord (11) Tree of Life

              G') Nephi prophesies about the New World and the Coming of the Lamb (12-14)

            F') The Tree of Life interpreted (15)

          E') The sons of Lehi marry the daughters of Ishmael and Ishmael Dies (16)

        D') The Brass Ball, the Liahona, a source of physical guidance as they traveled through the wilderness on their way to the promised land: America

    C') Nephi accomplishes a great feat by building a ship and the brothers are confounded (17)

  B') The departure from the Old World (18)

A') Nephi warns the Jews and quotes the prophecies of Isaiah (19-22)

John Welch, who was one of the first to identify and document the many chiasmi of the Book of Mormon, points out several interesting insights about this structure above:

"Should we consider it contrived that Ishmael is mentioned only twice in the entire Book of Mormon and that these two occurrences just happen to fall symmetrically around 1 Nephi 11 (chapters 7 and 16)? How else, except by chiasmus, can we explain the postponed interpretation of the vision of the tree of life? One would expect the interpretation to follow immediately after the dream, as most interpretive passages in the Book of Mormon do, and not several chapters later. Are we to believe that the unruly brothers of Nephi really waited nine chapters to marry the daughters of Ishmael: are we to neglect such specific parallels between the first half of 1 Nephi and its second half--e.g. 3:7 and 17:3--or again the fact that Nephi wrote two books (1 Nephi and 2 Nephi) instead of just running it all together into one, except by reference to the individual structure of each book?" [11]

Not only is the book of 1 Nephi a chiastic structure, but other entire books, such as Mosiah, have also been documented as chiasmi.[12] Because several books in the Bible are outlined chaistically (e.g. Jonah, Ruth), what Nephi has done may be more traditional than we might think.[13] However, as we will see, Nephi takes the poetry of parallelism to unprecedented heights by composing chiasmi which then parallel other chiasmi! For instance, Nephi will record the story of his family's preservation in the wilderness in 1 Nephi 5 as a chiasmus, whose climax or main point will parallel the apex of 1 Nephi 17. By such novel means, Nephi reveals insight otherwise concealed within his larger gospel message.

As we begin, please contemplate Neal A. Maxwell remarks below which I find to be relevant to the study pursued in this book:

Puzzlement, for instance, is often the knob on the door of insight. The knob must be firmly grasped and deliberately turned with faith. The harrowing of the soul can be like the harrowing of the soil to increase the yield with things being turned upside down.[14]

Along the way some taken-for-granted things might get turned upside down, but my hope is that the end result will be an increase in the spiritual yield of your life. On the following page is a diagram of Nephi's surprising book-wide parallel structure that will be discussed in this book. My proposed structure follows the general outline suggested by John Welch in his 1972 New Era article, though there are several significant additions and changes. For instance, Welch has chapter 2 parallel to chapter 18, and chapters 3 -5 parallel to chapter 17, whereas I find a chiasmus in chapter 4 specifically parallel to another in chapter 18, and chapter 5 chiastically parallel to chapter 17. In addition, I also find that chapters 3 and 19 have chiasmi that are parallel. In general terms, John Welch is correct, however, by using the very method that he pioneered it is possible to fine-tune the margins of his broader model, revealing more detail and insight concerning Nephi's message.

Nephi says of himself, "neither am I mighty in writing, like unto speaking" (2 Ne 33:1), but he is far too modest. The literary and poetical breadth of what Nephi has done is unprecedented and absolutely astounding. Like the movements of a symphony, entire chiasmi parallel other chiasmi, all under the umbrella of a larger book-wide chiastic structure, providing his work with unmatched poetic symmetry, all in celebration of Christ as the promised Messiah of prophecy.

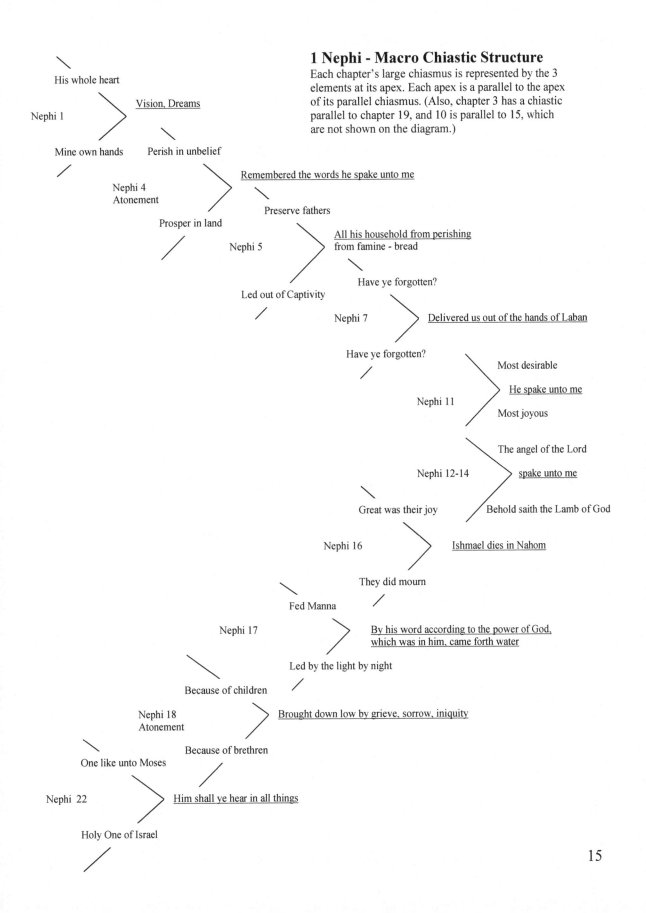

1 Nephi - Macro Chiastic Structure

Each chapter's large chiasmus is represented by the 3 elements at its apex. Each apex is a parallel to the apex of its parallel chiasmus. (Also, chapter 3 has a chiastic parallel to chapter 19, and 10 is parallel to 15, which are not shown on the diagram.)

His whole heart

Nephi 1

Vision, Dreams

Mine own hands

Perish in unbelief

Nephi 4
Atonement

Remembered the words he spake unto me

Prosper in land

Preserve fathers

Nephi 5

All his household from perishing
from famine - bread

Led out of Captivity

Have ye forgotten?

Nephi 7

Delivered us out of the hands of Laban

Have ye forgotten?

Most desirable

Nephi 11

He spake unto me

Most joyous

The angel of the Lord

Nephi 12-14

spake unto me

Great was their joy

Behold saith the Lamb of God

Nephi 16

Ishmael dies in Nahom

They did mourn

Fed Manna

Nephi 17

By his word according to the power of God,
which was in him, came forth water

Led by the light by night

Because of children

Nephi 18
Atonement

Brought down low by grieve, sorrow, iniquity

One like unto Moses

Because of brethren

Nephi 22

Him shall ye hear in all things

Holy One of Israel

15

1

Before the Throne

1 Nephi is a symmetrically constructed book of prophecy which relates the travels of Lehi's family in the wilderness. Remarkably, it begins where the New Testament ends, in the throne room of God, where Lehi (like John the Revelator) receives prophetic information and instruction. Along with his later revelatory vision of the tree of life (also a component of God's throne room found in Rev 22:2), this experience becomes a creative center and point of reference for the entirety of the Book of Mormon. 1 Nephi's ending is parallel to its revelatory beginning, with the visionary words of several prophets (Isaiah John, the Psalmist, and Nephi) who prophesy of end time events; when Israel is gathered, wrath is poured out, and Satan bound (ch 20-22). Below is a simple schematic of 1 Nephi, which highlights some fascinating relationships to be discussed in this chapter.

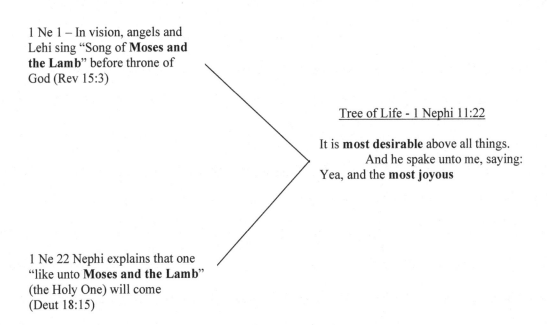

1 Ne 1 – In vision, angels and Lehi sing "Song of **Moses and the Lamb**" before throne of God (Rev 15:3)

Tree of Life - 1 Nephi 11:22

It is **most desirable** above all things.
And he spake unto me, saying:
Yea, and the **most joyous**

1 Ne 22 Nephi explains that one "like unto **Moses and the Lamb**" (the Holy One) will come (Deut 18:15)

After a brief introduction, in which Nephi states that he has knowledge of God's mysteries, Nephi recounts the heavenly vision of his father Lehi, in which he sees the Savior descend with a "luster above that of the sun," who gives him a book to read (vs 11). As Lehi reads the book, which our LDS scriptures chapter heading calls a "book of prophecy"; he is "filled with the Spirit of the Lord".[15] Though this book might be the Bible, we are not exactly informed. Nephi then tells us:

> 1 Ne 1:14 And it came to pass that when my father had read and seen many great and marvelous things, he did exclaim many things unto the Lord, such as: **Great and marvelous are thy works, O Lord God Almighty**. Thy throne is high in the heavens, and thy power, and goodness, and mercy are over all the inhabitants of the earth; and, because thou art merciful, thou wilt not suffer those who come unto thee that they shall perish!

Among several, this is one of the most intriguing verses we find in Nephi's first chapter, which upon closer examination also contains the exact words of John the Revelator as recorded in Revelation 15, which is the introduction to the song of Moses and the Lamb (originally sung in Exodus 15). Like Lehi, in a vision John was also taken up to the throne room of God. Below is the matching verse from Revelation to which Lehi alludes:

> 15:2 And I saw as it were a sea of glass mingled with fire: and them that had gotten the victory over the beast, and over his image, and over his mark, [and] over the number of his name, stand on the sea of glass, having the harps of God.
> 3 And they sing the song of Moses the servant of God, and the song of the Lamb, saying, **Great and marvellous [are] thy works, Lord God Almighty**; just and true [are] thy ways, thou King of saints.
> 4 Who shall not fear thee, O Lord, and glorify thy name? for [thou] only [art] holy: for all nations shall come and worship before thee; for thy judgments are made manifest.

We can readily make out the identical wording which begins both Lehi's and John's celebratory song; "great and marvelous are thy works, Lord God Almighty." Significantly, in all of scripture these exact words are used in only these two places, both accounts of God's throne room! We might be led to wonder, could these words be a part of what Lehi read in the book, and was the book of prophecy from which he read the Book of Revelation (we know that Nephi was aware of John's apocalyptic writings from 1 Ne 14:27), or was Lehi simply repeating what was sung by the angels and the saints who had "gotten victory over the beast"? In addition, whereas the rest of Lehi's words at the throne seem to emphasize the Lord's mercy and goodness, John's words (in opposing fashion) stress the fear of a just Lord and his judgments. With some analysis we can easily see several parallels between John and Lehi's versions of what is sung before the throne.

Lehi says:	John says
Throne (of King) is high	**King** of saints
power, **goodness, and mercy** are over all	**just and true** are thy ways
all the inhabitants of the earth	**all nations**
thou art merciful	for thou only art holy
will not suffer **those who come**	**all shall come** and worship
unto thee that they shall perish	for thy judgments are made manifest

Appropriately, the original Song of Moses at the Sea also expresses both of these; destruction of God's enemies (his "judgments made manifest"), and the merciful redeeming of his people ("not suffering those who come to him that they shall perish"). In a few pages we will look at Exodus 15 and the original Song of Moses.

In addition, there are other songs sung before the throne. For instance, Alma, a later Book of Mormon prophet, outlines a "song of redeeming love." In Alma 5 he highlights God's marvelous plan of salvation and identifies those who qualify to sing upon the sea of glass before the throne; having the image of Christ engraved on their countenance, having been spiritually born of God; having experienced a mighty change of heart.[16] Another song, also spoken of by John, is the new song. "And they sang a new song, saying, Thou art worthy to take the book, and to open the seals thereof: for thou wast slain, and hast redeemed us to God by thy blood out of every kindred, and tongue, and people, and nation" (Rev 5:9). Explaining how the new song and the song of Moses are essentially the same, one theologian comments, "The Psalmist tells us to sing a new song unto the Lord. This new song is not necessarily newly composed; rather it signifies the eternal song of salvation, a song that is ever ancient and always new. It was the song sung by Moses, Miriam and the angels, by Mary, Jesus and the apostles. It is sung in Heaven and even on earth by us. This New Song is personified in Christ, who has accomplished our salvation by virtue of His death, resurrection and ascension."[17] The lyric for another version of the New Song can be found in D&C 84:98-102, where the redemption of spiritual Israel is again celebrated in modern scripture.

- **Refrain for all the Book of Mormon – sung before the throne of God**

Perhaps not so remarkable, then, is that the refrain for all of 1ˢᵗ Nephi is originally sung in God's throne room – that those who come unto Him (keep his commandments) will not perish (vs 14). Indeed Nephi receives the same divine message in 1 Ne chapter 2 when he inquires of the Lord concerning his father's vision (vs 20-22), and again when he gets the plates of brass from Laban – with the addition that they will also prosper in the land (1 Ne 4:13-14). This message of perishing or prospering, tied to obedience, is recognizably the quintessence of God's direction throughout the Book of Mormon.

There are several interesting parallel elements to consider from Lehi's and John's vision of God's temple and throne room. Below are some of those:

◦ The sea of glass in Revelation is an allusion to the Red Sea in Exodus, where both groups (first Israel, then the heavenly host) celebrate God's miraculous deliverance and a glorious plan of salvation.

◦ The Israelites, saved and redeemed by the "marvelous" wonder of dividing the sea, are a pre-figure of those at heaven's sea of glass (see parallel B and B' below, pg 21).

◦ Likewise, as we stand before the throne of God (at the veil of the temple), in similitude of those redeemed, we celebrate the sentiment of the Song of Moses and the Lamb as we are instructed in the plan of salvation and redemption.[18]

◦ The unredeemed cannot join in the singing of this song because only the redeemed know the words. (Rev 14:4).[19] The words of this song are taught to the heart by the Holy Ghost (2 Ne 32:2-6).

◦ In the song, the celebration of the destruction of Pharaoh's army (Ex 15) is a celebration of overcoming death and sin, a parallel to man's deliverance by the Atonement of the Lamb.

◦ As we find in the modern temple, John and Lehi both also see the tree of life, which is near the throne (Rev 22:2, 1 Ne 8,11) in heaven's temple.

- **Song of Moses (and the Lamb) - Chiasmus**

Let's take a quick look at the main body of the original song of Moses sung at the sea, which is also chiastic. When I see these structures in the Old Testament, which would have also been preserved on the brass plates, I ponder that Nephi must have also paused from time to time to study them, using them perhaps as a guide for his composition. Because this is the blueprint for the song which his father Lehi sang with the angels in God's presence, such speculation seems plausible. Below is from Exodus 15 (parenthesis mine):

2 The LORD *is* my **strength** and song, and **he is become my salvation**: he *is* my God, and I will prepare him **an habitation** (nauvah) ; my father's God, and I will exalt him.

> 3 The **LORD** *is* a man of war: **the LORD** *is* his name.
>> 4 Pharaoh's chariots and his host hath he cast into the sea: (a wonder) his chosen captains also are **drowned in the Red sea.**

>>> 5 The **depths have covered them**: they **sank into the bottom as a stone.**

>>>> 6 Thy right hand, O LORD, is become glorious in power: **thy right hand, O LORD, hath dashed** in pieces **the enemy.**

>>>>> 7 **And** in **the greatness of thine excellency** thou hast overthrown them that **rose up** against thee: thou sentest forth thy wrath, *which* **consumed** them as stubble.

>>>>> 8 **And** with **the blast of thy nostrils** the waters were gathered together, the floods **stood upright** as an heap, *and* the depths were **congealed** in the heart of the sea.

>>>> 9 **The enemy** said.
I will pursue, I will overtake, I will divide the spoil; my lust shall be satisfied upon them; I will draw my sword, **my hand shall destroy them.**

>>> 10 Thou didst blow with thy wind, **the sea covered them**: they **sank as lead** in the mighty waters.

>> 11 **Who** *is* ᵃlike unto thee, **O LORD, among the gods**? who *is* like thee, glorious in holiness, fearful *in* praises, **doing wonders**? 12 Thou stretchedst out thy right hand, the **earth swallowed them.**

13 **Thou** in thy mercy hast led forth the people *which* **thou hast redeemed**: **thou** hast guided *them* in thy **strength** unto **thy holy habitation** (nauveh).

Please spend some time studying these verses and considering the many wonderful parallels. As suggested in this book's introduction, you may want to start in the middle and work outward, examining the parallels on either side as you go. I would like to comment on just a few things. First, the book-end verses (2 and 13) mention salvation and redemption in the context of the Lord's "holy habitation," which is a reference to the temple, and is the chiastic foundation upon which this song is composed. In fact, the Hebrew word for "habitation" in verse 2 (*nauvah)*, and its parallel in verse 13 (noun from *nauveh)*, are both related or cognate to Nauvoo, a beautiful "habitation" and temple city to which modern Israel was guided! Also, though Pharaoh's army is drowned, Moses' song unexpectedly indicates that it was equally done with heat (*charah*), which is the context many later prophets (like John) borrow to describe eschatological (end-time) events, when the earth is cleansed by fire. In Nephi's parallel chapter, 1 Nephi 22, there is no mention of the earth's final destruction by drowning, but "wrath" and consuming the wicked "as stubble" (also used by Isaiah) are mentioned several times. Surprisingly, this oft used biblical image's earliest roots originate from the ancient Song of Moses at the sea.

Finally, the word for "wonders" in verse 11, used in the phrase "who is like thee, glorious in holiness, fearful in praises doing **wonders**", in the Hebrew is *pele.* Here in Exodus 15 we find its first use in the Bible. When the heavenly hosts sing in praise before the throne, "great and marvelous (*pele*) are thy works", it is also a reference to these first great saving miracles, comparable to those the Lord will do in the earth's final days. This word *pele* is the same fascinating word which is rendered "wonderful" or "marvelous" in many other Old Testament verses, and is even used as a proper name to refer to the Messiah in Isaiah 9:6, "For unto us a child is born, unto us a son is given: and the government shall be upon his shoulder: and his name shall be called **Wonderful** (*pele*), Counsellor, The mighty God (*ale*), The everlasting Father, The Prince of Peace." As Jesus begins his ministry in Galilee, the first part of this verse from Isaiah is alluded to by Mathew (4:14-16) to introduce Jesus as the Messiah; "The people which sat in darkness saw great light; and to them which sat in the region and shadow of death light is sprung up." When we complete the Isaiah passage ("and his name shall be called Wonderful"), which Matthew through allusion no doubt hoped his readers would, we get a much fuller understanding of his testimony – that Christ is the one prophesied to be called Wonderful. Indeed, when the word "marvelous" is used in Lehi's and John's introduction of the Song of Moses and the Lamb, it is a reference not just to the miraculous destruction of the army of Egypt (the world), but is a celebration of God's greatest wonder, spiritual Israel's end-time deliverance through his Son; He is Wonderful, Marvelous (*pele*).[20]

- **1 Nephi 1 – a chiasmus**

It shouldn't surprise us that Nephi uses the literary pattern of Exodus 15, a chiasmus, to compose his first chapter. And if 1 Nephi 1 has chiastic elements, then it shouldn't be too astonishing that its parallel, chapter 22 is also chiastic. Further, because they mirror one another we might also expect to find as corroborating evidence more elements of the Song of Moses in chapter 22. However, let's start by first viewing the structure of chapter 1 (parentheses are mine):

1 Nephi Chapter 1 – Dreams and Visions

7 and he cast himself upon his bed, being overcome with the Spirit and **the things which he had seen**.

A 8 And being thus overcome with the Spirit, **he** (my father) was **carried away in a vision, even** that he saw the heavens open,

  B and he thought he saw **God** sitting upon his throne, **surrounded with numberless concourses of angels** in the attitude of singing and praising their God (chosen because of their faith).

    C 9 And it came to pass that he saw **One descending** out of the midst of heaven, and he beheld that his luster was above that of the sun at noon-day. (manifested plainly)

      D 10 And he also saw **twelve others** (prophets) following him, and their brightness did exceed that of the stars in the firmament. 11 And they came down and **went forth** upon the face of the earth;

        E and the first came and stood before my father, and gave unto him **a book**, and bade him that he should read.12 And it came to pass that as **he read**, he was **filled with the Spirit of the Lord.** (testified)

          F 13 And **he read**, saying: Wo, wo, unto Jerusalem, for I have seen thine **abominations**!

            G Yea, and **many things** did my father read **concerning Jerusalem - that it should be destroyed**, and the inhabitants thereof; many should perish by the sword, and many should be carried away captive into Babylon.

              H 14 And it came to pass that when **my father** had read and **seen** many **great and marvelous things**,

                I he did **exclaim many things** unto the Lord; *such as: Great and **marvelous are thy works**, O Lord God Almighty! Thy throne is high in the heavens, and thy power, and goodness, and mercy are over all the inhabitants of the earth; and, because thou art merciful, thou wilt not suffer those who come unto thee that they shall perish!*

                  J 15 And after this manner was the **language of my father** in the praising of his God; for his soul did rejoice, and **his whole heart** was filled, because of the **things which he had seen**, yea, which the Lord had shown unto him.

                    K 16 And now I, Nephi, **do not make a full account**

                      L of the things **which my father hath written,**

                        M for **he** hath **written many things** which he saw in

                          N **visions** and in

                          N' **dreams**; and

                        M' **he** also hath **written many things**

                      L' **which he prophesied and spake** unto his children,

                    K' of which I **shall not make a full account.**

                  J' 17 But I shall make an account of my proceedings in my days. Behold, I make an abridgment of **the record of my father**, upon plates which I have made with **mine own hands**; wherefore, after I have abridged the **record of my father** then will I make an account of mine own life.

              H' 18 Therefore, I would that ye should know, that after the Lord had **shown** so **many marvelous things** unto **my father**, Lehi,

           G' yea, **concerning the destruction of Jerusalem**, behold he went forth among the people, and began to prophesy

                I' and to **declare unto them concerning the things** which he had both seen and heard. (*see italicized portion in vs 14 for that which Lehi exclaimed*)

          F' 19 And it came to pass that the Jews did mock him because of the things which **he testified** of them; for he truly testified of their wickedness and their **abominations**;

        E' and **he testified** that the things which he saw and heard, and also the things which **he read** in **the book**,

  C' **manifested plainly of the coming of a Messiah**, and also the redemption of the world. 20 And when the Jews heard these things they were angry with him;

      D yea, even as with **the prophets of old**, whom they had **cast out**, and stoned, and slain; and they also sought his life, that they might take it away.

  B' But behold, I, Nephi, will show unto you that the tender mercies of **the Lord** are over **all those whom he hath chosen**, because of their faith, to make them mighty even unto the power of deliverance. (Those singing round the throne)

A' 1 Ne 2:1 For behold, it came to pass that the Lord spake unto **my father**, yea, **even** in **a dream**, and said unto him: Blessed art thou Lehi, because of **the things which thou hast done**;

As with the chiastic structure found in Exodus 15, I hope that you spend some time examining Nephi's thinking; the various elements and innovative ways he constructs his parallels. In a sense, many of these large compositions that Nephi composes could also be regarded as songs celebrating God's eternal redemptive plan. Time does not permit us to examine every relationship, but I would like to look at a few:

- The center is "dreams and visions", one of the miraculous ways in which God declares his word and promises.

- The small chiasmus "J" highlights the heart and J' highlights its compliment, the hands. Following the theme of these two symbols, the first half of the chiasmus (A-N) informs us of those things seen and shown to Lehi, which filled his "whole heart", and the last half (A'-N') is a history of what Nephi does "with mine own hands". For more context, the words of Psalm 24:3 express this relationship, "Who shall ascend into the hill of the LORD? or who shall stand in his holy place? 4 He that hath **clean hands, and a pure heart**; (Especially applicable because Lehi stands in the heavenly temple or "hill of the Lord")[21]

- B and B' is one of the most fascinating – it parallels those angels singing round the throne to "those whom he hath chosen, because of their faith, to make them mighty, even unto the power of deliverance!" I am reminded of Alma's words, "O that I were an angel". Alma sings that the "wish of his **heart**" (Alma 29:1) is to be "an instrument in the **hands** of God" (Alma 29:9). Certainly Alma would qualify to stand with those singing at the sea of glass.

Be aware that as you ponder the parallels that they are often antithetical, which was anciently a common method of construction. Ideas become clearer when juxtaposed to an opposite idea.

- **1 Nephi 22 – The Song of Moses and the Lamb is confirmed**

What Nephi begins in chapter 1, he compliments and wonderfully parallels in chapter 22. Expressing a comparable sentiment to the center of chapter 1, which is God's instruction through "visions and in dreams", chapter 22's center focus is, "him shall ye hear in all things he shall say unto you." This apex is particularly exciting as it relates to, and enhances the meaning of, the Song of Moses alluded to in chapter 1Ne 1! However, let's first look at the entire chiastic structure found in chapter 22 (parentheses mine):

A 12 Wherefore, he will bring them again out of captivity, and they **shall be gathered** together to the lands of their inheritance; and they shall be brought out of obscurity and out of darkness (Isa 29:18); and **they shall know** that **the Lord is their Savior** and their redeemer (Ex 29:46),

    B **the Mighty One of Israel** (Isa 1:24).

  C 13 And the blood of that great and abominable church, which is the whore of all the earth (Rev 17), shall turn upon their own heads (Psa 7:16); for they shall war among themselves, and the sword of their own hands shall fall upon their own heads, and they shall be drunken with their own blood. (Isa 49:26) 14 And every nation which shall war against thee, O house **of Israel**, shall be turned one against another, and they shall fall into the pit which they digged to ensnare the people of the Lord. (Psa 7:15)

   D And all that fight against Zion shall be destroyed, and that great whore, who hath perverted the right ways of the Lord, yea, that great and abominable church, shall **tumble to the dust** and great shall be the fall of it (Rev 17:5).

    E 15 For behold, **saith the prophet**, the **time cometh speedily** that Satan shall have no more power over the hearts of the children of men; for the day soon cometh that all the proud and they who do wickedly shall **be as stubble**; and the day cometh that they must be burned (Mal 4:1).

       F 16 For the **time soon cometh** that the

          fulness of the wrath of God shall be poured out

           upon all **the children of men**;

            for he will not suffer that **the wicked** shall destroy the righteous.

         b. 17 Wherefore, he will preserve **the righteous** by his power, even if it so be that the fulness of his wrath must come,

           and the righteous be **preserved,**

             even unto the destruction of their enemies by **fire**.

         b. Wherefore, **the righteous** need not fear; for thus saith the prophet,

           they shall be **saved,**

            even if it so be as by **fire**.

       F 18 Behold, my brethren, I say unto you, that these things **must shortly come**;

        yea, even **blood, and fire, and vapor of smoke** must come;

          and it must needs be **upon** the **face of this earth**; and it cometh **unto men** according to **the flesh**

           if it so be that they will **harden their hearts** against the Holy One of Israel.

            G 19 For behold, **the righteous shall not perish**;

              H for the time surely must **come** that all they who fight against Zion **shall be cut off.**

                I 20 And the Lord will surely prepare **a way (prophet)** for his people, unto the fulfilling of the words of **Moses,** which he **spake,** saying:

                  J **A prophet** shall the Lord your God raise up unto you, like unto me;

                    K. **him shall ye hear** in

                        all things (words-seed) whatsoever

                    K. **he shall say unto you**.

              H' And it shall **come** to pass that all those who will not hear that prophet **shall be cut off** from among the people.

              I' 21 And now I, Nephi, declare unto you, that **this prophet** of whom **Moses spake**

                  J' was the **Holy One of Israel** (prophet); wherefore, he shall execute judgment in righteousness.

            G' 22 And **the righteous** need not fear, for they are those who **shall not be confounded.**

      F' But it is the **kingdom of the devil**, which shall be built up among the children of men

        which **kingdom** is established among them **which are in the flesh**— 23 For the time speedily shall come that

          b'. all churches which are built up

            to get gain,

          b'. and all those who are built up

            to get power over the flesh**,**

          b'. and those who are built up

            to become popular in the eyes of the world,

        and those who seek the lusts of **the flesh** and the things **of the world** (kingdom of devil), and to do all manner of iniquity; yea,

      F' in fine, all those who belong to the **kingdom of the devil** are they who need fear, and tremble, and quake;

   D' they are those who must be brought **low in the dust**;

    E' they are those who must be **consumed as stubble**; and this is according to the **words of the prophet**. 24 And **the time cometh**

  C' that the righteous must be led up as calves of the stall, and the **Holy One of Israel** must reign in dominion, and might, and power, and great glory. (Malachi 4:2)

A' 25 And **he gathereth** his children from the four quarters of the earth; and he numbereth his sheep, and **they know him**; and there shall be one fold and one shepherd; and he shall feed his sheep, and in him they shall find pasture. (Isa 40:11, Jer 28:10) 26 And because of the righteousness of his people, Satan has no power; wherefore, he cannot be loosed for the space of many years (Rev 20:2-3); for he hath no power over the hearts of the people, for they dwell in righteousness,

    B' and the **Holy One of Israel reigneth** (Isa 49:7).

This chiasmus presents us with so many parallel elements to consider. Nephi, it seems, has saved a sort of parallelistic fireworks for this last chapter. I would have preferred to look at this chiasmus after spending some time with others that are less complex, but because it is the chiasmus which confirms what we suspect about Nephi's allusion to the Song of Moses and the Lamb from 1 Ne 1:14, we will evaluate it now.

- **Explanations about these parallels**

A,B,C and A',B',C' – At either end of this structure is a proliferation of scriptural quotation; a confluence of prophetic scripture taken from a variety of sources (this pattern is duplicated in 3 Ne 20-23, see pg 194). These bursts of end-time passages, which underpin the entire structure, allude to the events surrounding the gathering of Israel. Notice that I have placed their various sources in parenthesis. I might add that though many of these verses "feel" like the Book of Revelation with talk of wrath, destruction, burning and stubble, as we have examined, several of these terms originated in Exodus 15 and the Song of Moses.

B, B' - "Holy One of Israel" and the "Mighty One of Israel". These book-end proclamations assist in framing the center of this structure (H-K), repeating that the prophet like unto Moses is "the Holy One" or "Mighty One".

C, C' - A parallel that may not be apparent at first is verses 13 and 14, which speak of the destruction of the great and abominable church (Rev 17), which text is derived from a combination of several Old Testament authors (Psalms and Isaiah). It is antithetically parallel to verse 24, from Malachi, which conversely describes the salvation of the righteous: "But unto you that fear my name shall the Sun of righteousness arise with healing in his wings; and ye shall go forth, and grow up as calves of the stall" (Mal 4:2). [22]

F, F' On either side of chapter 22's apex there are two intricate **standalone** chiastic structures whose emphasis is upon the devil's kingdom and God's wrath to be poured out on the wicked participating in this worldly system. On the next page are these two complex structures placed side by side for comparison. Notice how the two centers (b, b') are antithetical; the preserved righteous (F, b), and those that build up to get gain, power, and popularity (F', b'). Also, observe how "the flesh" is found on either end, and at the center of this structure. In F and F' the phrase "the time soon cometh" (verse 16) is parallel to verse 23, "the time speedily cometh":

F 16 For the **time soon cometh** that the
   fulness of the wrath of God shall be poured out
    upon all **the children of men**;
     for he will not suffer that **the wicked** shall destroy the righteous.

  b. 17 Wherefore, he will preserve the righteous by his power, even if it so be that the fulness of his wrath must come,
    and the righteous be preserved,
     even unto the destruction of their enemies by fire.
  b. Wherefore, the righteous need not fear; for thus saith the prophet,
    they shall be saved,
     even if it so be as by fire.

F 18 Behold, my brethren, I say unto you, that these things **must shortly come**;
  yea, even **blood, and fire, and vapor of smoke** must come;
   and it must needs be **upon** the **face of this earth**; and it cometh **unto men** according to the flesh
    if it so be that they will **harden their hearts** against the Holy One of Israel.

   Apex – One like unto Moses, Him shall ye hear in all things

F' But it is the **kingdom of the devil**, which shall be built up among the children of men
  which **kingdom** is established among them **which are in the flesh**— 23 For the time speedily shall come that

   b'. all churches which are built up
    to get gain,
   b'. and all those who are built up
    to get power over the flesh,
   b'. and those who are built up
    to become popular in the eyes of the world,

  and those who seek the lusts of **the flesh** and the things **of the world** (kingdom of devil), and to do all manner of iniquity; yea,
F' in fine, all those who belong to the **kingdom of the devil** are they who need fear, and tremble, and quake;

- **Nephi precisely parallels the Song of Moses (ch 1) to "One like unto" Moses (ch 22) !!**

However, the most breathtaking parallel, which jumps across the length of Nephi's first book, is found in precisely the center of 1 Ne 22. If we had any doubts about Lehi hearing the Song of Moses and the Lamb in chapter 1, verses 19-22 in chapter 22 should assuage those reservations! Wonderfully, Nephi, who hasn't referred to Moses in three chapters, suddenly mentions his name, alluding to a famous verse from Deuteronomy 18:15 (a verse which was also used by Stephen in his chiasmus to prove Christ; see Appendix 1):

"The LORD thy God will raise up unto thee a Prophet from the midst of thee, of thy brethren, like unto me; unto him ye shall hearken."

Nephi then explains who that Prophet is! Below are those center verses from chapter 22 parentheses mine):

> G 19 For behold, **the righteous shall not perish**;
>> H for the time surely must **come** that all they who fight against Zion **shall be cut off.**
>>> I 20 And the Lord will surely prepare **a way** (a prophet) for his people, unto the fulfilling of the words of **Moses,** which he **spake,** saying:
>>>> J **A prophet** shall the Lord your God raise up unto you, **like unto me;**
>>>>> **him shall ye hear** in
>>>>>> all things (words-seed) whatsoever
>>>>> **he shall say unto you**.
>>> H' And it shall **come** to pass that all those who will not hear that prophet **shall be cut off** from among the people.
>>>> I' 21 And now I, Nephi, declare unto you, that **this prophet** of whom **Moses spake**
>>>>> J was the **Holy One of Israel**; wherefore, he shall execute judgment in righteousness.
> G' 22 And **the righteous** need not fear, for they are those who **shall not be confounded.**

What was promised to Lehi in song before the throne in 1 Nephi chapter one, chapter 22 repeats in verses 19 and 22; that the righteous will not perish nor be confounded. Nephi then compares "the way" prepared to fulfill the words of Moses (vs 20), to one like unto Moses, who is the Holy One of Israel (vs 21). In other words, a comparison of Moses to the Lamb! This is a distinct echo and reprise of the Song of Moses and the Lamb in chapter 1! These verses which compare Moses to the Holy One of Israel are placed twelve verses from the end of his book, whereas its parallel, the Song of Moses and the Lamb ("great and marvelous are thy works, O Lord God Almighty"), is placed by Nephi fourteen verses from the beginning of his book! (See the first illustration of this parallel on pg 24)

In a book so delightfully crafted, it is most fitting that Nephi should begin and end with such precise testimony and sacred jubilation. How wonderful it is to span the distance of time and pierce his mind; to discover his designed intention; joining with the Spirit in his remarkable poetic endeavor of adoration and praise to our Lord and Savior, the Lamb to follow Moses, even Christ the Messiah.

Newly "baptized" in the sea (1 Cor 10:1), standing at its shore and singing the song of Moses and the Lamb (a clear parallel of the angels upon the sea of glass), the children of Israel were a testament of God's promises made to the patriarchal fathers, which is that through Abraham all nations of the earth would be blessed. When we contemplate God's amazing plan of salvation, our hearts exalt as they turn to the same ancient promises, that as His spiritually begotten seed we shall be delivered, and that through our faith in Christ (the Lamb like unto Moses) we will be guided to a heavenly promised land. Israel's saving pattern is our pattern, and as we have seen, it is also the pattern of heavenly things found at God's throne. Even images such as the divided Red Sea, with life found exclusively in the middle, is a recapitulation of God's ancient covenant with Abraham (Gen 15), where the animal was divided and betwixt (with death on either side) Jehovah passed as a smoking furnace and burning lamp, a comparable image of Israel safely passing (with death on either side) betwixt the sea. These events are the "great and marvelous works" that Lehi and angels celebrate; they are the patterns of salvation to which our hearts it seems will be forever turned.

2

Preserved in the Wilderness – By the Word

Next, let's examine 1 Nephi chapter 3 and its parallel, chapter 19; both of which contain a chiasmus. The apex of each of these chapters is an exact and complimentary message; that Israel, as well as Lehi's remnant, will be preserved if they do not reject the words of the prophets! Let's begin with chapter 3:

A 5 And now behold **thy brothers murmur**, saying it is a hard thing which I have required of them; but behold I have not required it of them, but it is a **commandment of the Lord**. 6 Therefore go, my son, and thou shalt be favored of the Lord, because thou hast not **murmured**.

  B 7 And it came to pass that I, Nephi, said unto my father: I will go and do the things which the Lord hath commanded, for I know that the Lord giveth no commandments unto the children of men, save **he shall prepare a way for them** that they may accomplish the thing which he commandeth them.

    C 8 And it came to pass that when my father had heard these words he was exceedingly glad, for he knew that **I had been blessed of the Lord**.

      D 9 And I, Nephi, and my brethren **took our journey in the wilderness**, with our tents, to go up to the land of Jerusalem.

        E 10 And it came to pass that when we had gone up to the land of Jerusalem, **I and my brethren did consult one with another**.

          F 11 And we cast lots—who of us should go in unto the house of Laban. And it came to pass that **the lot fell** upon Laman; and Laman went in unto the house of Laban, and he talked with him as he sat in his house.

            G 12 And **he desired of Laban** the records which were engraven upon the **plates of brass**, which contained the genealogy of my father.

              H 13 And behold, it came to pass that **Laban was angry,** and thrust him out from his presence; and he would not that he should have the records. Wherefore, he said unto him: Behold thou art a robber, and **I will slay thee**.

                I 14 But **Laman fled out of his presence**, and told the things which Laban had done, unto us. And we began to be exceedingly sorrowful, and my brethren were about to return unto my father in the wilderness.

                  J 15 But behold I said unto them that: As the Lord liveth, and as we live, **we will not go down unto our father** in the wilderness until we have accomplished the thing which the Lord hath commanded us.

                    K 16 Wherefore, let us **be faithful in keeping the commandments of the Lord**;

                      L therefore let us go down to the land of our father's inheritance, for behold he left **gold and silver, and all manner of riches**. And all this he hath done because of the commandments of the Lord. 17 For he knew that Jerusalem must be destroyed, because of the wickedness of the people.

                        M 18 For behold, they have **rejected the words of the prophets.**

                          N Wherefore, if my **father** should dwell in the land after he hath been commanded to **flee out of the land,**

                            behold, he would also **perish.**

                        N' Wherefore, it must needs be that **he flee out of the land**

                            19 And **behold**, it is wisdom in God that we should obtain these records, that we may **preserve** unto our children the language of our fathers;

M' 20 And also that we may **preserve** unto them **the words which have been spoken by the mouth of all the holy prophets**, which have been delivered unto them by the Spirit and power of God, since the world began, even down unto this present time.

K' 21 And it came to pass that after this manner of language did I persuade my brethren, that they might be **faithful in keeping the commandments of God.**

L' 22 And it came to pass that we went down to the land of our inheritance, and we did gather together **our gold, and of silver, and our precious things.**

J' 23 And after we had gathered these things together, we **went up again unto the house of Laban**.

G' 24 And it came to pass that we went in unto Laban, **and desired him** that he would give unto us the records which were engraven upon **the plates of brass**, for which we would give unto him our gold, and our silver, and all our precious things.

H' 25 And it came to pass that when Laban saw our property, and that it was exceedingly great, **he did lust after it**, insomuch that he thrust us out, and sent his servants **to slay us**, that he might obtain our property.

I' 26 And it came to pass that we did **flee before the servants of Laban,**

F' and we were obliged to leave behind our property, and **it fell** into the hands of Laban.

D' 27 And it came to pass that **we fled into the wilderness**, and the servants of Laban did not overtake us, and we hid ourselves in the cavity of a rock.

E' 28 And it came to pass that Laman was angry with me, and also with my father; and also was Lemuel, for he hearkened unto the words of Laman. Wherefore **Laman and Lemuel did speak many hard words** unto us, their younger brothers, and they did smite us even with a rod.

C' 29 And it came to pass as they smote us with a rod, behold, an angel of the Lord came and stood before them, and he spake unto them, saying: Why do ye smite your younger brother with a rod? Know ye not that the **Lord hath chosen him** to be a ruler over you, and this because of your iniquities?

B' Behold ye shall go up to Jerusalem again, and **the Lord will deliver Laban into your hands**. 30 And after the angel had spoken unto us, he departed.

A' 31 And after the angel had departed, **Laman and Lemuel again began to murmur**, saying: How is it possible that the Lord will deliver Laban into our hands? Behold, he is a mighty man, and he can command fifty, yea, even he can slay fifty; then why not us? 4:1 And it came to pass that I spake unto my brethren, saying: Let us go up again unto Jerusalem, and **let us be faithful in keeping the commandments of the Lord.**

As is often the case, some of the parallels are antithetical, and others become more apparent with some explanation. To that end, let's examine some of these fascinating relationships:

A-A' The brothers murmur at the beginning and at the end of this chiasmus. Nephi, on the other hand, declares, both in the beginning and at the end, that they should be faithful to the Lord's commandments.

B-B' In B Nephi declares that he knows the Lord will prepare a way to fulfill his commandments. In B' the angel show Nephi the way the Lord has prepared, which is that Laban will be delivered into his hands.

C-C' In C Lehi declares that he knows Nephi is blessed of the Lord, and in C' the angel declares the way in which Nephi is blessed, which is that he has been chosen to rule over his brethren.

D-D' Both are journeys into the wilderness, one headed toward Jerusalem, and the other, fleeing Laban

E-E' In E the "consulting" is friendly and in E', Laman and Lemuel are doing the talking, speaking harshly to Nephi.

F-F' In these parallels are the only two usages of "fell" in this chapter. Coincidently they are spatially equidistant. In F the lot falls to Laman to seek the plates, and in F' their precious things fall into the hands of Laban.

H-H' There are also only two usages of "slay" in this chapter, and again they are equidistant. In both cases Laban seeks to slay the brothers, once after the first attempt and again after the second attempt.

I-I' In both parallels the brothers flee, Laman after the first attempt and all the brothers after the second

J-J' In J the brothers desire to return home, but after Nephi's pep talk which is the center of this chiasmus, they gather their possessions and in J' return to Laban's house.

Apex – The center of this chiasmus, K-N, is Nephi's declaring yet again to his brothers that they should be faithful in keeping the Lord's commandments. Nephi tells his brothers that because of their wickedness and rejection of the prophets' **words**, Jerusalem would be destroyed. Conversely, its parallel thought is that because the Lord had instructed them to flee, they will be able to preserve the **word** of the prophets and be faithful in keeping the commandments. This central thought is also a perfect parallel to the chiasmus of chapter 19, where the identity of the prophets who spoke these words is revealed!

- **Chapter 19 – Words of the Prophets**

As mentioned, Chapter 19 is Nephi's parallel response regarding the words of the prophets spoken of in chapter 3. Here he specifically mentions the exact words of these prophets as well as their names; Zenos, Neum, and Zenock.

Verses 1-6 Nephi writes about the plates he is commanded to make. Verse 3 states - **I, Nephi,** received a commandment that the ministry and the prophecies, the more plain and precious parts of them, should be **written upon these plates**; and that the things which were written **should be kept for the instruction of my people**, who should possess **the land**, and also for other wise purposes, which purposes are known unto the Lord.

A 7 For the things which **some** men esteem to be of **great worth**, both to the body and soul, **others** set at naught and trample under their feet. Yea, even the very God of Israel do men trample under their feet; I say, trample under their feet but I would speak in other words—they set him at naught, and hearken not to **the voice** of his counsels.

 B 8 And **behold he cometh,**

  C according to **the words** of the angel, **in six hundred years** from the time my father
  left **Jerusalem.**

   D 9 And the world, because of their iniquity, shall judge him to be a thing of
   naught; wherefore they scourge him, and he **suffereth it**;
    E and they smite him, and he **suffereth it.**
     F Yea, they spit upon him, and he **suffereth it,**
      G because of his loving kindness and his **long-suffering**
      towards the children of **men.**
       H 10 And the **God of our fathers,**
        I who were **led out of Egypt**, out of bondage, and also
        I' were **preserved in the wilderness**
       H' by him, yea, the **God of Abraham, and of Isaac, and the God of Jacob,**
      G' yieldeth himself, **according to the words** of the angel, as a
      man, into the hands of wicked **men,**
     F' to be lifted up, **according to the words** of Zenock,
    E' and to be crucified, **according to the words** of Neum,
   D' and to be buried in a sepulchre, **according to the words** of Zenos,

  C' which **he spake** concerning **the three days** of darkness, which should be a sign
  given of his death unto those who should inhabit the isles of the sea, more
  especially given unto those who are of the **house of Israel**.

 B' 11 For thus spake the prophet: The **Lord God surely shall visit** all the house of Israel at that day,

A' **some** with **his voice**, because of their righteousness, unto their **great joy** and salvation, and **others** with the thunderings and the lightnings of his power, by tempest, by fire, and by smoke, and vapor of darkness, and by the opening of the earth, and by mountains which shall be carried up.

A 12 And all these things must surely come, **saith the prophet Zenos.** And the rocks of **the earth** must rend; and because of the groanings of **the earth,**

 B many of the kings of the **isles of the sea** shall be wrought upon by the Spirit of God, to exclaim: The God of nature suffers.

  C 13 And as for those who are at Jerusalem, **saith the prophet**, they shall be scourged by all people,
  because they crucify the God of Israel, and **turn their hearts aside**, rejecting signs and wonders, and the
  power and glory of the **God of Israel**.

   D 14 And because they **turn their hearts aside, saith the prophet,** and have despised
   the **Holy One of Israel,** they shall wander in the flesh, and **perish,** and become a hiss
   and a byword, and be hated among all nations.

  C' 15 Nevertheless, when that day cometh, **saith the prophet,** that they **no more turn aside their hearts
  against** the **Holy One of Israel,** then will he remember the covenants which he made to their fathers.

 B' 16 Yea, then will he remember the **isles of the sea**; yea, and all the people who are of the house of
 Israel, will I gather in, saith the Lord,

A' according to the **words of the prophet Zenos,** from the four quarters of **the earth.** 17 Yea, and all **the earth** shall see the salvation of the Lord, saith the prophet; every nation, kindred, tongue and people shall be blessed.

Verses 18-24 Nephi writes again about the plates he was commanded to make. Verse 22 states - Now it came to pass that **I, Nephi,** did teach my brethren these things; and it came to pass that I did read many things to them, which were **engraven upon the plates** of brass, **that they might know concerning the doings of the Lord** in other **lands,** among people of old.

In verse 8 (C) we read, "according to the words of the angel". However, Nephi has not mentioned an angel to this point in chapter 19. We can only speculate that Nephi is referring to the angel that guided him during his vision of the tree of life, or perhaps the angel that visited him when he went to the mountain for instruction at the time he made a wooden bow (chapter 16), which was the last time we have an account of an angel visiting Nephi. Also, Chapter 19 begins and ends with Nephi talking about the brass plates. I have included it as a general block of parallel verses at either end of the chapter.

Two Centers

Noticeably, chapter 19 is comprised of two complimentary centers. The first chiastic center, from verses 7-11, is about Jehovah of the Old Testament who preserves Israel at the time of Moses, and then later yields himself as a mortal man to be crucified at the hands of the wicked; all according to the words of the angel and the prophets. Its accompanying center, verses 12-17, repeats the crucifixion of Christ as prophesied by the prophets, but also declares that after the Jews have been scourged, when their hearts are returned to him, he will remember his covenant and gather Israel. Generally speaking, the first chiasmus concerns the words of the prophets up to Christ, and the second chiasmus highlights the prophets' words from Christ until the millennial age. Let's look at some of the other parallels within the first chiasmus and then the second.

Verses 7-11

Further, the precise detail which Nephi provides of the Savior's suffering is striking. Nephi seems to be very intimate with the facts surrounding his death. In fact the phrase "suffers it" is used *three* times, each mentioning how Christ was scourged, smitten, and spit upon. Nephi then parallels these *three* usages of "suffer it" to *three* usages of the phrase "according to the words" of the prophet. With each usage of "according to" Nephi tells us more about Christ's suffering as revealed to specific prophets; lifted up according to Zenock, crucified according to Neum, and buried according to Zenos.

However, in the midst of these 6 sufferings of the cross (three on each side of the apex), Nephi reminds us that the crucifixion is only a part of the Lord's history of "long-suffering" and loving kindness for men. Nephi's center focuses on Christ's role as Jehovah, who was the "God of our fathers" (H), who led them out of Egypt (I, I'), yet "yielded himself" as a man (G')! Within those parameters is the pinnacle of this chiasmus, which is that by condescending to do so, not just ancient Israel but all mankind can be "preserved in the wilderness" of mortality.

Verses 12-17

As he did in the previous chiasmus, Nephi composes his second chiasmus repeating certain phrases *three* times. The phrases "saith the prophet", "Holy One of Israel", and "turn their hearts aside" are all mentioned *three* times in verses 13-15. Nephi use of this device might even be a commemorative of the three days of darkness that he mentions in verse 10, which we associate with the sign of Jonah, the sign that Christ is the Messiah. (In verse 7, "trample under their feet" and "set at naught" are also used *three* times!)

- **Possible meanings of the name Zenos, Zenock, and Neum**

Whereas in the first chiasmus we are told the name of each prophet, in the second chiasmus we are only told "saith the prophet". We are left to wonder what words regarding Christ could be attributed specifically to each prophet. Perhaps looking at the meaning of the names will shed some light.

Neum – is a Hebrew noun used hundreds of time in the Old Testament, though not known as a proper name. None the less, it means "saith" or "say", and is usually the noun used to describe when the Lord or prophet speaks. For example: thus saith (*neum*) the Lord.

Zenock – could likely come from the Hebrew verb *tsen* which means to hook or a thorn. Another possibility would be *tsanach*. In judges 4:21 it is used: "Then Jael Heber's wife took a nail of the tent, and took an hammer in her hand, and went softly unto him, and smote the nail into his temples, and **fastened** (*tsanach*) it into the ground: for he was fast asleep and weary. So he died."

Zenos – is a Greek work which means stranger. It is related to the Hebrew verb *zur*, which means to turn aside, depart, be a stranger.

If we apply these meanings to the three sayings of the prophets, perhaps the essence of what they said will match the meaning of the prophets' names. (Using names as part of the story happens often in ancient scripture.)

13 And as for those who are at Jerusalem, saith the prophet, they shall be **scourged** by all people, because they **crucify** the God of Israel, and turn their hearts aside, rejecting signs and wonders, and the power and glory of the God of Israel.

Zenock – hook thorn, fasten

14 And because they **turn** their hearts **aside**, saith the prophet, and have despised the Holy One of Israel, **they shall wander** in the flesh, and perish, and become a hiss and a byword, and be hated among all nations.

Zenos – to turn aside, depart
    be a stranger

15 Nevertheless, when that day cometh, **saith** the prophet, that they no more turn aside their hearts against the Holy One of Israel, then will he remember the **covenants** which he made to their fathers.

Neum – saith, The Lord will remember
    what he had said (covenanted)
    to the fathers.

3

Nephi and Laban

To help us more fully appreciate typology and symbolism in Book of Mormon stories such as Nephi and Laban, or Lehi's travels in the wilderness, the thoughts of a modern day apostle Bruce R. McConkie as he reflects upon the words of Malachi 4:5-6 are worth consideration:

> "He shall plant in the hearts of the children the promises made to the fathers." That immediately raises the questions: Who are the *children,* who are the *fathers,* and what are the *promises?* If we can catch a vision from the doctrinal standpoint that answers those questions—who the fathers are, who the children are, and what the promises were—**we can have our understanding of the gospel and our comprehension of the plan of salvation expanded infinitely**. We shall then catch a vision of what the whole system of salvation is all about. Until we do that, really, we never catch that vision.[23]

With respect to the identities of the "fathers", M. Catherine Thomas asserts, "Elder McConkie identifies "the fathers" as Abraham, Isaac, and Jacob, the fathers of the house of Israel on the earth. The promises have to do with the Abrahamic Covenant, which is the premortal covenant of godhood, named after Abraham because he would be one of the fathers of that great lineage."[24] An intimate understanding of the stories of the patriarchs is certainly also part of what Nephi meant by "learning of the Jews", which for centuries the ancient Jews passed on father to son.[25] Indeed, these histories, largely recorded in Genesis, contain a foundation for understanding all subsequent scripture. We might be led to ponder if our understanding, as Bro McConkie alludes, has been "expanded infinitely" by the stories of the patriarchs, such that the plan of salvation is unfolded for us. The implication here is that the pattern of the plan of salvation is interwoven into their stories. And what is the plan of salvation? --- that we start with our Father; that we spiritually die; we enter mortality; we physically die; and then we return to our Father. As well, what happens during mortality is of utmost importance – consisting of three periods; before we are reborn, our rebirth, and a spiritually fruitful time afterwards.

One of the best places to read several of these patriarchal patterns is in Acts 7 in the New Testament. There, Stephen tells the stories of Abraham, Joseph, and Moses, in which he repeats the same pattern three times; the plan of salvation which he interweaves into the life of each patriarch. (See Appendix 1 for a complete commentary.) In particular, at the heart of these stories is a revelation of divine promise and rebirth, meant to point the Sanhedrin to Jesus Christ. As well, these stories are chiastic. Below is a sample from the life of Joseph:

A 9 And the **patriarchs**, moved with envy (near **Sychem**), **sold Joseph into Egypt**: (near **Sychem**)
    B but **God was with him**, 10 And **delivered him out of all his afflictions**, and
        gave him favour and wisdom in the sight of Pharaoh king of Egypt; and he
        made him governor over Egypt and all his house.
            C 11 Now there came a **dearth over all the land** of Egypt and Chanaan,
                D and great affliction: and **our fathers** found **no sustenance.**
                    E 12 But when **Jacob** heard that there was corn (**seed**) in Egypt,
                        F he **sent out our fathers** first.
                            G 13 And at the second [time] **Joseph** was **made**
                              known to his brethren;
                           G' and **Joseph's kindred** was **made known unto**
                            Pharaoh.
                      F' 14 Then **sent Joseph, and called his father**
                  E' **Jacob** to [him], and all his kindred (**seed**), threescore and fifteen souls.
              C' 15 So Jacob went down **into Egypt**, and **died, he,**
                D' **and our fathers,**
A' 16 And were **carried over into Sychem**, and laid in the sepulchre that Abraham **bought for a sum** of money of the sons of Emmor [the father] of **Sychem.**
    B' 17 But when the **time of the promise** drew nigh, which **God had sworn to**
        Abraham, the **people grew and multiplied in Egypt,**

These verses give the story of Jacob and Joseph's descent into Egypt, and Israel's later return to Canaan. Below is a simplified chiasmus formed within these verses, with my comments included:

Joseph (sold for a price), "God was with him"– near Sychem in Canaan

  Dearth over Egypt – Famine, Death – fathers found no Sustenance

    Brothers first sent for wheat (seed), meet but do not know Joseph

      Brothers sent second time; Joseph is made known, (their redeemer)

    All of the kindred (seed) sent for by Joseph, are fruitful in new land

  All die in Egypt

Joseph (bought for a sum), "God had sworn" – Sychem in Canaan

As the days of creation (Genesis 1-2), this pattern is comprised of seven periods. Notice that it begins with God in a promised land and returns to God in that same promised land. Also, there is death upon leaving God's presence, as well as death before returning. Most importantly, there is a life-altering revelatory event in the middle (signifying rebirth) which is a typifying of Jesus Christ as the Savior. Jacob's family goes down (falls) into Egypt to be saved as a nation, which is a blessing and a curse. Paradoxically, Egypt (a type of the fallen world) saves the covenant seed of Abraham, yet it becomes a 400 year period of oppression and bondage. Just as Jacob's family needed Egypt to survive, grow, and perpetuate the covenant, we also need our probationary experience for a similar reason. Following this eternal covenant pattern, the road we travel in mortality is the same as the prophetic pattern that Stephen presents here to the Sanhedrin!

As mentioned, the center of this chiasmus about Joseph is a promise of salvation. If you recall, Joseph weeps and lovingly embraces his brothers when he reveals his identity – their brother who is able to save them (Gen 45:3). Below is a brief diagram of these three highly important phases of Joseph's life which parallel our mortal experience:

Brothers need wheat (seed), first attempt unsuccessful   *telestial*

   Brothers sent second time; Joseph is made known, (their redeemer) *terrestrial*

All of the kindred (seed) sent for by Joseph, are fruitful in new land *celestial*

You will notice that preserving Abraham's covenant depends upon the revelation of a Savior, and that fruitfulness is only possible if such a divine revelation has been received. This simple yet profound pattern is one of rebirth and is repeatedly found in scripture. For instance consider the story of Noah's dove which three times was sent to find a new land of promise after the flood:

Dove first attempt, not fruitful

Dove brings olive branch, the promise of new life (salvation)

Dove sent third time - fruitful in new land

Using this method (finding Christ and His plan of rebirth), let's now study the story of Nephi and Laban. Indeed, Nephi's courageous words as he embarks to recover the brass plates represent the sentiment of all those who enter into mortality with a determination to return to their Father. "And it came to pass that I, Nephi, said unto my father: I will go and do the things which the Lord hath commanded, for I know that the Lord giveth no commandments unto the children of men, save he shall prepare a way for them that they may accomplish the thing which he commandeth them." (1Nephi 3:7) In fact, if we chart Nephi's journey to get the plates we have the same 7 day creation pattern as the one viewed on the previous page:

Nephi in tent of father

    Sent into spiritually dead Jerusalem

        Laman (natural man) attempts but fails   *Telestial*

            Angel appears and promises deliverance   *Terrestrial*

        Nephi succeeds, yields to Spirit, slays Laban (sin) *Celestial*

    Leave Jerusalem (about to be physically destroyed)

Return to tent of Father

Nephi walks into Jerusalem without precise foreknowledge of how he will prevail against greatly overwhelming odds (Laban "can command fifty, yea, he can slay fifty" 1Ne 3:31). As pointed out earlier by Elder Jeffrey Holland (pg 2), Nephi's words at this time also wonderfully capture the character of Christ's actions as he obeyed and performed the Father's will in Gethsemane and on the cross; who also had never contended against such crushing odds - the sin and grief for innumerable mankind. (In Christ's defining hour, without previous experience from which to draw, we can only imagine how much or little he foreknew concerning his difficult mission, or the depth of pain that the Atonement would require of him.) Likewise, Nephi's narrative is a Christ-like story, one in which he travails in order to save his people from perishing. Once we permit ourselves to view Nephi's story as a figurative account of the Atonement (as we do the story of Abraham and Isaac for example), there are new and deeper insights for us to reflect upon.

- **1st of 3 attempts – unsuccessful** Telestial

Returning *three* days back to Jerusalem; in verse 3:10 the brothers cast lots to see who will go to the house of Laban to ask for the plates of brass. It should come as no surprise to us that Nephi, trained in the "learning" of his fathers, will use the narrative devices that he delights in, those which foretell Christ, dividing the story into *three* parts. And if we apply the pattern learned from Stephen (pg 40-42), then we might predict that their first attempt will be unsuccessful, like Noah's first dove that returned with nothing. We might also predict that someone with little appreciation for his spiritual birthright will be chosen, and Laman is an obvious perfect choice. The lots they cast to make this decision are reminiscent of the lots used by the ancient prophets, through whom, and with such devices as lots, God directed his affairs. For instance, Samuel used lots to select Saul as king (1 Sam 10:20-21). From the Smith's Bible dictionary we read, "The custom of deciding doubtful questions by lot is one of great extent and high antiquity. Among the Jews lots were used with the expectation that God would so control them as to give a right direction to them. They were very often used by God's appointment."[26] That Laman is selected first is surely by divine decree, preserving the biblical pattern of the carnal man preceding the re-born man, who will be Nephi. Nephi tells us of Laman's failure and what happened afterwards:

1 Ne 3:12 And he desired of Laban the records which were engraven upon the plates of brass, which contained the genealogy of my father. 13 And behold, it came to pass that Laban was angry, and thrust him out from his presence; and he would not that he should have the records. Wherefore, he said unto him: Behold thou art a robber, and I will **slay** thee. 14 But Laman fled out of his presence, and told the things which Laban had done, unto us. And we began to be exceedingly sorrowful, and my brethren were about to return unto my father in the wilderness. 15 But behold I said unto them that: As the Lord liveth, and as we live, we will not go down unto our father in the wilderness until we have accomplished the thing which the Lord hath commanded us. 16 Wherefore, let us be faithful in keeping the commandments of the Lord; therefore let us go down to the land of our father's inheritance, for behold he left gold and silver, and all manner of riches. And all this he hath done **because of the commandments** of the Lord.

Though Laman and Lemuel are disheartened by the failure of this first attempt, again Nephi resolutely declares that they need to be "faithful in keeping the commandments of the Lord." And so, Nephi formulates that they will use their physical inheritance, their riches of gold and silver, to purchase their spiritual legacy from Laban (vs 16). The trade-off of worldly wealth for spiritual inheritance is another common theme documented throughout the history of the Book of Mormon,[27] which test of pride the people often fail, prizing worldly riches over spiritual wealth. Like the earlier casting of lots for divine appointment, the Lord has foreseen the brother's second attempt, fore-guiding Lehi to leave behind his precious things just for the purpose of later offering them to Laban.

- **2nd of three attempts**   Terrestrial

Nephi next tells his readers about Laban's reaction when offered all their precious things:

3:23 And after we had gathered these things together, we went up again unto the house of Laban. 24 And it came to pass that we went in unto Laban, and desired him that he would give unto us the records which were engraven upon the plates of brass, for which we would give unto him our gold, and our silver, and all our precious things. 25 And it came to pass that when Laban saw our property, and that it was exceedingly great, he did **lust** after it, insomuch that he thrust us out, and sent his servants to **slay** us, that he might obtain our property. 26 And it came to pass that we did flee before the servants of Laban, and we were obliged to leave behind our property, and it fell into the hands of Laban.

This is the second time that Laban seeks to slay someone in Nephi's family. As author, Nephi gives his readers here more clues as to who/what Laban is a symbol of. We now know several disconcerting character traits; he is easily angered, he is lustful, a thief, and he has murder in his heart. For survival the brothers flee to the safety of a rock (which in scripture is often a symbol of Christ, 1 Cr 10:4). If we refer again to the patriarchal paradigm that Stephen gives us in Acts 7, and if Nephi and Laban's story is in fact such a presentation, then we might also expect a revelatory event or divine promise to occur sometime during this second of three typifying periods. And remarkably, as if on queue, an angel of the Lord appears to the brothers as they are smiting Nephi and Sam (Perhaps an allusion to Isaiah 53:1-5; Nephi is "despised and rejected" by his brothers; he is smitten, and bruised):

29 And it came to pass as they smote us with a rod, behold, an **angel of** the Lord **came and stood before them**, and he spake unto them, saying: Why do ye smite your younger brother with a rod? Know ye not that **the Lord hath chosen him to be a ruler over you**, and this because of your iniquities? Behold ye shall go up to Jerusalem again, and **the Lord will deliver Laban into your hands.** 30 And after the angel had spoken unto us, he departed.

The angel reveals to Laman and Lemuel the promise already made to Nephi in the wilderness, that he will be a ruler over them (1 Ne 2:22). As we read this account we might be reminded of Joseph in Egypt who was promised to be a ruler over his brethren (Gen 37:8), or Moses, who was asked by his brethren, "Who made thee a prince (ruler) and a judge over us?" (Exo 2:14) Now an angel, alluding to these same ancient events, intimates that Nephi be accorded comparable status to such hallowed figures. It is quite likely that father Lehi had taught them the stories of Moses and Joseph, and how these were types of the promised "deliverer" to come. The angel's prediction might have also reminded them of the repeated patriarchal pattern where the younger brother unexpectedly received the covenant promise of birthright and seed; e.g., instead of Cain it was Abel, instead of Ishmael it was Isaac, instead of Esau it was Jacob, instead of Reuben or Simeon it was Joseph, and instead of Manasseh it was Ephraim. Though Laman and Lemuel are oblivious and unmoved by any of this, the promise from the angel suggests to us a lot about who Nephi represents in this story. Joseph and Moses were figures like unto the Lamb – is Nephi?

- **Promise of Deliverance**

In addition to designating Nephi as their ruler, the angel promises them; "go up to Jerusalem again, and the Lord will deliver Laban into your hands." Isn't it interesting that the angel doesn't promise that they will get the plates, which seem to be secondary at this point? Removing the obstacle that Laban has become is now the key to securing the plates (the word). However, Laman and Lemuel's lack of faith so soon after such an experience is as surprising as anything that has happened thus far. We ask ourselves, how could they so immediately doubt the angel's promise?

> 31 And after the angel had departed, Laman and Lemuel again began to murmur, saying: How is it possible that the Lord will deliver Laban into our hands? Behold, he is a mighty man, and he can command fifty, yea, even he can slay fifty; then why not us?

We perhaps are reminded of the words of Christ the day after he has fed the 5,000. Many, who had seen with their own eyes the miracle, come the next day to Capernaum for more food. After Christ tells them that he is the bread of life, and that they must partake of his flesh and blood, many are offended by such "hard sayings", failing to understand its symbolic and spiritual meaning. In John 6 we read:

> 60 Many therefore of his disciples, when they had heard [this], said, This is an hard saying; who can hear it? 61 When Jesus knew in himself that his disciples murmured at it, he said unto them, Doth this offend you? 62 **What] and if ye shall see the Son of**

man ascend up where he was before? 63 It is the spirit that quickeneth; the flesh profiteth nothing: the words that I speak unto you, [they] are spirit, and [they] are life. 64 But there are some of you that believe not. For Jesus knew from the beginning who they were that believed not, and who should betray him.

Notice what Christ tells the unbelievers (many of whom had seen the earlier miracle), that even if they saw him rise up in front of them and ascend into heaven, they still wouldn't believe (vs 62). No doubt, if Laman and Lemuel had been there they would have been among those that "went back and walked no more with him." (We also find in Jn 7:5 that Christ also has kinsmen who do not believe.) Only those that were "quickened by the Spirit" (vs 63), and comprehended with their hearts and not their eyes, understood that Jesus' word was the true nourishment which could sustain them.

Without faith, miraculous events are not valued or appreciated. Archeological evidence from the jungles of South or Central America will never convince most people of the Book of Mormon's divine origins, which should come as no surprise - "For we walk by faith, not by sight." (2 Cor 5:7)

- **3rd Attempt - Let us go up! Laban paralleled to Egypt**   Celestial

Having obtained the angel's promise, in chapter 4 we next read Nephi's words of renewed hope and encouragement to his brothers:

1 AND it came to pass that I spake unto my brethren, saying: **Let us go up** again unto Jerusalem, and let us be faithful in keeping the commandments of the Lord; for behold he is mightier than all the earth, then why not mightier than Laban and his fifty, yea, or even than his tens of thousands? 2 **Therefore let us go up**; let **us be strong like unto Moses**; for he truly spake unto the waters of the Red Sea and they divided hither and thither, and our fathers came through, out of captivity, on dry ground, and the armies of Pharaoh did follow and were drowned in the waters of the Red Sea. 3 Now behold ye

know that this is true; and ye also know that an angel hath spoken unto you; wherefore can ye doubt? **Let us go up;** the Lord is able to deliver us, even as our fathers, **and to destroy Laban, even as the Egyptians.**

Nephi begins the narration of the *third* attempt to obtain the word of God contained on the brass plates by *three* times using the phrase, "Let us go up". In these verses Nephi bolsters his brother's confidence by continuing to develop the angel's reference to Moses, recounting the story of Moses leading their fathers through the parted Red Sea and preserving them in miraculous fashion. Nephi then concludes (vs 3) by drawing a fascinating and clear parallel of Laban to Egypt, "the Lord is able to **deliver us, even as our fathers,** and to destroy **Laban**, **even as the Egyptians.**" For Nephi's ancient fathers, Egypt represented captivity, bondage, and death, which symbolism Nephi now categorically equates\parallels to Laban! Moreover, whereas Egypt in the days of Joseph's famine represented life, 400 years later it conversely symbolized death - the Hebrew meaning of Laban's name, as we will see, shares this same duality of life and death. [28]

- **Meaning of Laban – White and Death**

If you will recall, Jacob the patriarch had a Laban to contend with in Haran (Gen 29-31), as does Nephi now in Jerusalem, and we might consider that in a spiritual sense we do as well. Before looking at what Laban means in Hebrew, I should point out that another aspect of Jewish scripture is the importance of names and their Hebrew meanings. In stories of the Old Testament, most of the time a person's name will have particular meaning as it pertains to the story in which he/she is involved. In his book on gospel symbolism, Joseph McConkie states that, "Names play a *significant* role in the scriptural history. This is true of both place-names and personal-names." He calls this device a "story within a story."[29] For example, we all know that Abraham is from the Hebrew meaning father of many nations or a multitude, which coincidently is an important part of his covenant promise. A Hebrew name can also be a play on words, or can even mean two opposite things. For instance, Joseph's name – "taken away and added to" [30] seems to foretell the way his life would paradoxically unfold (sold into slavery, only to become a ruler in Egypt). In fact, Joseph's name also captures the essence of Christ's ministry and the gospel; that to save one's life, one needs to lose it.

Let's consider Laban in Hebrew. In the Hebrew lexicon we find:

לָבָן—(1) adj. f. לְבָנָה *white*, Ex. 16:31; Levit. 13:3, seq.
(2) pr. n. *Laban*, the son of Bethuel, an Aramæan, the father-in-law of Jacob, Gen. 24:29, 50; chapters 29—31. [31]

How do we determine the fullest meaning of Laban's name from this innocuous looking explanation, especially when his character is certainly quite the contrary of what we usually interpret white to symbolize. Though nothing may be readily apparent from this lexicon explanation, and while it seems reasonable to associate "white" with purity or light, in the ancient Hebrew culture, white (like the lifelessness of winter) can also symbolize death. For instance, leprosy was a condition that manifested itself by a skin of white appearance.[32] "In Leviticus 13 we find this word (laban) used sixteen times as the key indicator of leprosy – the sore or hair became white or "laban" (in the Hebrew). For example, consider that Miriam the wife of Moses was thought of as "one dead":

Num 12:12-14 And the cloud departed from off the tabernacle; and, behold, Miriam [became] **leprous, [white] as snow**: and Aaron looked upon Miriam, and, behold, [she was] leprous. And Aaron said unto Moses, Alas, my lord, I beseech thee, lay not the sin upon us, wherein we have done foolishly, and wherein we have sinned. **Let her not be as one dead**, of whom the flesh is half consumed when he cometh out of his mother's womb.

Or, consider how the prophet Joel uses white to describe the destruction to come upon Israel:

Joel 1:7 He hath laid my vine waste, and barked my fig tree: he hath made it clean bare, and cast [it] away; the branches thereof are made white (*laban*).

When Naaman the Syrian is sent to be healed by Elisha, a distressed king of Israel exclaims:

2Kings 15:7 And it came to pass, when the king of Israel had read the letter, that he rent his clothes, and said, **[Am] I God, to kill and to make alive,** that this man doth send unto me to recover a **man of his leprosy**? wherefore consider, I pray you, and see how he seeketh a quarrel against me.

Making Naaman whole is like raising a man from the dead. The cure for Naaman's affliction of leprosy, which is a symbol of sinfulness[33] and living death,[34] is to be reborn, like unto a "little child":

2Kings 15:14 Then went he down, and dipped himself seven times in Jordan, according to the saying of the man of God: and his flesh came again like unto the flesh of **a little child**, and he was clean.

From the CES Old Testament manual we read: "Leprosy in its various forms was a disease that involved decay and putrefaction of the living body; also, because of its loathsomeness, it required the person to be ostracized and **cut off** from any fellowship with the rest of the house of Israel. Because of these characteristics, leprosy was seen as an appropriate type or **symbol of what happens to a man spiritually when he sins**. Sin introduces decay and corruption into the spiritual realm similar to what leprosy does in the physical realm. Also, a sinful person was **cut off** from a fellowship with spiritual Israel and could not be a part of the Lord's true covenant people. So the **leper himself provided a type or similitude of what King Benjamin called the 'natural man.'**"[35] Laban, therefore, is also such a representation, of the carnal man, separated from God, a figure of the internal leprosy or sinfulness in each of us. And as indicted, it was required that he be "cut off" (even as the Laban in Nephi's story).

Consequently, white can be used to symbolize death, depending on scriptural context. Other examples would include - Mat 23:27 where Christ describes the Pharisees as "**whited** sepulchers, which indeed appear beautiful outward, but are within full of dead [men's] bones, and of all uncleanness." Likewise, in Acts 23:3 Paul also refers to inner corruption, calling the wicked high priest who falsely accused him a "whited wall". Coincidently, the white bricks used to build the tower of Babel (confusion) were called "lebenahs" (a noun from the word laban), as were the bricks which the Israelite slaves toiled to make in Egypt (Gen 11:3, Ex 5:8).[36] In the view of the world these white bricks appeared as grand monuments, while to God's people they represented death and bondage. Even the prince of darkness, we are told in 1 Cor 11:14, can appear as an angel of light (white). Hence "Laban", according to the "learning of the Jew," could represent purity and good, or ironically it's opposite, darkness and death.

- **Drunkenness - another indicator of fallen man**

When Nephi comes upon Laban in verse 3:9 he tells us, "I beheld a man, and he had fallen to the earth before me, for he was drunken with wine". There are a couple of additional symbols in this short verse which indicate what Laban represents. First of all, we are told that he has "fallen to the earth". While this is a literal description, it is also figurative of his spiritual condition – a fallen man. Further, Laban's drunkenness is a common symbol in scripture for someone who is spiritually asleep or dead.

In the garden, symbolically there were two fruit trees (vines) of which Adam and Eve could partake. Each produced a particular wine from its fruit - one to intoxicate with the love of God which awakened the soul, and the other that intoxicated the mind of man with darkness or spiritual sleep.[37] Thus, when Adam and Eve partook of the wine\fruit of the second tree it produced spiritual sleep and separation from God. They fell from the garden, and their posterity continues spiritually fallen as well; seed of the fruit of that forbidden tree. To reverse its effects, as Lehi's dream describes, all need to partake of the fruit of the first tree, the tree of life and healing, who is Christ.

For an example of the good wine, remember the day of Pentecost when the Holy Ghost filled the upper room and the disciples prophesied and spoke in tongues? They were accused of being drunk, but it was the fruit of the tree of life which intoxicated them (Acts 2:15). Jeremiah is filled with the Spirit and writes: "Mine heart within me is broken because of the prophets; all **my bones shake**; I am like a **drunken** man, and like a man whom **wine hath overcome, because of the LORD**, and because of the **words** of his holiness." (Jer 23:9) Interestingly, the phrase "shake" in this verse, which Jeremiah uses to describe the Spirit's effect on him, is the same Hebrew word (*rachaph*) which we examined earlier in Genesis 1:2 where the Spirit "moves" or flutters upon the waters! Used only two other times in scripture, Jeremiah's intoxicated "feeling" alludes to the same divine creative power which helped to form the earth - the Holy Ghost! (You might also notice how Jeremiahs points to the "word" as the cause of this drunken state.)

The scriptures, however, are also full of examples supporting the bad spiritual effects of drunkenness caused by the fruit of the malignant vine:

Job 12:25 They grope in the dark without light, and he maketh them to stagger like [a] drunken [man].

Isa 29:9 Stay yourselves, and wonder; cry ye out, and cry: they are drunken, but not with wine; they stagger, but not with strong drink. 10 For the LORD hath poured out upon you the spirit of deep sleep, and hath closed your eyes: the prophets and your rulers, the seers hath he covered.

Jer 51:7 Babylon [hath been] a golden cup in the LORD'S hand, that made all the earth drunken: the nations have drunken of her wine; therefore the nations are mad. 39 In their heat I will make their feasts, and I will make them drunken, that they may rejoice, and sleep a perpetual sleep, and not wake, saith the LORD.

Thus, drunkenness can be used to symbolize either fallen man, or quite the opposite, a man intoxicated (moved) with the Spirit of God. In the same way, the dual (and contradictory) meaning in Laban's name literally builds tension into Nephi's story, even as discerning good from evil creates tension in our lives. We are often challenged by Satan's deceptions, which outwardly entice, yet are "full of dead bones, and of all uncleanness." As a precedent, in the biblical story of

Jacob, his uncle Laban "appeared" to be his friend, when in fact his continual deception proved him to be the exact opposite. For this reason God ultimately commands Jacob to completely cut himself off from Laban in order to be fruitful and prosper (Gen 31:11-18), which clearly is what Nephi must also do to the Laban (also kindred) in his life.

We might also contemplate that just as the fruit of the tree of life was "white", it is highly likely that so was the fruit of the Satan's tree of knowledge of good and evil. Lehi tells us that the tree of life and the fruit on it "exceeded all the whiteness that I had ever seen" (Ne 8:11). When Nephi sees the tree of life in chapter 11 he also comments that "the beauty thereof was far beyond, yea, exceeding all beauty; and the whiteness thereof did exceed the whiteness of the driven snow." For Eve to have considered eating of the forbidden tree of knowledge of good and evil, it must have been comparable. Indeed, in Gen 3 we are told that Eve is deceived when she sees that the forbidden tree is "pleasant to the eyes, and a tree to be desired." Satan knew better than to beguile Eve with a tree that outwardly seemed any less glorious than the true and living tree, and his tactics have not changed.

- **Meaning of Nephi's name – A type of Christ**

If Jacob's uncle Laban, and Nephi's uncle Laban are symbols of death (false symbols of light) in their respective stories, then who does Nephi represent? At this point it should be apparent that Nephi is Laban's antithesis, and like his ancestor Jacob, he is also a type of Christ. If we examine the meaning of Nephi's name we find some startling, but not unexpected results. Nephi's name is from:

> "a possible wordplay in the first verse of the Book of Mormon that provides internal textual evidence that the name *Nephi* derives from the Egyptian word *nfr*. While *nfr* denotes "good, fine, goodly" of quality, it also signifies "beautiful, fair" of appearance."[38]

The word play referred to concerns his "goodly" parents. Nephi (in 1 Nephi 1:1) is comparing his beauty or fair appearance to that of his parents. In the 1828 Webster's Dictionary the primary definition of "goodly" is given as, "being of a handsome form; **beautiful**"[39] Thus Nephi is a seed begotten after its own kind – beautiful or goodly, like his parents. In fact, Lehi's name in the Hebrew Lexicon is defined as, "the cheek, so called as being the **seat of beauty**."[40] Later, in 1 Ne 13:15 Nephi describes his people using three synonyms: "and I beheld that they were **white**, and **exceedingly fair** and **beautiful**", another word play on his name.[41] A primary definition of "fair" in the same 1828 dictionary (the language of Joseph Smith's time) is "white". Nephi's people (Nephites) are forever after identified with this main sense of his name.

Why would Nephi begin with such word-play so early in his writing if it wasn't important? Clearly he wants his readers to consider the meaning of his name, so that when they encounter the name of the antagonist Laban they will feel the tension between two names which seemingly express the same thing. Yet, it doesn't take his readers long to discover that Nephi and Laban could not be more different; one who is truly white and the other a counterfeit.

- **Nephi is a type of Christ – "One" who should perish, yet live**

Before continuing, a review of the three phases of Nephi and Laban's story, which is also a pattern of man's mortal journey, will be very helpful:

The first of the three attempts to recover the records is done by Laman, a conflicted and carnal man who seems to have no abiding witness of his Savior. This is also the case with the first period of Moses or Jacob's stories, where they are self-interested and spiritually unproductive.

In the second period, Nephi and his brothers give away their temporal possessions to Laban. In so doing their spiritual "soil is fallowed", as Brother Maxwell might say. Those with ready hearts are receptive and the Savior's promise of redemption is revealed. An angel is sent, just as there was an angel to direct Moses on Sinai in his second 40 years. (See page 228-230 for the story of Moses' 40-40-40 pattern.)

During Nephi's third attempt, Nephi walks by faith, as do all who have experienced a revelation of Christ as the promised Savior. This comes after baptism and, and if not at that time, then whenever a spiritual witness is received and the new man is being formed through God's Spirit. Nephi tells us in Nephi 4:6 – "And I was led by the Spirit not knowing beforehand the things which I should do. Nevertheless I went forth". We are all led to the same place Nephi was led, which is to a confrontation with the Laban (sin,death) within us. Fruitfulness is the result.

Thus, a prophetic or patriarchal pattern is revealed in Nephi's story. Laban, as a figure of death, is ultimately delivered to Nephi that he might obediently slay him on the third attempt (*third day*), thereby delivering his people. Temporally and spiritually, his family's fruitfulness hangs in the balance. And, in 1 Nephi 4:13 we read the reason why Nephi is divinely constrained to slay Laban:

> 13 Behold the Lord slayeth the wicked to bring forth his righteous purposes. It is better that **one** man **should perish** than that a nation (mankind) should dwindle and perish in unbelief.

Like the dual meaning of Laban's name, this somewhat ambiguous statement is also instructive on various levels. At face value, certainly "wicked" refers to Laban, and therefore Laban is also the "one man" who needs to perish. However, there is also a deeper spiritual sense to the Spirit's statement. In fact, Christ personally "entices" his disciples in Mat 5:30 with almost the same words that the Spirit uses to constrain Nephi! Alluding to a personal sacrificial offering, he reminded them:

> And if thy right hand offend thee, cut it off, and cast [it] from thee: for it is profitable for thee that **one** of thy members **should perish**, and **not [that] thy whole body** should be cast into hell.

Teaching on the mount (a symbol of the temple and its sacrifices), Christ is contrasting here the higher spiritual law to the temporal Law of Moses. While there are medical reasons for removing parts of our body that are diseased or cancerous, Christ is obviously speaking of the spiritual surgery required to rid ourselves of the wickedness in our lives. The sacrifice of our offending habits and desires (laid as the animal on the altar) emulates the pattern of Christ's selfless atoning sacrifice, wherein he was made "sin for us" (2 Cor 5:21) and the "one" to perish, so that the whole body of mankind might not be "cast into hell."

Indeed, the pattern of one's carnal nature **perishing** in order to **prosper** spiritually is required of all who desire to reflect His image and truly enter His kingdom. In Luke 17:33 Christ rephrases this somewhat paradoxical principle to his disciples, "Whosoever shall seek to save his life shall lose it; and whosoever shall lose his life shall preserve it."

Remarkably, Christ's atoning struggle is prefigured in Nephi's story by its two main characters, Laban as death and Nephi as Christ - who is life. Together they represent the two conflicting and embattled elements which intersect in Gethsemane, and in all of our lives, which only Christ (the one who could die yet live, be crucified yet resurrect, perish yet prosper) can resolve.[42] And, as Christ allowed his will to be swallowed up by the Father's in Gethsemane and on the cross (Mosiah 15:7), Nephi's will is "swallowed up" by the Spirit's constraint. Symbolically, the "one man" in Nephi's story represents the carnal man in each of us.

For a scriptural story with a similar interpretation, consider the story of Joseph. In that story, the baker of **bread** who is slain (perishes) and the cup bearer of **wine** who rises out of prison (lives), are two people who *simultaneously* personify Christ; one his death and the other his resurrection! Only because Joseph correctly understands the meaning of the bread and the wine (that because one dies, one lives) does the Pharaoh ultimately notice him and *raise him up* from prison - to nourish and save the world from perishing. If Moses (who wrote Genesis) could compose patriarchal history with such imaginative foreshadows of Christ, mightn't Nephi also?

- **Nephi constrained *three* times – a similitude of Gethsemane**

In the New Testament, Christ reveals that Abraham rejoiced to see his day, "and he saw [it], and was glad" (Jn 8:56). How much detail Abraham was privileged to see 2,000 years before the fact, we don't entirely know. In a similar way, we also know that Lehi was given a book by the angel to read (1 Ne 1:11), and that afterwards he exclaimed that it "manifested plainly of the coming Messiah. Nephi himself is shown the vision of the tree of life and the "Lamb of God going forth among the children of men", healing the sick and casting out devils. Nephi also sees that "the Son of the everlasting God was lifted up upon the cross and slain for the sins of the world" (1 Ne 11:33). Nowhere, however, in the Book of Mormon is Christ's struggle in the Garden of Gethsemane discussed. Still, Nephi's struggle with Laban in Jerusalem dramatically parallels the accounts we have of Christ in Gethsemane.[43]

For instance, both stories can readily be broken into *three* distinct parts. Indeed, before slaying Laban, Nephi is constrained three times by the Spirit, which is similar to the three prayers of the Savior in Gethsemane as recorded by Mathew, Mark, and Luke. Below is a summation of Nephi's three reactions to the Spirit's three constraints:

1 Nephi 4 Verse 11-13 – Nephi is constrained by the Spirit, he "shrinks" *telestial*

Verse 14 – Nephi hears the "word", that it is better for one to perish, and remembers the "words" spoken to him in wilderness, that if he keeps the commandments he would prosper. *terrestrial*

Verse 15-18 – Nephi says that he now knows that Laban has been delivered into his hands "for this cause", to obtain the commandments (word), so that they can prosper. Nephi is obedient and slays Laban. *celestial*

Though Nephi does not tell us that he is praying, we might safely assume that on that night, fraught with peril, he was. In Mathew and Mark's version of Gethsemane we are also told that Jesus prayed *to* the Father *three* times with an identical prayer; "O my Father, if it be possible, let this cup pass from me: nevertheless not as I will, but as thou [wilt]." We might consider, based on Nephi's difficulty in doing the Spirit's will, that this was also his prayer. Luke, on the other hand, does not specify that there were three prayers, but instead he divides the Savior's praying into three stages; Christ begins to pray, then an angel appears to comfort him (even as the angel came in the 2nd stage of the brothers quest for the plates), and finally, as Christ prays more earnestly, he sweats great drops of blood.

Perhaps we could liken the third stage of Christ's prayer to Nephi's submission to the Spirit, and also to the third period of all our lives, when sanctification and transformation is possible through strict obedience to the Spirit's voice. This 3rd period is when our faith and desire to obey is ultimately tried and refined. While some of the sins of mankind for which Christ atoned may have occurred in the first two prayers (or in Luke's account, earlier in the prayer), it seems obvious that the final period required increased faith, and was the most difficult and agonizing. Applying these verses to our fallen nature, in our lives we all have impure desires that are more difficult, even with the aid of the Holy Ghost, for us to overcome. We might compare these to the third or more agonizing part of Christ's prayer in Gethsemane when he shed great drops of blood. Surely these tightly held sins might represent the last of the embedded dross of wickedness that persistently remains in us, and are the most difficult to dislodge from the heart, and which would be impossible to eliminate without the deepest sufferings of the Atonement.

- **Nephi shrinks – as the Savior (verse 10)**

Also very much like Gethsemane, Nephi records, "And I shrunk and would that I might not slay him." Like the Savior in the garden, Nephi shrinks because of the severity of God's command. Referring to this event in Gethsemane, in D&C 19:18 we read: "Which suffering caused myself, even God, the greatest of all, to tremble because of pain, and to bleed at every pore, and to suffer both body and spirit—and would that I might not drink the bitter cup, and **shrink**." But just as Christ would do the Father's will and endure the Atonement for all his children, so Nephi faithfully follows the Spirit's constraint, slaying death's figure (Laban), which preserves his posterity. It is wondrous to ponder Nephi's apparent insight into Gethsemane, as well as his willingness (perhaps even eagerness) to also cast himself in the same role as his Savior in the midst of his personal challenge. From Jeffrey R. Holland we read:

"A bitter test? A desire to shrink? Sound familiar? We don't know why those plates could not have been obtained some other way—perhaps accidentally left at the plate polishers one night, or maybe falling off the back of Laban's chariot on a Sabbath afternoon drive. For that matter, why didn't Nephi just leave this story out of the book altogether?… It is not intended that either Nephi or we be spared the struggle of this account.

"I believe that story was placed in the very opening verses of a 531-page book and then told in painfully specific detail in order to focus every reader of that record on the absolutely fundamental gospel issue of obedience and submission to the communicated will of the Lord. If Nephi cannot yield to this terribly painful command, if he cannot bring himself to obey, then it is entirely probable that he can never succeed or survive in the tasks that lie just ahead.

"'I will go and do the things which the Lord hath commanded.' (1 Nephi 3:7.) I confess that I wince a little when I hear that promise quoted so casually among us. Jesus knew what that kind of commitment would entail and so now does Nephi. And so will a host of others before it is over. That vow took Christ to the cross on Calvary and it remains at the heart of every Christian covenant. 'I will go and do the things which the Lord hath commanded'? Well, we shall see."[44]

As Brother Holland so aptly attests, Nephi's struggle is indeed a parallel or allusion to Christ's atoning struggle. The bitter choice that each of them must make will have far-reaching consequences; peoples will perish or prosper based upon their decision. And as Brother Holland affirms, their situation is one common to all of us – will we be obedient and prosper, or will we follow the devil's temptation and perish. The Book of Mormon is a mighty record of antiquity like no other, and when interpreted by modern apostles, with some of the "learning of the Jew," as Nephi has set forth, I hope it takes you, as it does me, to new levels of appreciation, gratitude, and wonder. However, there are yet more astounding witnesses to consider. To completely understand Nephi's message, let's take a look at a couple of Old Testament stories which crystallize Nephi's struggle with Laban as an ancient foreshadow of the Atonement. The first is about Phinehas, who obediently slays a sinful Israelite and then receives Christ-like recognition for his act.

- **Old Testament precedent - The story of Phinehas as a patterned story of Atonement**

In the book of Numbers 22-25 there is a story with very distinct connections to the story of Nephi and Laban, along with some significant clarification. In fact, this story is a scriptural litmus corroborating the contention that the story of Nephi and Laban foreshadows the Savior's Atonement. It involves Phinehas who follows the Lord's command to slay rebellious Israelites who have pulled others into sin. Most noteworthy, Phinehas is afterwards explicitly told by the Lord that his severe, yet obedient, actions have served as a saving "atonement"!

The story begins with Balaam, the son of Beor, who is coincidently reported in the Targum to be the son of Laban! [45] We are told that he is responsible for teaching the "doctrine of Balaam" (Rev 2:14), which caused Israel to sin through idolatry and fornication. In Numbers 25 we read that the Lord has commanded Moses to slay all those who had "joined to Baal" in committing whoredoms or sacrificed to false gods. We also find an account of how the use of Balaam's doctrine to enslave Israel was ultimately defeated and atoned for by Phinehas:

5 And Moses said unto the judges of Israel, Slay ye every one his men that were joined unto Baalpeor. 6 And, behold, one of the children of Israel came and brought unto his brethren a Midianitish woman in the sight of Moses, and in the sight of all the congregation of the children of Israel, who *were* weeping *before* the door of the tabernacle of the congregation. 7 And when Phinehas, the son of Eleazar, the son of Aaron the priest, saw *it,* he rose up from among the congregation, and took a javelin in his hand; 8 And he went after the man of Israel into the tent, **and thrust both of them through, the man of Israel, and the woman through her belly**. So the plague was stayed from the children of Israel. 9 And those that died in the plague were twenty and four thousand. 10 And the LORD spake unto Moses, saying, 11 Phinehas, the son of Eleazar, the son of Aaron the priest, hath turned my wrath away from the children of Israel, while he was zealous for my sake among them, that I consumed not the children of Israel in my jealousy. 12 Wherefore say, Behold, I give unto him my covenant of peace: 13 And he shall have it, **and his seed** after him, *even* the covenant of an everlasting priesthood; because he was zealous for his God, and **made an atonement**

for the children of Israel. 14 Now the name of the Israelite that was slain, *even* that was slain with the Midianitish woman, *was* Zimri, the son of Salu, a prince of a chief house among the Simeonites. 15 And the name of the Midianitish woman that was slain *was* Cozbi, the daughter of Zur; he *was* head over a people, *and* of a chief house in Midian.

Like the story of Nephi and Laban, we are perhaps shocked by Phinehas' sudden brutality, even more so because a woman is also slain, and we are again left to wonder if such harsh action was necessary. However, we also read that Phinehas' zealous actions are highly cherished by the Lord, who promises him and his seed a covenant of peace and everlasting priesthood because he made "**an atonement**" for the children of Israel. Indeed, by describing what Phinehas did as "an atonement", Phinehas' actions prefigure Christ who will also slay death and sin, preserving all of mankind from "perishing". Because Israel had broken their Mosaic covenant they were under God's curse, but by the actions of "one man", God restores their covenant of peace. (The restitution of a "covenant of peace" might perhaps remind us that after Laban is slain, Nephi also establishes a covenant of peace with Zoram and his seed [1 Ne 4:32-35]).

Like Nephi, Phinehas is carrying out the "constraints" of the Lord when he slays Zimri and Cozbi, who are classical representations of carnal man. In fact, in the Hebrew Zimri means to be plucked or cut off, and Cozbi means liar or deceiver![46] Also, Cozbi is a Midianite, which means strife or contention. Thus we see again how interpreting the Hebrew meaning of the names helps us to better understand ancient scripture. In particular, Phinehas has an interesting meaning in Hebrew which further deepens our appreciation of his role as a type of the Savior.

Phinehas' name in the Hebrew is understood to be a combination of two Hebrew words – *peh,* which is mouth, and *nachash,* which means either serpent or brass. Combined, the interpretation would be "mouth of brass" or "serpent's mouth".[47] Such ambiguity in the meaning could be intentional, and a clever allusion to the "brass serpent", which also comes from the Hebrew *nachash*. Coincidently, the story of the brass serpent is told just prior to Phinehas', in Numbers 21. Most notably, both Phinehas and the brass serpent (who is also Christ) heal Israel's curse, saving her from destruction.[48]

- ## David and Goliath – Common Characteristics with Nephi and Laban

Another excellent and often acknowledged parallel to the story of Nephi and Laban is the Old Testament story of David and Goliath. As in the other stories, David slays the incarnation of carnal sin and destruction, who is Goliath. Indeed, if David hadn't been successful the Israelites would have become slaves of the Canaanites (they would have perished). It is interesting, however, that when Goliath is killed and his head cut off, our reaction does not seem to be as gut-wrenching as when Nephi slays and beheads Laban. Perhaps because David is young, and Goliath a giant, our recoil at the carnage is somehow diminished. Also, it seems that we never stop to consider that David could have perhaps just wounded Goliath or incapacitated him in some manner other than killing him (as we do with Nephi). Indeed, when Goliath is struck by the stone, which was surely guided by the Spirit, we don't know that he is necessarily dead until his head is removed. And so, in spite of our failure to emotionally respond in the same way, the elements used to second guess Nephi also exist for questioning David's seemingly brutal actions. And, like Phinehas and Nephi, for David's act to be considered an atonement, it required that blood be spilt through an act of sacrificial obedience in order to preserve Israel.

David, which means "beloved" in Hebrew, in this story is a type of Christ; and Goliath, which is rooted in the Hebrew word for "naked" or "shame" (*galah*), is a type of man's shame and sin, which has been the scriptural interpretation of nakedness ever since Adam and Eve's transgression caused them to feel shame for their nakedness in the garden (Nah 3:5, Isa 47:3). Conversely, the Hebrew word for Atonement is *kaphar*, which means to cover or wrap around, which is what was done for Adam and Eve after their sin – an animal was sacrificed to make them a covering for their shame\sin\nakedness (Gen 3:21). Just as Nephi removes all of Laban's clothing, in essence exposing his shame, so Goliath, as his name indicates, is stripped by David of his armor and clothing, exposing him for who he was – a type for sin.

Poignantly, in the story of Goliath, though he caused the armies of Israel to flee in disgrace, in miraculous and ironic fashion, the giant ultimately becomes the one shamed. Also, the greatest becomes the least, and the least (David) the greatest; king and savior at that time to all Israel. Alonzo Gaskill, in his book The Lost Language of Symbolism, describes Goliath's typological meaning:

Curiously, Goliath was said to be six cubits and six inches tall (see Samuel 17:4). He is described as wearing six pieces of armor, of which was a spear whose head weighed six hundred shekels of iron. The man was no doubt, the height of opposition to the independence of God" and served well as the proverbial "**manifestation of evil.**"[49]

Six in Hebrew scripture is considered a symbol for fallen and corrupted man, and as Gaskill points out, there are many references to the number six used to describe Goliath, which further establish him as a "manifestation of evil". (See Appendix 2 for the story of Samuel slaying Agag - also about the Atonement.)

- **Verse 11, "Never at any time have I shed the blood of man" – The Atonement**

When Nephi is constrained to kill Laban his heart responds that he has never "shed the blood of man". It would be safe to assume that neither had Phinehas or David before they slew their adversaries in acts which preserved Israel. As mentioned, if we regard these accounts as foreshadows of Christ's saving Atonement, then it is significant that Nephi also sheds blood. Let's consider for a moment longer what blood is a symbol of, and how it relates to the heart of Nephi's struggle to obey the Spirit's constraint.

Yom Kippur, the Day of Atonement, required blood to atone for Israel. Even as a lamb was sacrificed to provide Adam and Eve with coverings, or Abraham's covenant (Gen 15) was accomplished by the spilling of animal blood, so Jesus' blood shed in the garden and on the cross was also requisite. In Leviticus 17:11 we read:

For the life of the flesh [is] in the blood: and I have given it to you upon the altar to make an atonement for your souls: **for it [is] the blood [that] maketh an atonement for the soul.**

Commenting on this exchange of animal blood for the cleansing of sin, a contemporary theologian explains:

A blood sacrifice is required by the Lord for the issue of sin. Leviticus 17:11 agrees with the teaching in the B'rit Chadashah (Holy Covenant) in Hebrews 9:22: "Without the shedding of blood there is no remission." The substitutionary shedding of blood, the **"life-for-life"** principle, is **essential to the true "at-one-ment"** with the Lord God. The Levitical system of animal sacrifices, including the elaborate Yom Kippur ritual, was meant to foreshadow the true and abiding sacrifice of Yeshua as the means of our reconciliation with God. The Old Covenant provides a **shadow of the substance revealed** in the New Covenant. [50]

The sacrament reminds us that an obedient sacrifice is still required. As partakers of the New Covenant, the sacrament water we drink remains a symbol of His blood (Mat 26:28 – "this is my blood of the New Covenant"), pointing us backward to the "substance revealed" in Christ. In fact, if we were to graph how the blood of Old Covenant pointed forward, and how the blood of the New Covenant points back, it would produce a familiar pattern:

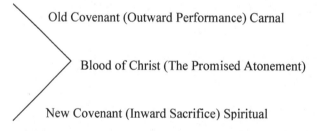

Old Covenant (Outward Performance) Carnal

Blood of Christ (The Promised Atonement)

New Covenant (Inward Sacrifice) Spiritual

This pattern of rebirth is also the pattern of Noah's dove, which we examined briefly on page 42 of this book. Its hinge-point is the blood of the promised Atonement, which was wrought by Christ's perfect obedience and love. In fact, exact obedience is what qualified Christ as the "one man" who was worthy to atone for all mankind. Exodus 12 is an excellent early example of how the blood of the Lamb has the power to save. Israel was told that their lives would be spared by placing the blood of a lamb on their door posts. Those that failed to obey God's direction suffered the consequences of their faithless disobedience – death. The lesson is applicable to Christ himself; if he had failed to submit fully to the will of his father, his blood would be powerless to deliver, and there would be no Atonement. Adam's disobedience, which brought death, is therefore reversed by Christ's obedience, which brings life (Rom 5). Just as obedience to the word of God was a focal point in the stories of Eden, Egypt, Nephi and Laban, and Gethsemane and the cross, it continues to determine whether we perish or prosper.

- **Obedience, sacrificial offering of a broken heart and contrite spirit**

King Benjamin also spoke about the sacrificial and "atoning blood of Christ," and its power to make us "saints through the Atonement." In Mosiah 3:18-19 we read, "Salvation was, and is, and is to come, in and through **the atoning blood of Christ**, the Lord Omnipotent. For the natural man is an enemy to God, and has been from the fall of Adam, and will be, forever and ever, unless **he yields to the enticings of the Holy Spirit,** and **putteth off the natural man** and becometh a saint **through the atonement of Christ** the Lord." In terms of Nephi's story, the "natural man" which needs to be "put off" (sacrificed) is the Laban in each one of us, which is done by obeying the "constraint (enticings) of the Spirit." Importantly, following the Spirit's guidance to do the Father's will, and not that of our own carnal nature, mirrors our personal offering to Christ's atoning sacrifice.[51]

As our atoning partner Christ has already experienced in Gethsemane and on the cross the trying and defining moments of our lives, and as the great high priest has promised to be with us in our hour of struggle with the natural man, which hour is a type of His atoning struggle. Though literal blood sacrifice is no longer required, its spiritual counterpart, laying our carnal nature upon the altar, is. Like King Benjamin, Paul also uses sacrificial imagery in Romans 12:1-2 to illustrate how we spiritually contend with the world. He reminds us to not be "conformed to this world" (the natural man), but rather to offer ourselves as "living sacrifices" (allusion to blood of the sacrificial Lamb). He then tells us how this is done, which is also very similar to what we just read from King Benjamin - to be "**transformed by the renewing** of your mind, that **ye may prove what [is] that good, and acceptable, and perfect, will of God.**" Paul contends that when our minds and hearts are "transformed" and renewed by the Holy Ghost (the only power able to change and transform us spiritually) we can know and act in concert (obediently) to "that good and acceptable, and perfect will of God." Paul calls this obedient response to the Spirit, "proving" God's perfect will. And doesn't it make sense, that when we follow the Spirit's voice (no matter the cost), and unite our will with the Father's, there is at-one-ment? (Importantly, the rest of Romans 12 summarizes how those with "one mind", who are "many members in one body" and "one body in Christ," will conduct their lives according to God's perfect will, serving and loving one another.)

Elsewhere, in Galatians 5, Paul outlines the fruits of the Spirit, such as love, joy, peace, meekness, as well as the elements of the flesh that contend with the Spirit, which are hatred, strife, murders, and drunkenness; all characteristics exhibited by Laban. Paul then (once again) uses an image of Christ's Atoning blood, personalizing its operation in our lives:

Gal 5:24 And they that are Christ's have **crucified the flesh with the affections and lusts**. 25 If we **live in the Spirit**, let us also walk in the Spirit.

Paul calls the process of crucifying (sacrificing) the flesh to - "live in the Spirit", which highlights the Holy Ghost's crucial role in overcoming the natural man.

Consequently, after his crucifixion, Christ also tells the inhabitants of the Americas about the new "offer for a sacrifice" which replaces the literal shedding of blood:

3 Ne 9:17 And as many as have received me, to them I have given to become the sons of God; and even so will I to as many as shall believe on my name, for behold, by me redemption cometh, and in me is the law of Moses fulfilled. 18 I am the light and the life of the world. I am Alpha and Omega, the beginning and the end. 19 And ye shall offer up unto me **no more the shedding of blood**; yea, your sacrifices and your burnt offerings shall be done away, for I will accept none of your sacrifices and your burnt offerings. 20 And **ye shall offer for a sacrifice unto me a broken heart and a contrite spirit**. And whoso cometh unto me with a broken heart and a contrite spirit, him will I baptize with fire and with the Holy Ghost

Verse 17's mention of the "law of Moses" is a reference to the Old Covenant and its preparatory ordinances of blood sacrifice which pointed forward to Christ. This instruction is also chiastic. Notice below how the Old Covenant is parallel to the New Covenant; outward and the inward symbols of His great sacrifice:

19 And ye shall **offer** up unto me no more **the shedding of blood**;
>> yea, your sacrifices and your burnt offerings
>>> shall be done away,
>>>> for I will accept none
>>> of your sacrifices and your burnt offerings.
20 And ye shall **offer** for a sacrifice unto me **a broken heart and a contrite spirit**.

Christ is quoting from Psalm 51:17, which indicates that the true symbolism of sacrifice was understood long before His coming (see also Alma 25:15). And if you are wondering exactly what it means to offer a broken heart and contrite spirit, Elder Neal Maxwell astutely explains: "So it is, that real, personal sacrifice never was placing an animal on the altar. Instead, it is a willingness **to put the animal in us** upon the altar and letting it be consumed! Such is the "sacrifice unto the Lord … of a **broken heart and a contrite spirit**."[52] Thus, Nephi's obedience (symbolically laying Laban on the altar) is a wonderful example of the sacrifice of a broken heart and a contrite spirit. In the New Testament, Peter calls this "obeying truth through the Spirit", or, "sanctification of the Spirit unto obedience and the sprinkling of the blood of Christ" (1 Pet 1:2,22).

- **Three Levels of Applying 1 Nephi 4**

As we have seen, there are multiple levels of meaning to be mined in the story of Nephi and Laban. Let's analyze what we have learned.

1. Outward Appearance of Story – Flesh and blood Nephi slays Laban, a bad man who has sought to kill him and his brothers. This is the Law of Moses level, or the "eye for an eye and tooth for a tooth". We might question – where is the lesson of the Atonement?
2. Type and Shadow – Nephi is a type of Christ who slays death (Laban), shrinking to drink the bitter cup, but nonetheless doing the Father's will.
3. Us as type of Christ – we are His type and must overcome sin\death by yielding to the "enticings of the Holy Spirit"; we must be an active participant in slaying the

Laban in us that would rob us of our seed and fruitfulness. As King Benjamin explains, this is how we "become saints through the Atonement."

If we choose to operate only on a Mosaic Law level, most of the preceding makes little sense. However, with spiritual eyes, Nephi's story rises to another stratum. The New Covenant, like its predecessor the law, still requires an obedient Christ-like offering. There are Labans, Goliaths, and Zimris that assail us, that would take our promised inheritance, and which must be slain. In this sense, Laban exists not outside of, but within each one of us. He is the darkness of the adversary that reaches into our hearts at times, keeping us from association with the Lord and the joyous and desirable fruit of his love.

4

Nephi's Atoning Chiasmus

How we respond, therefore, to God's word (in obedience or disobedience) indicates how effectively the Atonement is functioning in our lives. Indeed, God's word has the power to transform us if we act in faith and follow its instruction. In this regard, Nephi articulates his transformative experience with Laban in Jerusalem in a wonderful parallel pattern. Below is a condensed version of these parallelisms with just the main points:

5 By night, Nephi with his brothers

  7 Goes unto House of Laban

    8 Finds Laban

      9 Unsheathes Laban's sword

        10 *Spirit* constrains Nephi to slay Laban

          11 *Spirit* said – Lord **delivered Laban** into thy hands, **I also knew** he would not hearken unto the commandments of the Lord

            12 *Spirit* said – slay him, the Lord hath delivered him

              13 **Perish** – better for one man to perish than a nation to dwindle

              14 I heard the **word** (seed),

              14 I remembered the **words** (seed) which the Lord spake unto me

              14 **Prosper** in the land – inasmuch as they keep my commandments

            15 *I thought* – they could not keep commandments of Lord without the law

          16-17 *I knew* – the Lord **delivered Laban** into my hands, **I also knew** that they could not keep the commandments of the Lord without the law

        18 *I did obey* the voice of the Spirit, and smote off Laban's head

      19 Unclothes Laban

    20 Finds servant of Laban

  20 Goes into the treasury of Laban

22 By night, Laban was with elders

And, here are the actual verses, arranged in their chiastic form:

1 Nephi 4 – Constrained Three Times

A 5 And it was **by night**; and I caused that they should hide themselves without the walls. And after they had hid themselves, I, Nephi, crept into the city and went forth towards the house of **Laban**. 6 And I was led by the Spirit, not knowing beforehand the things which I should do.

B 7 Nevertheless I went forth, and as I came near **unto the house of Laban** I beheld a man, and he had fallen to the earth before me, for he was drunken with wine.

C 8 And when I came to him **I found that it was Laban**.

D 9 And I beheld **his sword,** and **I drew it forth from the sheath** thereof; and the hilt thereof was of pure gold, and the workmanship thereof was exceedingly fine, and I saw that the blade thereof was of the most precious steel.

E 10 And it came to pass that **I was constrained by the Spirit** that **I should kill Laban**; but I said in my heart: Never at any time have I shed the blood of man. And I shrunk and would that I might not slay him.

F 11 And the **Spirit said unto me again**: Behold the Lord hath **delivered him into thy hands**. Yea, and **I also knew that** he had sought to take away mine own life; yea, and he would **not hearken unto the commandments** of the Lord; and he also had taken away our property.

G 12 And it came to pass that **the Spirit said unto me again**: Slay him, for the Lord hath delivered him into thy hands;

H 13 Behold the Lord slayeth the wicked to bring forth his righteous purposes. It is better that one man should perish than that a nation **should dwindle and perish** in unbelief.

J 14 And now, when I, Nephi, had heard these **words,**

J I remembered the **words** of the Lord which he spake

H unto me in the wilderness, saying that: Inasmuch as thy seed shall keep my commandments, **they shall prosper** in the land of promise.

G 15 Yea, and **I also thought** that they could not keep the commandments of the Lord according to the law of Moses, save they should have the law.

F 16 And **I also knew** that the law was engraven upon the plates of brass.

17 And again, **I knew that** the Lord had **delivered Laban into my hands** for this cause— that I might obtain the records **according to his commandments.**

E 18 Therefore **I did obey the voice of the Spirit**, and took **Laban** by the hair of the head, and **I smote off his head** with his own sword.

D19 And after I had smitten off his head with **his own sword, I took the garments of Laban and put them upon** mine own body; yea, even every whit; and I did gird on his armor about my loins.

B 20 And after I had done this, I went forth **unto the treasury of Laban**.

C And as I went forth towards the treasury of Laban, behold, **I saw the servant of Laban** who had the keys of the treasury. And I commanded him in the voice of Laban, that he should go with me into the treasury.

A 21 And he supposed me to be his master, **Laban**, for he beheld the garments and also the sword girded about my loins. 22 And he spake unto me concerning the elders of the Jews, he knowing that his master, Laban, had been out **by night** among them.

Notice that the Spirit's constraints symmetrically align to Nephi's thought process – he thought, he knew, and he "did obey." As discussed previously, the *three* constraints are also reminiscent of Christ's three prayers in the garden, wherein he prays for strength to obey the Father's will. Fittingly, in the center-most parallel Nephi highlights God's word, by which his seed will either perish or prosper.

> J 14 And now, when I, Nephi, had heard these **words** (of the Spirit),
>
> J I remembered the **words** of the Lord which he spake

The Spirit's words spark a recollection, and it then occurs to Nephi that in order for his family to prosper they are going to need the scriptures, which contain the commandments (word of God). Remarkably, as Nephi contemplates the word's importance to his posterity, his personal obedience (to slay Laban) is simultaneously being tested by the words of the Spirit (a dynamic lesson on how God's word functions in combination with the Spirit). As we did with the blood in the last chapter, let's expand upon what the word signifies and how it operates.

We might start by again considering the Garden of Eden, which is an early example of God's word given to man, which served to test Adam and Eve. How they complied with God's instruction determined whether they prospered ("be fruitful and multiply") or perished ("thou shalt surely die"). Not that much has changed. As in Eden, we still have approved and forbidden choices – symbolized by the two trees. And like Adam and Eve, if we eat of the forbidden tree (what God has prohibited), the sentence is still death and spiritual separation. Because all have been tempted and failed to keep God's word, Jesus Christ was sent to atone for our disobedience and its consequences. However, in order to qualify as our Savior, even Jesus had to be proven by God's word. His submission and perfect obedience to his Father's will secured an eternity of prospering; and by his words, "not my will, but thine be done", death is conquered and man is set free. In this regard, though we can't fully comprehend the pain that Christ endured, all who follow Him, who have sacrificed their will to obey His word, participate in and grasp a deeper gratitude of His atoning sacrifice and love.

Another characteristic of the word is its strong relationship to faith. As we hear or remember what God has said, and exercise faith on it, we experience the transforming power of the

Atonement. In Romans 10:10, Paul tells us that "with the heart man believeth (has faith)", and then in verse 17 he tells us how this heart-felt faith begins.

> So then **faith** [cometh] by
> hearing,
> and hearing
> by the **word of God**.

Here Paul parallels faith to the word of God, connecting them by the experience of "hearing" (in our ears, and in our hearts). This close association is delightfully represented by Lehi's iron rod, where the word can take us to the tree of life only if we exercise faith in it. We need both to get there. In 2 Nephi 33:1, Nephi confirms Paul's teaching and also explains how the word gets from our ears to our hearts: "for when a man speaketh (the word) by the power of the Holy Ghost the power of the Holy Ghost carrieth it unto the hearts of the children of men."

This brings us to another important feature of the word, its close connection to the Spirit. Eph 6:17, for instance, tells us that we should arm ourselves with the "sword of the Spirit, which is the word of God". Similarly, in Jn 6:63 Jesus tells his disciples that, "the words that I speak to you are Spirit, and they are life." There is also an interesting verse in 1 Pet 1:23, which is chiastic:

> Being born again,
> not of corruptible seed,
> but of incorruptible, by the word God,
> which liveth and abideth for ever.

We know that we are not necessarily born again by the incorruptible word of God, but more precisely through the Spirit of God. (Jn 3:7-8, "Ye must be born again . . . born of the Spirit.") In the same way, the Spirit is coupled to the word when Christ tells his disciples that they are "clean through the word which I have spoken unto you" (Jn 15:3). Again, it isn't the word that cleanses, but the Hoy Ghost. For this reason, when we read in Hebrews 4:12 that the word is "quick (living) and powerful", we know that it is alive only because of the Spirit which testifies of its truth.

Truth communicated to our hearts **by the Holy Ghost** is what causes **faith** to grow, manifesting itself in **obedience** (obedience to the word demonstrates an active faith). By this standard, Nephi correctly designates "the word" as the multifaceted hinge upon which Nephi's struggle, and God's great plan, swings. All of these elements – the word, the Spirit, faith, obedience – work in concert to form the new creature in Christ (his seed). And ultimately, those who obey his truths ("thy word is truth", Jn 17:17) are those who love God. Christ tells his disciples in Jn 14:23, "If a man love me, he will keep my words," and in 1 Jn 5:3 we read, "For this is the love of God, that we keep his commandments." Indeed, God's word presents us with an opportunity – to act in faith, to experience his Spirit, to obey, and know the joy of His great love.

- **What transformed Nineveh? A word of change**

To help us better understand the word's transformative and restorative power; let's return briefly to the life of Jonah. As a figure of Christ's resurrection after three days in the tomb, Jonah emerges from the belly of the whale to deliver a life-changing "word" to Nineveh. It probably shouldn't surprise us too much that the Book of Jonah is also considered to be arranged chiastically. As a side note, we might again imagine that Nephi at some time read and perhaps studied its design:

A Jonah's commission (1:1-2)
  B Jonah vs. the LORD: Jonah's flight and the LORD's storm ("anger") (1:3-4)
    C Dialogue between sailors and Jonah: "fear" motif (1:5-13)
      D The sailors' prayer (1:14a)
        E The LORD's sovereign freedom (1:14b)
          F The sea ceased its raging ("anger") (1:15)
            G The men feared the LORD with a great fear (1:16)
              H LORD appoints great fish to change Jonah's mind (2:1-2)
                I Song of Jonah (2:3-10)
                  J Jonah's deliverance (2:11)
                    K Jonah delivers word of "change" (3:1-4)
                  J' Nineveh's repentance (3:5-7a)
                I' Decree of king of Nineveh (3:7b-9)
              H' God changed His mind (3:10)
            G' A great evil came to Jonah (4:1a)
          F' Jonah became angry (4:1b)
        E' The LORD's sovereign freedom (4:2)
      D' Jonah's prayer (4:3)
    C' Dialogue between the LORD and Jonah (4:4-9)
  B' The LORD vs. Jonah: the LORD's justification of His compassion (4:10-11)
A' Jonah/Israel's response needed (implied) [53]

At the center (K) is the divine promise that Jonah prophesies to Nineveh, and it is upon this "word" Nineveh will prosper or perish. What did Jonah say to Nineveh, or what seed could he possibly have planted that it would produce such a powerful result? (While looking at this verse, keep in mind that Jonah in the Hebrew means "dove", which as we previously discussed is the sign of the Holy Ghost):

3:4 And Jonah began to enter into the city a day's journey, and he cried, and said, Yet forty days (*three* days in the Septuagint)**, and Nineveh shall be overthrown.**

Surprisingly, this abbreviated message is the extent of Jonah's preaching. However, there is more here than meets the eye. In the Hebrew the word for overthrown is *haphak*, which means:

הָפַךְ *to turn, to convert, to change,* Ps. 105:25; followed by לְ *into something,* Psal. 66:6; 105:29; 114:8; Jerem. 31:13. Intrans. (like No. 1) *to be changed,* followed by an acc., into something. Lev. 13:3, שֵׂעָר בַּנֶּגַע הָפַךְ לָבָן

54

There are many other verbs that Jonah could have used had his only intent been to declare destruction on Nineveh (such as *abad* or *shamad*). For broader context, this same Hebrew word which Jonah delivered is also used to describe what happened to the Nile when Moses "changed" or "transformed" the water to blood (Ex 7:20). Most especially, it is used by Samuel when telling Saul of his spiritual rebirth - "And the Spirit of the Lord will come upon thee, and thou shalt prophecy with them and [you] shalt be turned (*haphak*) into another man." (1 Sam 10:6) By using the ambiguous word *haphak*, Jonah's prophecy is guaranteed to be accurate. Indeed there will be change, one way or another, physical or spiritual, good or bad. By the brevity of the word which Jonah delivered, we also know that Nineveh's decision to repent could not have been based on an intellectual argument. Rather, its decision to repent, and the miraculous and wonderful transformation\change which occurred, could only be attributed to the power of the Holy Ghost; the gentle movement of the dove, the Spirit of God, Jonah. The people of Nineveh felt Jonah's message swell within their hearts, exercised a particle of faith, and the seed of his word took root

(Alma 32). Alma perfectly describes how this process happens, which is by the restorative and illuminating power of the word:

Alma 5: 7, 12-14, 26

7 Behold, he **changed** their hearts; yea, he awakened them out of a deep sleep, and they awoke unto God. Behold, they were in the midst of darkness; nevertheless, **their souls were illuminated by the light of the everlasting word**; yea, they were encircled about by the bands of death, and the chains of hell, and an everlasting destruction did await them. 12 And **according to his faith** there was **a mighty change** wrought in his heart. Behold I say unto you that this is all true.

13 And behold, he preached **the word** unto your fathers, and **a mighty change** was also wrought in their hearts, and they humbled themselves and put their trust in the true and living God. And behold, they were faithful until the end; therefore they were saved. 14 And now behold, I ask of you, my brethren of the church, have ye spiritually been born of God? Have ye received his image in your countenances? Have ye experienced this **mighty change** in your hearts? 26 And now behold, I say unto you, my brethren, if ye have experienced a **change** of heart, and if ye have **felt to sing the song of redeeming love, I would ask, can ye feel so now**?

If you are like me, these have to be some of your favorite verses in the Book of Mormon. They are majestic, and somehow I am transformed by just reading them! Though we don't know all the details, this "mighty change of heart" is what also happened to those in Nineveh. And though we may not have considered it before, in some way, because they allowed their darkened souls to be "illuminated by the light of the everlasting word", they experienced this transformation, were spiritually born of God, and felt to sing the song of redeeming love! Indeed, Nineveh comes to the tree of life and tastes its delicious fruit. I know what you are thinking - really, Nineveh? We might imagine that at some point the fullness of the gospel message was preached to Nineveh, but even if it wasn't, the story of its mighty transformation (overthrowing) preserves for us an example of how powerful even a small portion of God's word is. And even though we know that Nineveh's conversion over time faded as pride crept back into people's lives, it does not negate their initial miraculous "change".

Without a doubt, the capacity of the Atonement to produce fruit and transform lives depends first on all men hearing "the word." We might also ponder Christ's supernal faith in Gethsemane, supported by God's word. In the garden, on whose words did Christ reflect? When the angel came to comfort him, what words did he speak? We might guess that they were Jehovah's own promises spoken in the wilderness to righteous patriarchs and the many prophets throughout the ages, harkening back to the preexistence. Were they not the words of the Father, whose covenant plan of mercy Christ came to fulfill? Were they just as delicious and joyous to His soul as they were to Nephi's, or yours and mine? Sustained by wonderful and powerful promises, preserved in holy and ancient words, Christ faithfully drank the bitter cup and performed the promised Atonement.

As Alma aptly exclaimed, "Behold, how many thousands of our brethren has he loosed from the pains of hell; and they are brought to sing redeeming love, and **this because of the *power of his word*** *which is in us*, therefore have we not great reason to rejoice?" (Alma 26:13) Is there anything more powerful than God's word!

- **Feasting and Enduring**

Nephi's final thoughts recorded in 2 Nephi perhaps take on new meaning in light of his emphasis on "the word" as a central component of the Atonement. In 2 Nephi 31 we read of the "doctrine of Christ":

19 And now, my beloved brethren, after ye have gotten into this strait and narrow path, I would ask if all is done? Behold, I say unto you, Nay; **for ye have not come thus far save it were by the word of Christ** with unshaken **faith** in him, relying wholly upon the merits of him who is mighty to save. 20 Wherefore, ye must press forward with a steadfastness in Christ, having a perfect brightness of hope, and a love of God and of all men. Wherefore, **if ye shall press forward, feasting upon the word of Christ**, and endure to the end, behold, thus saith the Father: **Ye shall have eternal life.** 21 And now, behold, my beloved brethren, this is the way; and **there is none other way nor**

name given under heaven whereby man can be saved in the kingdom of God. And now, behold, **this is the doctrine of Christ**, and the only and true doctrine of the Father, and of the Son, and of the Holy Ghost, which is one God, without end. Amen.

The "straight and narrow path" which begins these verses is a reference to baptism, and Nephi asserts that only by the "word of Christ" does one come that far. But Nephi also contends that it is by thereafter continually feasting on the word that man maintains his bright hope, unshaken faith, love for God and man, and is saved and gains eternal life. Indeed, this "doctrine of Christ" prescribes what Nineveh needed to do for permanent change, but over the long haul failed to remember. (For more on the Doctrine of Christ see pages 211-212.)

"Feasting upon the word" also reminds us of what we studied earlier, the word's close association to the Spirit. Significantly, when one feasts on the word he\she is filled with not just the word, but the Holy Ghost. "Feasting on the word" also alludes to the renewal of sacrament covenants; figuratively partaking Christ's flesh and drinking his blood in remembrance of his atoning sacrifice. As previously discussed (pg 46), long before the last supper Jesus first spoke of his flesh and blood as important nourishment on which his disciples needed to feast (Jn 6:54-56). At that time Christ called himself the bread of life, and compared his flesh and blood to his words, saying "unto you [they] are Spirit, and [they] are life." This comparison (of his word to the Spirit) is the great lesson of the Bread of Life sermon, which is subsequently communicated in our sacrament prayer. As we partake of the sacrament each week and take his name upon us, we promise to obey **his word** or "commandments which he has given them", that in so doing we will "have **his Spirit**." To feast upon and follow the covenant words of Christ, we keep the Spirit in our lives.

Finally, let's take a look at D&C 84:45-46 concerning the pivotal nature of the word in our lives. "For you shall live by every word that proceedeth forth from the mouth of God. For the word of the Lord is truth, and whatsoever is truth is light, and whatsoever is light is Spirit, even the Spirit of Jesus Christ." The following equation is clearly understood:

$$\text{The word} = \text{truth} = \text{light} = \text{the Spirit}$$

5

Nephi and Zoram - In the tomb

Because the sword anciently was a symbol of authority, when Nephi takes his vanquished enemy's sword, he also symbolically takes the power of his defeated adversary.[55] Earthly kingdoms, such as the one that Laban administrated, were usually obtained and maintained by use of the sword. However, Christ's kingdom, which will "overthrow" all such worldly principalities, will do so by means of the sword of his word - the measure by which all people will be judged. In a spiritual sense, because the sword is also a symbol of the word (Eph 6:17, "the sword of the Spirit, which is the word of God"), when Nephi takes possession of Laban's sword, he notably takes control of the words (seeds) to be planted in the hearts of his people, preparing them for divine judgment. (And as discussed, David's taking of Goliath's sword represents the same thing; by it he will teach, rule, and judge Israel.)

As a type of Christ, and to complete the victory over sin and death, Nephi must also be clothed for a time in death's (Laban's) raiment, "even every whit" (verse 19). It is odd that Nephi tells us "every whit" unless he wants to emphasize how totally Nephi becomes as Laban. I am reminded again of Paul's words in 2 Cor 2:5, "For he hath made him [to be] sin for us, who knew no sin; that we might be made the righteousness of God in him." Though we might contend that Christ did not necessarily "become sin", the point remains that he was a total sin offering, "every whit".

So that we might be "clothed in garments of salvation and robes of righteousness" (Isa 61:10), Christ will fully experience what every mortal man does, which is to put on death. We are reminded in Heb 4:15 that in so doing Christ became "the great high priest after the order of Melchizedek" (King of Righteousness), who was "touched with the feelings of our infirmities .... on all points" (every whit). During those three days in the tomb we are told that Jesus "went and preached to those spirits in prison" to deliver his seed from the chains of death (1 Pet 3:19). In the story of Nephi and Laban we also find an element similar to death's prison, which is represented by Laban's treasury. Likewise, as we will examine, the name of the servant with the key to the prison is appropriately named Zoram. In 1 Nephi 4 we read:

20 And after I had done this, I went forth unto the treasury of Laban. And as I went forth towards the treasury of Laban, behold, I saw the servant of Laban who had the keys of the treasury. And I commanded him in the voice of Laban, that he should go with me into the treasury. 21 And he supposed me to be his master, Laban, for he beheld the garments and also the sword girded about my loins. 22 And he spake unto me concerning the elders of the Jews, he knowing that his master, Laban, had been out by night among them. 23 And I spake unto him as if it had been Laban. 24 And I also spake unto him that I should carry the engravings, which were upon the plates of brass, to my elder brethren, who were without the walls. 25 And I also bade him that he should follow me. 26 And he, supposing that I spake of the brethren of the church, and that I was truly that Laban whom I had slain, wherefore he did follow me.

Just as knowing the Hebrew meaning of Laban helps us to better understand the first part of Nephi's story, so the Hebrew meaning of Zoram's name will open new windows of understanding. It has been suggested that Zoram is a cognate of the Hebrew verb *zara,* meaning to scatter or sow seed.[56] In the Hebrew lexicon there is a protracted definition of this verb along with a lengthy list of related words from this root.[57] For instance; zera is the noun for seed, zaraq means to sprinkle or scatter, zirmah means flow of seed, zaram means to pour out rain, zarach means to scatter the rays of sunlight, zarah means to scatter, winnow, disperse (seed, people), and zerem means a powerful rain (rain drops scattered like seed). Hugh Nibley suggests the meaning of Zoram to be from this last cognate – Zerem. "The name Zoram is again one of those desert names. It's from the eastern half of Manasseh. It means a welcome, refreshing, powerful rain."[58] However, the underlying association of all these words, including Zerem, remains rooted in the basic concept of sowing or scattering seed. Though there is no way at present to be absolutely sure that Zoram's name means seed, Nephi's storyline strongly supports that this is the case.

Again you may ask, why it is important for Zoram's name to have any extra meaning? The answer once more is that it was the Jewish custom of Nephi's day, and a measure of the "learning of the Jew" which one would expect to find if Nephi's writing is ancient. Thus, the fact that we can identify highly likely Hebrew cognates for Zoram as they relate to the story is very exciting and hints at its comparative antiquity. You might also ask - how would Zoram's parents know before hand what to name their son? A possible explanation might be found in a Jewish midrash where we read: "The ancients, because they could avail themselves of the Holy Spirit, named themselves in reference to forthcoming events…" (Genesis Rabbah on Genesis 10:25).[59] With names that looked to the future, inspired ancient parents created the means whereby scripture purposed to foreshadow Christ and his divine attributes could be produced.

As a figure of Christ who suffered the Father's will in Gethsemane and the Cross, Nephi now goes to the treasury to gather his seed; the seed of the word (the brass plates), and Zoram (the covenant seed of posterity). Both are equally important, and as Nephi was reminded by the Spirit in Jerusalem, if one perishes so does the other (4:14).

- **God's Treasury**

It is perhaps a misnomer to call the place where the dead go "spirit prison." We might contemplate that God's greatest treasure is his seed wherever it is found, still in mortality or passed on and waiting to be called forth in the resurrection. Since most people in the world live and die without hearing the gospel, we should expect that God's treasury of those waiting to accept the gospel message is large and immensely valuable. Sensing that Zoram represents more than a single individual, others have accurately nuanced Zoram the "people's proxy"[60], which would be especially accurate in light of the likely meaning of his name and its application in the context of Nephi's story. In Mosiah 15 there is a scripture that becomes particularly interesting when set against the figurative backdrop of Nephi's recruitment of Zoram (parenthesis mine):

10 And now I say unto you, who shall declare his generation? Behold, I say unto you, that **when his soul has been made an offering** for sin **he shall see his seed**. And now what say ye? **And who shall be his seed?** 11 Behold I say unto you, that whosoever has heard the **words (seed)** of the prophets, yea, all the holy prophets who have prophesied concerning the coming of the Lord—I say unto you, that all those who have hearkened unto their **words** (planted their seed**)**, and believed that the Lord would redeem his people, and have looked forward to that day for a remission of their sins, I say unto you, that **these are his seed**, or they are the heirs of the kingdom of God. 12 For these are they whose sins he has borne; these are they for whom he has died, to redeem them from their transgressions. **And now, are they not his seed?**

Alluding to Isaiah 53:10, the prophet Abinadai confirms that, "when his soul has been made an offering for sin, **he shall see his seed**." This of course is what Christ does while in the tomb, which is to visit the spirit world (1 Pet 3:19), but it is also a figure of what Nephi does when he visits the treasury and offers covenant promises to Zoram (seed). Likewise, Abinadai also ties together the two kinds of seed; of the word and of posterity (whosoever hears and hearkens to the word, these are his seed, vs 11).

As further evidence that Zoram's name means seed, in Alma 32, which is Alma's sermon about the seed of the word that grows into a tree of life, Alma is addressing the rebellious Zoramites who are of course Zoram's descendants! In this sermon Alma uses the word "seed" 17 times, more times than any other chapter in the Book of Mormon (sermon includes Alma 33:1) Alma, it seems, has chosen the most poignant metaphor and word-play with which to teach the Zoramites, especially so if "seed" is also the meaning of their name!

- **Tension – Life and Death, verses 28-29**

After Nephi slays Laban, the first person to be confused by Nephi dressed in Laban's clothes is Zoram, who follows Nephi (life) falsely believing he is Laban (death). We have discussed that Zoram is a characterization of the scattered seed that Christ (Nephi) has come to release from prison (the treasury). It makes sense that those in prison only know spiritual death, or at least they are confused and seem willing to follow what they are accustomed to. This confusion is precisely the reason that most are in prison, because in ignorance (not having as yet heard the words of Christ) they are still willing to follow sin and death! Nephi (Christ) will lead them out of prison, instruct them, and covenant with them (vs 32-35) before returning with them to the dwelling place (tent/tabernacle) of his father.

Conversely, when Nephi, dressed as Laban, is seen by his brothers, they flee. As Zoram's heart was confused, so are Nephi's brothers'. Remember that these are the same brothers that feared because Laban could "command fifty and slay fifty" (3:31). But now we might ask, where are all those soldiers? Isn't Laban, without an army, walking right into their hands? Weren't their words, "How is it possible that the Lord will deliver Laban into our hands?"(3:31). Also, since they don't yet know what has happened to Nephi, where is their worry for him? In effect, Laban (Nephi dressed as Laban) has been delivered into their hands just as surely as he was earlier to Nephi (vs 7-8).

Can you imagine their surprise and joy if they had remembered the angel's promise (word) and hurried to subdue who they thought was Laban, only to discover that it was their brother Nephi? Many esteem Christ in the same way as the brothers outside the wall, the wrong way, relying on worldly vision, confused by what their eyes see or think they see (sight is not faith). Our spiritual vision becomes clear only as we act in obedience, out of love (the tree of life) and not fear (the mixed seed\fruit of Satan's tree). Putting Nephi's boldness and Laman and Lemuel's fear into perspective, John tells us that the love of God is perfected by obedience (1 Jn 2:5), and that perfect love gives us boldness (1 Jn 4:17), and "casteth out fear" (1 Jn 4:18). A vibrant spiritual life is possible only to those who "fear not" and obey.

- **Covenant Seed**

In verse 31 Nephi's large stature is emphasized as Zoram attempts to flee. Others have suggested that by accomplishing this feat of obtaining the plates, Nephi attains kingly status,[61] because in the Hebrew tradition most kings were big in physical stature. For instance, Saul the first king of Israel was a head taller than the rest of the men of Israel (1Sam 9:2). However, in Nephi's case, it is actually his regal word (seed) that calms and convinces Zoram, not his imposing physical presence:

32 And it came to pass that I spake with him, that if he would hearken unto my words, as the Lord liveth, and as I live, even so if he would hearken unto our words, we would spare his life.

There is a short chiasmus in this verse. My comments are in parenthesis:

I spake with him

    If he would hearken unto my words

        As the Lord liveth

        As I Live

    If he would hearken to our words

We would spare his life (what I spake)

Notice that a promise of life is found betwixt the dual phrase "hearken unto my\our words". Also notice that Nephi, speaking in first person at the apex/center, is definitely identifying (or paralleling) his life with the Lord's, each reflecting the other (as the Lord live, as I live)! Such a comparison, Nephi as the Lord's proxy, further adds to the possibility that he has purposefully written this entire account with himself typified as Christ. Also, notice that the first and last legs reflect the thought that Zoram's (seed) life would be spared by the words that Nephi (as a type of Christ) spoke. (Again, this is an exact chiastic reflection of what Christ told his disciples in John 6:63, that His "word is life".) If you think about it, this chiasmus is also a repetition of what the Spirit told Nephi when it constrained him to slay Laban, which is that his seed would not perish, but prosper if they kept the commandments (hearkened to the word).

- **Covenant brings peace**

Finally, in verses 33-36 Nephi takes an oath, Zoram is calmed and also pledges an oath. These verses have been noted by many to exemplify the Lord's pattern for covenant making. The Lord (Nephi as type of the Lord) puts forth the covenant unilaterally, with its associated promises, and we (Zoram, God's treasured seed) covenant in return to obey in expectation of fulfilled promises. This reflects the ancient Near-Eastern king and vassal covenant pattern where; 1. the great king identifies himself (Nephi, the Lord), 2. an outline of promises by king and obligations by treaty partner (obey commandments, go down into wilderness), 3. consequences or stipulations (if he hearkens life is spared, he is a free man, has place with their father), 4. covenant is ratified (Zoram takes an oath as a sign or token of the covenant, and they return to the tent of the father).[62] We are not told there was a feast, which is usually associated with ratification of treaty or covenant, but we can perhaps assume there was a great feast as Lehi is "filled with joy" upon their return:

33 And I spake unto him, even with an oath, that he need not fear; that he should be a free man like unto us if he would go down in the wilderness with us. 34 And I also spake unto him, saying: Surely the Lord hath commanded us to do this thing; and shall we not be diligent in keeping the commandments of the Lord? Therefore, if thou wilt go down into the wilderness to my father thou shalt have place with us. 35 And it came to pass that Zoram did take courage at the words which I spake. Now Zoram was the name of the servant; and he promised that he would go down into the wilderness unto our father. Yea, and he also made an oath unto us that he would tarry with us from that time forth.

Verse 37 tells us that after the covenant has been made, their "fears did cease". Resolving their differences is important, for only love can abide where God is, and Lehi in this narration is a figure of God the Father, to who's tent (tabernacle in Hebrew) they all return — the treasured seed and word preserved, all covenant promises performed and administered by Nephi (Christ), the giver and fulfiller of the covenant.

- **More chiastic evidence that Zoram means seed**

There is also another way to estimate the meaning of Zoram's name. Below is a diagram of how the meaning of Zoram's name is likely confirmed by the sequential parallels of Nephi's book-wide chiastic structure:

Chapter 4 Great Feat - Nephi in faith struggles to slay Laban and get plates
   Ch 4 Zoram (seed) collected
      Ch 5 Lehi searches plates – "the genealogy of his fathers"

 Ch 11 Tree of Life

Chapter 18 Great Feat – Nephi in faith struggles on the ship to lead family to Promised Land
   Ch 19 Plant seeds (Zera) in promised land
      Ch 19 Nephi makes new plates – "the genealogy of his fathers"

After Nephi's struggle with Laban, we first encounter Zoram (seed), with whom Nephi makes a covenant. In parallel (1 Ne 18), again right after Nephi has struggled with his brothers to cross the great waters, we find Nephi planting seeds (zera) in the Promised Land.[63] In addition, right after each of these great feats in chapters 4 and 18, we also read the parallel accounts of metal plates which Nephi is keeping, or preparing to keep. In Nephi's writing the exact phrase, "the genealogy of his fathers", is only used in these two distant, though parallel, instances; 1Ne 5:14-16, and 1Ne 19:2! Because all of the other parallels surrounding Zoram (1 Ne 4-5) and seed (1 Ne 18-19) sync up so well, it is very possible that there is also a connection in meaning.

Digressing for just a moment, we also find another Hebraism here which testifies that Nephi's record is ancient. Consider the word in Hebrew for genealogy, which is *yachas*. From the Lexicon we read:

יַחַשׂ m. a word of the silver age, A RACE, A FAMILY. Found once Neh. 7:5, סֵפֶר הַיַּחַשׂ *pedigree, genealogy* (Chald. יְחַס is used in the Targums for Heb. מִשְׁפָּחָה and תּוֹלְדוֹת. Simonis also compares اِخَاس *nature, origin;* but this word properly signifies *brass*, i. q. נְחֹשֶׁת and the phrase كَرِيم النّكَاس of a liberal and generous disposition, is figurative, and properly signifies *of fine brass*). Hence there is formed a denom. verb in —

HITHPAEL הִתְיַחַשׂ *to cause one's name to be recorded in genealogical tables,* ἀπογράφεσθαι, *to be enrolled,* 1 Chron. 5:1, 7, 17; 9:1; Neh. 7:5. Inf. הִתְיַחֵשׂ is often used as a noun, and signifies *register, table of genealogy,* 1 Ch. 7:5, 7, 9, 40; 2 Ch. 31:16, 17; 2 Ch. 12:15, "the acts of Rehoboam — are recorded in the commentaries of Shemaiah — לְהִתְיַחֵשׂ so that the particulars are related in the manner of a genealogical table."

[64]

If we wonder why the plates were made of brass, this explanation provides us with a perfect understanding. We discover here that genealogical records were engraved on brass, and because of this, the word to describe a genealogy was derived from the Hebrew word for brass! Anciently speaking, the most accurate way for Lehi and Nephi to depict the "genealogy" of their fathers, was to describe them as plates of brass, which were one in the same! In addition, notice that in the case of Rehoboam (above), his genealogy in brass also included his acts "recorded in a commentary", which sounds like what Nephi is doing. The Greek word used in this definition, $\dot{\alpha}\pi o\gamma\rho\dot{\alpha}\phi\epsilon\sigma\theta\alpha\iota$, means "to engrave upon", which is also how Nephi many times tells us they wrote on their brass plates (1Ne 3:3,12,24; 1Ne 5:10; 1Ne 19:1).

6

1 Nephi Chapter 5 – More Chiastic Emphasis on Seed

While Nephi and his brothers are in Jerusalem, Nephi's parents have anxiously waited in the wilderness. Their worry, which turns to prophetic celebration, is recorded in Chapter 5, which chapter is also a chiasmus, the apex of which again emphasizes seed – "that he might preserve Jacob (seed) and all his household from perishing with famine (of the word)." Filled with the Spirit, Lehi in 1 Ne 5 commemorates Joseph's family's preservation from famine, comparing it to his own family's obtaining God's word in Jerusalem. Such a figurative interpretation of famine is attested in Amos 8:11, "Behold, the days come, saith the Lord GOD, that I will send a famine in the land, not a famine of bread, nor a thirst for water, but of hearing the words (seed) of the LORD." Joseph's provision of bread in Egypt is also a shadow of Christ, who will come in a later time of famine, offering the seed of truth, his word, to a hungry world. Let's take a look at the chiastic structure found in 1 Ne 5 and then discuss its immense value.

A 5 I have obtained a **land of promise**

   B 5 **Bring them** (seed,word) down to us **in the wilderness**

      C 6 to **obtain the record** (seed) of the Jew (seed)

         D 8-9 I know that **the Lord hath commanded** my husband to flee into the wilderness, protected my sons, delivered then out of the hands of Laban (death), that they might **accomplish** the thing (word) **the Lord has commanded them**

            E 10 Lehi took the record upon **the plates of brass** (word,seed) and searched from **the beginning**

               F 11-12 They **(plates of brass)** contain an account of the creation, and Adam and Eve **(seed)**, first parents; and also a record of the Jews, even down to Zedekiah, king of Judah (**people of his seed**);

                  G 13 And also the **prophecies** of the holy prophets to Zedekiah; and also many prophecies spoken by **Jeremiah**

                    H 14   a. Lehi also found a **genealogy** of his **Fathers**,
                             b. **descendent of Joseph,**
                               c. son of **Jacob**
                                  d. **sold into Egypt** (life),
                                    e. **who** was **preserved**
                                      f. **by** hand of the **Lord** that he might
                                        g. **preserve** his father Jacob

                                    Vs 14 and all his **household** (seed) from perishing with **famine** (seed of the word)

                                    g. They were **led out of captivity**
                                  d. **out of the Land of Egypt** (death)
                                f. **by** that same **God**
                              e. **who** had **preserved them.**
                         c. And **Laban** was a
                     b. **descendent of Joseph,** wherefore
                 H 15-16 a. he and his **fathers** had kept the **records**

                  G 17 **My father** was filled with the spirit and began to **prophesy** concerning his seed

               F 18 That these **plates of brass** (word,seed) should go forth unto all nations, kindreds, tongues, and **people, who were of his seed**

            E 19 these **brass plates** should never perish, neither be **dimmed by time**

         D 20 I and my father **kept the commandments** (word) wherewith the **Lord had commanded us**

      C 21 We had **obtained the records** (seed) which the Lord commanded

   B 22 That we **should carry them** (word) with us as we journey **in the wilderness**

A 22 Towards **the Land of Promise** (fruitfulness)

88

As we observed previously, by analyzing the mirrored legs of the chiasmus, further insight into the writer's thinking is often gleaned. For instance, verse 13 reflects verse 17, wherein Nephi compares his father Lehi to the prophets that had prophesied up to Zedekiah and Jeremiah! And lest we wonder if Nephi is aware of Laban's symbolic significance, he has placed historical Jacob (vs 14) parallel to Laban (vs 16), perhaps playing on the antithetical sense of their biblical relationship in Genesis, which makes our estimation of who/what Laban represents in chapter 4 all the more tenable.

Egypt is also used in parallel, reprising the tension that was a theme in the story of Laban and Nephi, which is that one must perish in order to prosper. Though slightly out of place, flanking the apex on either side, Egypt first represents saving life during the time of Joseph, but will later become a representation of death and captivity from which Israel must be redeemed! If you recall, Joseph who saves his family into Egypt, and Moses who saves Jacob's descendents out of Egypt, is also a part of Stephen's parallelistic articulation in Acts 7:9-16. (On page 40 of this book we see that Stephen also frames the apex of his chiasmus with Egypt.)

Most importantly, at the apex Lehi draws upon the story of Joseph who was divinely fore-sent into Egypt and "preserved by the hand of the Lord" so that his father's seed could be saved from famine (a lack of seed, bread). Similarly, God's foreknowledge is also evident in Nephi's going into Jerusalem, which was equally divinely appointed by the Lord and pre-purposed to avert a drought of the word in Lehi's group. In fact, as told to Nephi at the apex of 1 Ne 4, their seed would perish in unbelief without it. As previously mentioned, this is the second time that Lehi has read a book, this time the brass plates, which has filled him with the Spirit. In this case it is specifically the story of Joseph, a patriarch whose story in so many ways prefigures Christ.

As told by one author, "Consider the majesty of Joseph's deliverance. He saved Israel from physical death, and *will* save Israel from spiritual death. In overcoming the two deaths, the beloved son of Israel is in similitude of the Beloved Son of the Father. This deep similitude is but the last in a life that was in nearly every respect parallel to the Master's. As the chosen instrument of temporal and spiritual deliverance, Joseph's path of preparation points in striking similitude to the path of paths – the solitary way of the Savior of all."[65] In the Spirit, Lehi likewise seems to be well aware how the story of Joseph into Egypt is a portrayal of their plan of salvation.

- **A Sacrament Emblem - Bread**

In Genesis, Joseph prepares the granaries with seed (bread) that saves Israel, and later in Exodus, Israel is saved again by manna or bread in the wilderness. As the antitype (fulfillment) of these events, when Christ comes he proclaims that He is the Bread of Life which fed the Israelites in the wilderness (Jn 6:48-51). He also breaks bread as an emblem of his new covenant and commands his disciples to eat in remembrance of him. As we shall see, Nephi is using the focus of this chapter, an allusion to Joseph's bread, to express the first sacrament emblem. And, as evidence that this is his intent, in the chiasmus parallel to this chapter (1 Ne 17), Nephi will construct a chiasmus which wonderfully centers its focus on Moses' striking the rock to bring forth water - the other emblem of the sacrament! Think of it — 600 years before Christ, Nephi had an astonishing understanding of the sacrament's meaning, structuring his writing so as to emphasize and pay tribute to its symbolic and covenant importance.

Just as the bread and water miraculously preserved ancient Israel, as modern Israel, if we understand its significance and to whose sacrifice it points, the bread and water of the sacrament will also save us!

Note: To see Nephi's parallel chiasmus you will need to go to chapter 11 of this book, which examines 1 Ne 17. However, I would recommend that you don't rush ahead.

7

1 Nephi 7 – Ishmael's Seed Recovered

Let's next turn our attention to 1 Nephi 7. The brothers return to Jerusalem one last time with the same purpose as the first, to secure seed. Only on this occasion it is seed of another variety, the household of Ishmael, and especially his daughters, without which they would surely perish as a nation. Ultimately, both trips to Jerusalem are important to their survival, but we might observe that preservation of physical posterity is done after safeguarding the word has been accomplished, indicating that Abraham's physical seed is little if nothing without the word (seed), its spiritual counterpart. Nephi begins chapter 7:

> 7:1 AND now I would that ye might know, that after my father, Lehi, had made an end of prophesying concerning his **seed,** it came to pass that **the Lord spake** unto him again, saying that it was not meet for him, Lehi, that he should take his family into the wilderness alone; but that his sons should take daughters to wife, that they **might raise up seed** unto the Lord in the land of promise.

Remarkably, the general character of chapter 7 follows the pattern of Nephi's first journey into Jerusalem, which we have already identified as one of type. It also follows the general pattern of other stories; Lehi's voyage to the new world and the wilderness journey to Bountiful. Consider the following elements from 1 Nephi 7 that are clearly parallel to Nephi's first journey into Jerusalem:

They leave from the tent of father Lehi.

Their mission is from the Lord

Their task is to secure seed

They go to a house, this time Ishmael's

The older brothers rebel

Nephi exhorts his brothers – instead of "let us go up" *three* times, uses "have ye forgotten" *three* times

Emphasis on remembering the word (seed) at climax of the story

The Spirit of the Lord constrains Nephi in each account.

Nephi physically suffers, is afflicted – instead of being beaten is bound

Nephi is miraculously delivered – not by angel, but he speaks the word and his bands are loosed

Similar to Zoram's covenant, rebels ask forgiveness and receive it

Peace restored

Return to the tent of father Lehi

And of course, Nephi has constructed this chapter as a chiasmus to highlight the events of this story. Below is chapter 7's chiastic form (condensed to fit on page), followed by my observations:

A 1 Lord speaks to **father Lehi** to raise up seed in land of promise

  B 2 Lord commands that **I Nephi and my brethren** bring **down Ishmael** and his family

    C 4 *Came to pass* that Nephi and brethren go to Ishmael's household and **speak words of the Lord to them**

      D 5 *Came to pass* the Lord **did soften the heart** of **Ishmael** and also **his household**

       E 5 *Came to pass* that we journeyed **in the wilderness**

        F 6 *Came to pass* that **Laman and Lemuel**, Ishmael's 2 daughters and sons **did rebel** against us

         G 7 *Came to pass* that they were desirous to **return to the land of Jerusalem**

          H 8 Being grieved for **the hardness of there hearts** I spake unto **them:** **Behold ye** are mine elder brethren, and how is it that **ye** are so hard in your hearts and so blind in your minds, and **ye** have need that your younger brother should speak unto **you** and set an example

           I 9 How is it that ye have not hearkened unto **the word of the *Lord*?**

            J 10 **How is it ye have forgotten** that ye have seen an angel of the *Lord*?

             K 11 Yea and how is it that ye have forgotten what *great things* the Lord hath done for us,

             K in *delivering us out of the hands of Laban*, and also that we should obtain the record (word)?

            J 12 Yea and **how is it that ye have forgotten** that the *Lord* is able to do all things according to his will, for the children of men, if it so be that they exercise faith in him?

           I 13 If it be so that we are faithful, we shall obtain the land of promise; and ye shall know at some future period that **the word of the *Lord*** shall be fulfilled concerning the destruction of Jerusalem

          H 14 For **behold the Spirit ceaseth to strive** with **them, they** have rejected the prophets, and Jeremiah **they** cast in prison, and **they** sought to kill my father, insomuch that **they** have driven him out of the land

         G 15 Behold I say unto you that if ye **return unto Jerusalem** ye shall also perish

        F 16 *Came to pass* **my brethren** were **angry** with me, and did lay there hands on me, and they did bind me with cords, for they sought to take away my life

       E 16 *Came to pass* that they sought to leave me **in the wilderness** to be devoured

    C 18 *Came to pass* that when I has **said these words**, the bands were loosed, I stood before my brethren and **spake unto them** again.

      D 19 *Came to pass*, that the mother, a daughter, and one of the sons of **Ishmael** (his household) did plead, they **did soften their hearts;** and they did cease striving 20 They were sorrowful 21and I did forgive them

A 22 We did come down unto the tent of our **father**

  B And after **I and my brethren** and all the house of **Ishmael** had come **down,** they did give thanks

Apex, Verse 11 - It's curious that in a chapter about the gathering of Ishmael's daughters for seed, Nephi's centermost thoughts return to the obtaining of the word from Jerusalem. Not forgotten by Nephi, and important to his chapter-wide chiasmus, is Nephi's emphasis on their deliverance from Laban, celebrating his act of obedience to the Spirit's constraint, a happening that is given equal importance to the obtaining the plates (word) - "delivering us out of the hands of Laban, and also that we should obtain the record." As we will see, Nephi's placement of Laban at the apex of this chiasmus forms an essential and enlightened witness to the parallel apex found in 1 Ne 16 (covered in chapter 10 of this book)!

Verses 10,11,12 - Notice the *three* uses of the question at the center of this chapter - "Have ye forgotten?" In ancient literary terms this repeated pattern of three is called a cycloid, which device Nephi uses many times. It is a reminder of what occurred earlier at the center of Nephi's chiasmus in 1 Ne 4, when he was constrained three times by the Spirit. However, here Nephi plays the role of the Spirit and is the one constraining three times, just as he was constrained. Nephi's intent is certainly the same as was the Spirit's, which is that his brother's should slay the anger and rebellious desires within themselves which continually resisted the word of the Lord - the sin and death that corrupts their souls and the leprosy of Laban within. In fact, they have become no better than Laban and seek Nephi's life (vs 16), even as Laban sought theirs in Jerusalem!

Verses 7 and 15 (G) - Further emphasizing the pull between the carnal and spiritual man, verse 7 tells us that members of Ishmael's household desire to return to Jerusalem. The verse that parallels this desire is verse 15, where Nephi is constrained by the Spirit to tell them that they will perish if they do return to Jerusalem, a worldly place whose apostate inhabitants are spiritually dead. Unfortunately, such a place is where members of Ishmael's family, as well as Laman and Lemuel, feel most acclimated; enjoying the pleasures of the world. Nephi constrains that to return is certain death, and assuredly, Babylon does destroy Jerusalem and carry her inhabitants away into captivity (2 Ki 25). Comparatively, spiritual death will do even worse, slaying and taking captive their immortal souls. Coincidently, in chapter 16 Laman and Lemuel will again want to return to Jerusalem. The rebellious sentiment and phrase, "desire to return unto Jerusalem" is mentioned in only these two parallel chapters of 1 Nephi!

Verses 8 and 14 (H) - Nephi uses the adjoining parallel verses, 8 and 14, to continue comparing his brothers to those in Jerusalem. In verse 8 he outlines his brothers' behavior, addressing them with "**ye**" before each point – "how is it that *ye* are so hard in your hearts, and so blind in your minds, that *ye* have need of that I, your younger brother, should speak to you, yea, and set an example for you? How is it that *ye* have not hearkened unto the word of the Lord?" Its parallel, verse 14, compares the wicked of Jerusalem, using the same device only repeating "they" with each point made – "For behold the Spirit of the Lord ceaseth soon to strive with them; for behold, *they* have rejected the prophets, and Jeremiah have *they* cast into prison. And *they* have sought to take away the life of my father." We quickly recognize that Laman and Lemuel, as well as the those in Ishmael's family, point for point (ye for they) are doing the same things to Nephi as those without the Spirit in Jerusalem have done to the prophets – they have rejected Nephi, they bind him (type of prison), and they seek to take away his life, contemplating leaving him to be devoured by wild beasts (vs 16). (Curiously, the phrase "wild beasts" is used only twice by Nephi. The other use is found in chapter 16, the parallel chapter to this chapter!)

Verses 4 and 17-18 (C) - Finally, let's look at a unique and fascinating parallel. Notice that in verse 4 Nephi "speaks the word of the Lord" to Ishmael and his **heart is softened**. This thought is parallel to verses 17-18 where Nephi has prayed for strength to "**burst these bands** from which I am bound". He notes that after he "had said these **words**", that the "bands were loosed from off my hands and feet." Nephi again does something amazing by comparing the power of the word to soften Ishmael's heart, to the word's power to physically and miraculously burst his bonds. Certainly the spiritual implication is that we all are bound with bonds of sin by our carnal and self-centered desires. The power to accomplish the spiritual feat of breaking free from the chains of sin and death comes via the sanctifying and cleansing power of the Holy Ghost, whose power is felt through God's word.

- **Ishmael**

In 1 Ne 7 we encounter a new character, Ishmael. Since the name of Ishmael is biblical we can easily ascertain its basic meaning and historical precedent, and therefore assess with some accuracy how Nephi might interweave it into his story. The Hebrew meaning of Ishmael's name is "God will hear".[67] If you recall, the Old Testament Ishmael was Abraham's son through Hagar, and was cast out on the day Isaac was weaned because he laughed at (mocked) his brother, which God, as well as Sarah, heard, even as his name predicted. We might ponder if the Ishmael of the Book of Mormon also had at some point mocked Lehi for his visions and prophesying. As mentioned, Ishmael heart appears to have initially been hard, needing to be softened by the Lord before he would go with Nephi. Further, as happens so often in the wilderness, members of Ishmael's household align with Laman and Lemuel, rebel and want to return to Jerusalem, which, as we have also discussed, is a representation of those spiritually asleep.

Thus, out of a *physical* necessity, Ishmael's household is recruited. Initially they had been left behind with the likes of Laban. We might naturally wonder why, if they were equipped spiritually, they didn't go with Lehi in the first place? If you recall, Nephi's uncle Laban has all of the attributes of the biblical uncle Laban in Genesis - both Labans seeking to steal from and kill their nephews. Is it possible that Lehi's Ishmael is also a depiction of the biblical Ishmael of Genesis? If this is the case, then how might this relate to Nephi's story? Nephi has done it once with Laban, and in a narration so full of parallels it is not hard to imagine that he will do it again (use the Book of Mormon Ishmael as a figure or type). Though not readily apparent in this chapter, Nephi will make his intentions regarding Ishmael clearer when Ishmael and his daughters are mentioned again, which of course is the chiasmus parallel to this chapter, 1 Ne 16. And, as Laban is the center-most focus of this chapter, Ishmael will be the focus in chapter 16. Ishmael's meaning, now concealed, will be revealed. You can always skip to that section for those parallels, but before Nephi's record takes us there he has other delights for us to consider.

Chapter 8 – Lehi's Vision of Tree of Life
The Olive Tree – Chapter 10

Immediately before his own vision (in chapters 11-14), Nephi relates the words of his father concerning two trees, the tree of life (chapter 8) and the olive tree (chapter 10). Upon his return (chapter 15), Nephi finds his brothers still talking about these two trees. All of which might lead us to wonder, how long did Nephi's vision last? It certainly couldn't have been too long if he returns to find Laman and Lemuel still in discussion on the same subject. Regardless, this prolonged conversation by his brothers conveniently helps to preserve Nephi's chiastic narration! Below is a diagram of this chiastic series of events, in which trees (and fruit) are intriguingly a center of discussion:

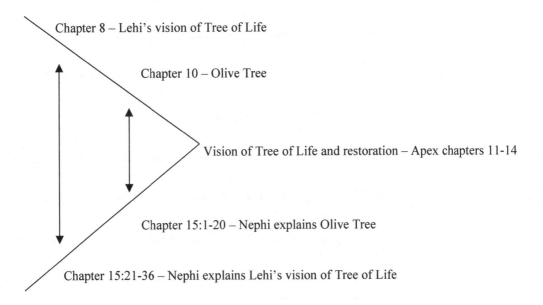

Based on the many other chiasmi we have discussed, we might wonder if either Lehi's vision in chapter 8, and its explanation in chapter 15:23-36 are chiastic? Let's start with Lehi's vision from chapter 8 and then look at its parallel in chapter 15:

Lehi's Vision of the Tree of Life – 1 Nephi 8

A 2 It came to pass that while **my father** tarried in the wilderness, he spake saying, I have **dreamed a dream**

  B 3 I have reason to rejoice because of Nephi and Sam, I have reason to suppose that they will **be saved**

    C 4 But Laman and Lemuel, I fear **exceedingly** because of you; for behold I saw in my dream a dark and dreary wilderness

      D 5 I saw a man in white robe, he came and **stood** before me

        E 6 Bade me to **follow him**

          F 7 **Dark and dreary** waste

           G 9 **Large and spacious field**

          H 11 I did **go forth**

            I 10 I beheld a **tree**, with fruit to make one happy

              J 11 White to **exceed all white**, sweet, 12 filled with joy, desirable

                K 13 **River** of water, it **ran along**

                  L 14 **Head** thereof

                    M 14 I beheld your mother **Sariah, Sam, Nephi**

                      N 15 I beckoned with my voice, **come unto me**

                        O and partake of the **fruit**

                          which was desirable

                        O above all other **fruit**

                      N 16 They did **come unto me** and partake

                    M 17 I was desirous that **Laman and Lemuel** should come

                  L 17 wherefore, I cast my eyes to **head** of the river

                K 19 I beheld a rod of iron, and it **extended along** the bank of the **river**

            G 20 It led unto a **large and spacious field**, as if it had been a world

          H 21 I saw people **pressing forward**

            I 21 That they might obtain the path to **the tree**

              J 23 A mist of darkness arose, **exceedingly great mist of darkness**

         F 24 Others caught hold of the iron of in the **mist of darkness**

        E 24 Clinging to the **rod of iron** (following it) until they did come unto the tree and partake

      D 26 And I beheld a great and spacious building; and it **stood** in the air, high above the earth

    C 27 And it was filled with people, their manner of dress was **exceedingly** fair, they were mocking, pointing fingers at those partaking of the fruit

  B 28 And after they tasted they were ashamed, and fell into forbidden paths and **were lost**

A 29 And now I, Nephi, do not speak all the words (**dream**) of **my father.**

There are several very interesting parallels in Lehi's chiasmus, many of them juxtapositions.

B,B' Lehi antithetically parallels Nephi and Sam, who would be **saved** (B), to those who fall into forbidden paths and are **lost** (B').

C,C' Lehi refers to his sons Laman and Lemuel almost as if they are the cause of the dark and dreary wilderness (C). Notice that Laman and Lemuel are parallel to "the people" that are mocking in the spacious building.

D,D' The great and spacious building which stood in the air is antithetically parallel to the man in white (Christ) who stood before Lehi.

E,E' Following the man in white is parallel to clinging to the iron rod!

J,J' Nephi, who is recording his father's dream, astonishingly juxtapositions the exceeding whiteness of the tree of life to the exceeding great mists of darkness which arose! This affect wonderfully builds tension between these opposites. In J, verse 12, Nephi partakes and is filled with great joy. In contrast, in J', verse 23, instead of joy, because of the mists of darkness, people lose their way and wander off and are lost.

M,.M' Sariah, Sam, and Nephi are juxtapositioned to Laman and Lemuel.

O,O' The center of Lehi's vision tells us that the fruit is "desirable above all other fruit". When Nephi has his vision of the tree of life in chapter 11, he describes the same thing at the apex of his chiasmus, that the fruit was "most desirable above all things" (11:22)!

If we consider the centers of Lehi and Nephi's (see next chapter) dreams we find that both have seed; Nephi's center has "the children of men" while Lehi's center has his family; Sariah, Sam, Nephi, Laman, and Lemuel. Both visions describe the fruit as desirable, and both describe "partaking" the fruit. However, Nephi never actually tells us that this (partaking) is what he is doing. Filled with the love of God, he simply describes how it tastes to his soul.

Next let's look at the chiastic parallel to Lehi's vision of the tree of life. In 1 Nephi 15:21-25 Laman and Lemuel ask Nephi the meaning the tree of life and the iron rod. However, verses 26-36 contain Nephi's explanation of a river of water which his father almost failed to notice during his vision because his mind was "swallowed up in other things." Wonderfully, Nephi's explanation to his brothers is chiastic, also possessing a parallel which clarifies the thing upon which Lehi's mind was focused. You will notice that this chiasmus represents the antithesis of Lehi's tree of life, the awful hell prepared for the wicked.

A 26 And **they said unto me**: What meaneth the river of water which our father saw?

B 27 And I said unto them that the water which my father saw was filthiness; and so much was **his mind swallowed up in other things** (the fruit of tree of life) that he beheld not the filthiness of the water. 28 And I said unto them

C that it was an awful gulf, which **separated the wicked**

D from the **tree of life**, and also from **the saints of God**.

E 29 And I said unto them that it was a **representation of that awful hell**, which **the angel** said unto me was **prepared for the** wicked. 30 And I said unto them that our father also saw

F that **the justice** of God

G did **also divide the wicked**

H from **the righteous**;

I and the brightness thereof was like unto the brightness of a flaming fire, which **ascendeth up unto God** forever and ever, and hath no end.

31 And they said unto me: Doth this thing mean the torment of the body in the **days** of **probation**,

or doth it mean **the** final state of the soul after the death of **the temporal body**,

or doth it speak of the **things which are temporal**?

32 And it came to pass that I said unto them

J that it was a representation of **things both temporal and spiritual**;

for the day should come that they must be judged of their works,

yea, even the works which were done by **the temporal body**

in their **days** of **probation.**

G' **33** Wherefore, if they should die in their **wickedness** they must **be cast off also**,

H' as to the things which are spiritual, which are **pertaining to righteousness**;

I' wherefore, they must be brought to **stand before God**, to be judged of their works; and if their works have been filthiness

they **must needs be filthy**;

and if they **be filthy**

it must needs be that **they cannot dwell** in the kingdom of God;

If so, the kingdom of God

must **be filthy** also.

J' 34 But behold, I say unto you,

the kingdom of God

is **not filthy**,

and there **cannot any unclean thing enter** into the kingdom of God;

wherefore there **must needs be** a place of **filthiness** prepared for that which is **filthy.**

E' 35 And there is a place **prepared**, yea, even that **awful hell** of which I have spoken, and **the devil** is the **preparator** of it; wherefore the final state of the souls of men is to dwell in the kingdom of God, or to be **cast out** because of

F that **justice** of which I have spoken.

C' Wherefore, the **wicked are rejected**

D' from **the righteous**, and also from **that tree of life**,

B' whose fruit is most precious and most desirable above all other fruits; yea, and it is the greatest of all the gifts of God. (this thought swallowed up Lehi's mind)

A And thus **I spake unto my brethren.** Amen.

Opposed to the tree of life, which we are told in 1 Ne 11 represents the "fount of living waters" (as well as the love of God), the river of filthy waters represents death or "that awful hell." We can assume that the source of this polluted river is from the forbidden tree, of which Satan is the well-spring. In addition, consider some of the other parallels:

I, I' These parallels tell us that the wicked (I') will "stand before God" to be judged, and that the fire of hell will "ascend unto God" for ever and ever (I) because of their filthy works. There is imagery here that parallels the tree of life – a fiery brightness which is reminiscent of the "exceeding" beauty and whiteness of the tree of life, (1Ne 11) and the eternal nature of this fiery torment, which is parallel to the eternal life given to those who partake of the fruit of the tree of life and drink from its living waters.

J, J' These are the two centermost individual chiasmi. The first (J) is an explanation concerning the spiritual and temporal torments of hell, whereas it's parallel (J') is about the kingdom of God (its antithesis), which is also temporal and spiritual. At the center of each of these small chiasmi is the apex "I said unto them" (J) and "I said unto you" (J'). This is very similar to the center of Nephi's vision of the tree of life, which is the title of this book, "he spake unto me." However, what is spoken here by Nephi to his brothers is not desirable or joyful, but it's opposite – the torment of the soul.

B, B' Verse 27 tells us that Lehi failed to notice that the river of water was filthy because his mind was "swallowed up" in other things. It's parallel (B') provides the cause of Lehi's mind distraction; because it was focused on the tree of life, "whose fruit is most precious and most desirable above all other fruits," and the greatest gift of God. The joy that Lehi experienced in is heart at that time is antithetical to the bitterness of the fruit of the forbidden tree, which he later explains in 2 Ne 2:15.

- **Olive Tree Parallel, Chapter 10 and Chapter 15:1-20**

Chapter 10 begins with Nephi telling his readers that his father has just finished relating his dream of the Tree of Life, after which he continues narrating new revelatory information. Lehi prophesies that; Babylon will carry Jerusalem away captive (vs 3), that a Messiah will be raised up among the Jews (vs 4), that a prophet will precede the Messiah (vs 7-8), that he will be baptized in Bethabara (vs 10), that he will be slain and resurrect (vs 11), and that Israel will be scattered like the broken branches of an olive-tree to later be gathered along with the Gentiles (vs 11-15). Nephi then tells us of his own desire to "see, hear, and know of these things" (vs 17). It is while Nephi is pondering his father's words that he too is carried away in the Spirit and his personal vision of the tree of life begins. Nephi's vision will include not just the tree of life, but the other elements of Lehi's prophesying as well, such as the scattering and gathering of Israel. In addition, Nephi will receive more detail concerning the Messiah, along with more information concerning the events leading up to the restoration; e.g. Columbus, the pilgrims, and the revolutionary war. It is no wonder that Nephi is able to explain fully the meaning the olive-tree upon his return. The explanation he provides his brothers in chapter 15 comes directly from the high mountain and the throne of God.

Marvelously, there are also large chiasmi in 1 Nephi 10 and in 1 Nephi 15:1-20 which reflect each other. Let's first look at the olive tree chiasmus found in chapter 10, and then its parallel in chapter 15:

A 1 AND now I, Nephi, proceed to give an account upon these plates of my proceedings, and my reign and ministry; wherefore, to proceed with mine account, **I must speak somewhat** of **the things** of my father, and also of my brethren. 2 For behold, it came to pass after my father had made an end of speaking the words of his dream, and also of exhorting them to all diligence, he spake unto them concerning the Jews—

B 3 That after **they should be destroyed**, even that great city Jerusalem, and many be **carried away** captive into Babylon,

C according to the **own due time** of the Lord, they should **return again, yea, even be brought back out** of captivity; and after they should be **brought back out of captivity they should possess again** the land of their inheritance. 4 Yea, even six hundred years from the time that my father left Jerusalem, a prophet would the Lord God raise up among the Jews—even a Messiah, or, in other words, a Savior of the world. 5 And he also spake concerning the prophets, how great a number had testified of these things, concerning this Messiah, of whom he had spoken, or this Redeemer of the world.

D 6 Wherefore, all **man**kind were in a lost and in **a fallen state**, and ever would be save they should rely on this Redeemer.

E 7 And he spake also concerning a prophet who should come before the Messiah, to **prepare the way** of the Lord— 8 Yea, even he should go forth and cry in the wilderness: Prepare ye the way of the Lord, and **make his paths straight**; for there standeth one among you whom ye know not; and he is mightier than I, whose shoe's latchet I am not worthy to unloose.

F And much spake **my father concerning this thing**. 9 And my father said he should baptize in Bethabara, beyond Jordan; and he also said he should **baptize with water**; even that he should baptize the **Messiah** with water. 10 And after he had baptized the Messiah with water, he should behold and bear record that he had baptized the Lamb of God, who **should take away** the sins of the world.

G 11 And it came to pass **after my father** had spoken these words he **spake unto my brethren** concerning the gospel which should be preached among the Jews, and also concerning the dwindling of the Jews in unbelief.

H And after they had slain **the Messiah**, who should **come**, and after he had been slain he should rise from the dead, and should make himself manifest, by the Holy Ghost, unto the Gentiles.

I Yea, even my father spake much concerning the **Gentiles**,

J and also concerning the **house of Israel**, that they **should be**

K compared like unto an **olive-tree**,

L whose branches **should be broken off**

M and should be **scattered** upon **all the face of the earth**.

13 Wherefore, he said it must needs be that we should be led

N with one accord into the land of promise, unto the fulfilling of **the word** of the Lord,

M' that we should be **scattered** upon **all the face of the earth**.

L' 14 And after the house of Israel **should be scattered** they should be gathered together again; or, in fine,

I' after the **Gentiles** had received the fulness of the Gospel,

K' the natural branches of the **olive-tree**,

J' or the remnants of the **house of Israel**, **should be** grafted in, or

H **come** to the knowledge of the **true Messiah**, their Lord and their Redeemer.

G' 15 And **after** this manner of language did **my father** prophesy and **speak unto my brethren**, and also many more things which I do not write in this book; for I have written as many of them as were expedient for me in mine other book. 16 And all these things, of which I have spoken, were done as my father dwelt in a tent, in the valley of Lemuel.

F' 17 And it came to pass after I, Nephi, having heard all the words of **my father, concerning** the **things** which he saw in a vision, and also the things which he spake by the power of **the Holy Ghost**, which power he received by faith on the **Son of God**—and the Son of God was **the Messiah** who should come—I, Nephi, was desirous also that I might see, and hear, and know of these things, by the power of the Holy Ghost, which is the gift of God unto all those who diligently seek him, as well in times of old as in the time that **he should manifest** himself unto the children of men.

E' 18 For he is the same yesterday, to-day, and forever; and **the way** is **prepared** for all men from the foundation of the world, if it so be that they **repent** and come unto him.

C' 19 For he that diligently seeketh shall find; and the mysteries of God shall be unfolded unto them, by the power of the Holy Ghost, as well in these **times as in times of old**, and as well **in times** of old as **in times** to come; **wherefore, the course of the Lord is one eternal round.**

D' 20 Therefore remember, O **man**, for all thy doings thou shalt be brought into **judgment** (fallen state).

B' 21 Wherefore, if ye have sought to do wickedly in the days of your probation, then ye are found unclean before the judgment-seat of God; and no unclean thing can dwell with God; wherefore, ye must be **cast off forever** (carried away).

A' 22 And the Holy Ghost giveth authority that **I should speak these things**, and deny them not.

Based on Nephi's consistent pattern, once again we find the "word" of God as the central focus of this chiasmus, which prophesies the scattering and gathering of Israel and the grafting-in of the Gentiles. Though the center-most parallels are fairly apparent, the outer parallels contain some very interesting revelations:

C – C'

In verse 3, Nephi relates Lehi's words concerning Jerusalem being destroyed, the Jews being carried away captive, and their eventual returning to possess again their land of inheritance. If you notice this is a complete circuit. The parallel to this verse is verse 19, wherein we find the famous quote by Nephi that the course of the Lord is one eternal round (a complete circuit). To the inside of these parallel verses, moving toward the apex, is an explanation of how this circular pattern occurs, pointing to verse 13, wherein we are told that through the "fulfilling of the word of the Lord" (that a Messiah should come) we are able to return (go round) to the promised land.

Further confirming this circular idea, there is a small poetic pattern common to verses 3 and 19. Poetically called an anabasis, in verse 3 we find:

> they should **return again**,
>
>> Even be **brought back out** of captivity
>>
>> and after they be **brought back** out of captivity
>
> they should **possess again** the land of inheritance

And it's parallel in verse 19

>> as well as in these **times**
>>
>>> as in **times of old**
>>>
>>> and as well as in **times of old**
>>
>> as in **times** to come;

If we had ever wondered about the meaning of Nephi's words in verse 19, that by the power of the Holy Ghost the mysteries of God are unfolded, and consequently that "the course of the Lord is one eternal round", then by means of a little literary analysis our understanding is wonderfully amplified.

E – E'

Also parallels, E and E' (verses 7 and 18) tell us that "a way is prepared", and that by repentance man can return, or rather, make the round back to the Lord – collectively, as in Israel's case, or in our individual lives.

F – F'

Though we may not have noticed it before, Lehi's parable of the olive tree is structured like his vision of the tree of life from 1 Ne 11. Obviously both structures narrow their focus to a tree. Further, one must be affiliated with the tree, be it the tree of life or the olive tree, if they desire to be preserved. The alternative, in the case of the tree of life, is to "fall away" or "wander off" and be lost, and in the case of the olive tree is to be "cast off" forever. However, in Nephi's vision of the tree of life there is another marked similarity to the account of the olive tree. In 1

Ne 11 on either side of Nephi's Apex is the parallel question, "knowest thou the condescension of God", wherein Nephi first sees Christ's birth, and then its parallel, where he beholds Christ's second birth or baptism. In the account of the olive tree we have something similar, which are parallel verses which discuss aspects of the Messiah's condescension. In verses 9-10 (F) we find another small poetic form which, like the tree of life, also recounts Christ's baptism:

> he should **baptize** in Bethabara, beyond Jordan;
> > and he also said he should **baptize with water**;
> > > even that he should **baptize the Messiah** with water.
> > 10 And after he had **baptized the Messiah** with water,
> he should behold and bear record that he had **baptized** the Lamb of God,

It's parallel, F' (verse 17), tells us of the power which a person receives when baptized, which is the Holy Ghost. Nephi makes it clear that by this "gift of God" the Messiah is manifest, even in vision.

> the things which he **saw in a vision**,
> > and also the **things** which he spake by the **power of the Holy Ghost**,
> > > which power he received by faith on the **Son of God**—
> > > and the **Son of God** was **the Messiah** who should come—
> > I, Nephi, was desirous also that I might see, and hear, and know of these **things**, by the **power of the Holy Ghost**,
>
> which is the gift of God unto all those who diligently seek him, as well in times of old as in the time that **he should manifest** himself

Thus we find the manifestation of the earthly Messiah and his baptism (or rebirth) on either side of the olive tree, just as we found it in Nephi's vision of the tree of life (1 Ne 11). Is it possible to draw any conclusions from these structural similarities? Is Nephi suggesting that the tree of life is an olive tree, that both are representations of Christ, to whom we must come, or be grafted into, in order to be saved?[68]

- **Chapter 15**

Wonderfully, chapter 15, the parallel to chapter 10, has a chiasmus (though smaller), which is also about the olive tree, which also narrows its focus to the same treasured thought – "the things (words) which Lord hath said." Did we imagine that it could be otherwise.

A 4 And now I, Nephi, was grieved because of the hardness of their hearts, and also, because of the things which I had seen, and knew they must unavoidably come to pass because of the great wickedness of **the children of men**.
  B 5 And it came to pass that I was overcome because of my afflictions, for I considered that mine afflictions were great above all, because of **the destruction of my people**, for I had beheld their fall. 6 And it came to pass that after I had received strength I spake unto my brethren, desiring to know of them the cause of their disputations.
    C 7 And they said: Behold, we cannot understand **the words which our father hath spoken concerning** the **natural branches**
      D of the **olive-tree**, and also concerning **the Gentiles**.
        E 8 And I said unto them: Have ye inquired of **the Lord?** 9 And they said unto me:
          F We have not; for the Lord **maketh no such thing known** unto us. 10 Behold, **I said unto them**:
            G How is it that ye do **not keep the commandments** of the Lord?
              H How is it that **ye will perish**, because of the
                I **hardness of your hearts**?
                  J 11 Do ye not remember **the things (words)**
                  J which the Lord hath said (words)? —
                I' If ye will not **harden your hearts**,
              H' and ask me in faith, believing that **ye shall receive**,
            G' with diligence in **keeping my commandments**,
          F' surely these **things shall be made known** unto you. 12 Behold I say unto **you**
        D' that the **house of Israel** was compared unto **an olive-tree**, by
        E' the Spirit of **the Lord** which was in our father;

      C' **and behold** are we not broken off from the house of Israel, and are we not **a branch** of the house of Israel? 13 And now, the **thing which our father meaneth concerning the** grafting in of the **natural branches** through the fulness of the Gentiles,
  B' is, that in the latter days, when **our seed shall have dwindled in unbelief**, yea, for the space of many years, and many generations after the Messiah shall be manifested in body
A' unto **the children of men**, then shall the fulness of the gospel of the Messiah come unto the Gentiles, and from the Gentiles unto the remnant of our seed—

Many of the parallels near the center of these verses are antithetical (D,F,G,H). And though not as extensive as the chiastic structure of chapter 10, we do see all of the same elements represented; e.g. the olive tree, "fallen" man and a fallen people, a manifestation of the Messiah, natural branches, the house of Israel, and the gentiles. In addition, Nephi admonishes his brothers to keep the commandments and not harden their hearts.

9

1 Nephi 11 - Revelation of Seed through Chiasmus

69

Mircea Eliade talks of the "symbolism of the Centre," and mankind's intense desire to grasp the essential reality of the world and his origin. The center is where the God of religion, first created humankind and the world. In symbolic language the center is imagined as the cosmic axis, or Axis Mundi, or the Tree of Life.[70]

In her book called "Thinking in Circles", Mary Douglas, the English anthropologist who wrote about ring composition (chiasmus) in ancient literature, addresses how we cannot know the chiastic author's meaning without understanding his structure:

It sounds simple, but, paradoxically, ring composition is extremely difficult for Westerners to recognize. To me this is mysterious. Apparently, when Western scholars perceive the text to be muddled and class the authors as simpletons it is because they do not recognize the unfamiliar method of construction. Friends ask me, what does it matter? **Why is it important to know the construction**? This leads to another point: **in ring composition the meaning is located in the middle. A reader who reads a ring as if it were a straight linear composition will miss the meaning. Surely that matters!**[71]

As we have arrived at Nephi's middle we might ask, what is it that "surely matters" most to him? Nephi's book-wide center is a vision of the tree of life, which Nephi ultimately learns is a "representation of the love of God". Unquestionably Nephi could not have captured a grander thought than this upon which to centerpiece his composition. In addition, the appearance of the tree of life also turns our minds from Nephi's middle to reflect on Genesis, the beginning, and the tree of life found there. We might ponder how Nephi's tree of life, which is a representation of the love of God, can be applied to the story of Eden. It is not hard to understand that when Adam and Eve fell they were cut off from the tree of life and separated from the "love of God". Further, we might also move forward to the end of the Bible, in Revelation, where John sees the tree of life beside God's throne. Here we become aware that the redeemed are reunited with the tree of life and are once again immersed in the "love of God." That mankind will not perish, but ultimately return and prosper in God's presence, is the pattern of resurrection from death unto life.

Thus, the tree of life, placed at the fulcrum of Nephi's book, is a powerful symbol which sends us back to the beginning as well as forward to the end. In fact, the preface to Nephi's dream, which is found in the last verses of chapter 10:19, reads – "and the mysteries of God shall be unfolded unto them, **by the power of the Holy Ghost**, as well **in these times as in times of old, and as well in times of old as in times to come**; wherefore, the course of the Lord is **one eternal round**." Nephi then sees these aforementioned mysteries in a vision - the tree of life (chapter 11) accompanied by an arch of unfolding events until the end of the world (chapters 12-14)! Together with the brass plates, Nephi's vision gives him a complete picture of the world from "times of old" to "times to come"; the beginning to the end; one eternal round moving around a center, which Nephi tells us is the "most desirable above all things", and "the most joyous to the soul", who is Jesus Christ (the Tree of Life).

- **Chiasmus within Chiasmus – Chapter 11**

Upon examination, Nephi has composed his center, chapters 11-14, as a double chiasmus, with two complimentary apexes (see the macrostructure illustration on page 13). We might also expect this dual center to accentuate the other foci that we have previously examined, which are the seed of the word and the seed of temporal posterity. We will first look at the chiasmus in chapter 11, and then its parallel, chapters 12-14. As the epicenter of his writing we will find the concentrated quintessence of Nephi's thinking, repeated twice for our benefit. Below is a condensed version of this first chiasmus, with my notes in parenthesis:

A 1 I was caught up into **exceeding high** mountain – (Temple of God)

   B 2 -5 Spirit said unto me what **desirest? Believest thou** that **thy father saw the tree?** Thou knowest I belief.

      C 6 The **Spirit rejoices**: Hosanna to the Lord, the most high God. **Blessed** art thou because thou believest in the Son of the most high God, thou shall behold the things thou desirest.

         D 7 And behold this thing will be unto thee for a sign; ye **shall bear witness that it is the Son of God**

            E 8 Spirit said: Look! And **I beheld a tree**, the beauty thereof exceeding all beauty, the whiteness thereof exceeding the **whiteness of the driven snow**

               F 9 I said unto the Spirit: **I beheld** that **thou hast shown me the tree** which is precious above all.

            G 12 **Spirit** of Lord – **I saw him not,** for he had **gone** from my presence

               H 13 And I looked and beheld the **great** city of Jerusalem, and also other cities, and Nazareth.

                  I 14 The **heavens open** and an **angel came down** and stood before me

                     J 16 Knowest thou **the condescension of God**?

                        K 17 And I said: I know that he loveth his children. 18 And he said unto me: Behold the virgin whom thou seest is the mother of the Son of God, after the manner of the flesh. 19 And it came to pass that I beheld that she was carried away in **the Spirit**; 20 And I looked and beheld the virgin again, bearing a child in her arms. 21 And the angel said to me, behold **the Lamb of God**, yea even the Son of the Eternal Father!

                        L 21 Knowest thou the **meaning of the tree**?

                           M 22 And I answered him: It is the **love of God** which **sheds abroad** in the hearts of **the children of men (seed).**

                              O 23 wherefore, it is **the most desirable** above all things
                              And he spake unto me saying
                              O 23 yea, and **the most joyous** to the soul

                           M 24 I beheld the **Son of God** (love) **going forth** among **the children of men (seed);** and I saw many fall down and worship him.

                        L 25 And I beheld that the rod of iron, which my father had seen, was the word of God, which led to the fountain of living waters, or to the tree of life; which waters are a representation of the love of God; and I also beheld that **the tree of life was a representation of the love of God.**

                     J 26 Behold **the condescension of God!**

                        K 27 And I looked and beheld the Redeemer of the world, and the prophet who should prepare the way before him. And **the Lamb of God** went forth and was baptized of him; and after he was baptized I beheld the heavens open, and **the Holy Ghost** come down out of heaven and abide upon him in the form of a dove.

                  H 28 And I beheld that he went forth ministering unto the people in power and **great** glory. And I beheld that **they cast him out.** (Nazareth is where Christ was cast out).

               G 29 The twelve following are **taken away** in **the Spirit** from before my face**, I saw them not.**

                  I 30 And I looked and beheld the **heavens open** again and **angels descending** upon the children of men

            E 31-32 And **I looked and beheld the Lamb (white)** of God going forth healing the sick, afflicted and diseased. The angel spake and showed all these things to me. And he was taken by the people.

         D 32 yea, the **Son of God** was judged of the world; and **I saw and bear record**

               F 33 And **I, Nephi, saw** that **he was lifted up upon the cross** and slain for the sins of the world.

   B 34-35 And the multitude of the earth were in a large and spacious building, which **my father saw**

A 36 I saw that the spacious building was pride of the world, whose fall was **exceeding great** (Temple of Pride)

      C 36 The **Angel warns**: Thus shall be the **destruction** of all nations that fight against the Lamb.

As an aid I have provided a side by side comparison of Nephi's chiastic parallels in a format that is perhaps easier to follow. The events are paraphrased, and I have also added brief commentary in parenthesis:

1 Mountain – Temple of God	34-36 Spacious Building – Worldly Temple
1 **Exceedingly high**	34-36 Fell, and the **fall was exceedingly** great
3 Nephi has righteous desire	34-36 World has pride
4-6 Nephi's believes father's words and in the Son of Most High God	34-36 Multitudes in building believe in wisdom of the world
7 Spirit says that Nephi will see Son of God and bear record	32 Nephi sees Son of God and bears record
8 I beheld a tree exceeding all beauty, exceeding whiteness of the driven snow	31 Nephi sees the Lamb of God (snow and lamb are white) going forth healing the sick, casting out devils
9 **I beheld**, thou hast shown me **the tree** that is precious above all.	33 **I Nephi saw** that he was lifted up upon **the cross** and slain for the sins of the world. (Acts 5:30 The God of our fathers raised up Jesus, whom ye slew and hanged on **a tree**.)
12 Spirit disappears from his presence "saw him not"	29 Twelve carried away in Spirit, disappear from his presence, "I saw them not"
14 Heavens open and an angel came down	30 Heavens open and angels descend upon children of men
13 Nephi sees the **great** city of Jerusalem, and other cities, and the city of **Nazareth** and in Nazareth a fair virgin.	28 Nephi sees Christ going forth ministering unto the people with power and **great** glory. The multitudes Gathered to hear and cast him out. (**Nazareth** casts out Christ – Luke 4:28-29)
16 Knowest thou the condescension of God?	26 Behold the condescension of God!
18 Nephi beholds the **virgin**, the mother of the Son of God who is **carried away in the Spirit**, and then sees the child. The angel says; behold **the Lamb of God.** (Christ's mortal birth)	27 Nephi beholds the baptism of the **Lamb of God**, and the **Holy Ghost** (Spirit) descends and abides in the form of a **dove.** (Rebirth, anointing from on high)
21 Knowest thou the meaning of the **tree of life**?	25 Nephi sees the rod of iron, which is the word of God, which goes to the **tree of life** or to the fountain of water, both of which he beheld represent the love of God.
22 And I answered him: It is the **love of God**	24 I beheld the **Son of God** (love) **going forth among**

which **sheds abroad in the hearts of the children of men. (seed)**	**the children of men. (seed)**
23 Wherefore, it is **the most desirable** above all things.	23 Yea, and **the most joyous** to the soul

23 **And he spake unto me, saying:**

Nephi distills the entirety of his thoughts in his first book to a delicious and joyous center; that "he spake unto me"! And what has been "unfolded" to him? - There is a God in heaven that loves his children, who has sent his Son, who has condescended to atone for and save them, and who wants them to have faith in this life-changing truth. This is the fruit of the tree of life and means whereby man might gain eternal life. There are so many wonderful parallels to consider in Nephi's vision of the tree of life, and I find each relationship from beginning to end desirable and joyous to my soul! Please take the time to contemplate each one, faithfully preserved for our day, and able to fill us with his Holy Spirit.

- **Commentary on Parallels - The Tree of Life is Christ**

1 Mountain – Temple of God 1**Exceedingly high**	36 Spacious Building – Worldly Temple 36 Fell, and the **fall was exceedingly** great

Nephi starts by being taken to the *high* mountain, which is antithetical to the end of his vision, the *fall* of the spacious building.[72] I can't help but be impressed by the distance used to geographically separate these two antitheticals, one representing His very dwelling place which is placed at the beginning, the heights of all heights, and the other as far away as could be placed, at the end, the depths of all depths. These two states of mind and heart, in fact, could not be farther apart.

9 Nephi beholds **a tree** (Hebrew – *ets*) which is precious above all.	33 Nephi sees Son of God taken, lifted up on **cross** (also *ets*) and slain for the sins of the world. (Acts 5:30 The God of our fathers raised up Jesus, whom ye slew and hanged on **a tree**.)

This fascinating parallel is the one of several that directly relates the tree of life to Christ, and in this case his cross. As noted in the italics, the Hebrew word for tree is *ets*, and though the word "cross" is not mentioned in the Old Testament, the Hebrew apostles of the New Testament comfortably referred to the cross as a tree (Acts 5:30, 10:39, 13:29, Gal 3:13, 1 Pet 2:24). A parallel such as this provides ancient testament to Nephi's writing.[73] (See picture at the start of this chapter.) And, because Nephi esteems the tree of life as precious above all, the inference is that the cross is also precious above all. Indeed, Christ's willing death and resurrection is the height of God's love for man.

| 21 Knowest thou the meaning of the **tree of life**? | 25 Nephi sees the rod of iron, which is the word of God, which goes to the **tree of life** or **to the fountain of water**, both of which represent the love of God. |

Within the parallel verses, 21 and 25, there is an additional enlightened ingredient. Verse 25 tells us that the tree of life is also the fountain of waters, "which waters are also a representation of the love of God". This being the case, it behooves us to reflect for a moment on what we know about waters and fountains as symbols in scripture. Jeremiah, for instance, uses this exact phrase "the fountain of living waters" as a name of the Lord, who is Christ!

> Jer 17:13 O LORD, the hope of Israel, all that forsake thee shall be ashamed, [and] they that depart from me shall be written in the earth, because they have forsaken **the LORD, the fountain of living waters.**

Or, perhaps we could refer to story of the Samaritan woman in John's gospel:

> Jn 4:14 Jesus answered and said unto her, Whosoever drinketh of this water shall thirst again: 15 But whosoever drinketh of the water that I shall give him shall never thirst; but the water that I shall give him shall be in him a well of water springing up into everlasting life.

As water is life to the thirsty in the wilderness, so Christ quenches our spiritual thirst. We might remember that Israel questioned in the wilderness if the Lord was "among" or within them (as it could be translated – perhaps a wordplay), and so that it might be "revealed" to them that He was indeed "among" (within) them, water flowed from the Rock for them to drink. When we partake of the water during the sacrament, in a spiritual sense the water we drink is from that same fount of living water, shed from the same Rock for his people Israel, to preserve and heal them. By this same token, the bread of which we partake is the fruit of the tree of life. (See Nephi's next parallel for further explanation on this point.)

This "fountain of water" could also be thought of as the source of the river of water that John saw in the temple of God in the Book of Revelation 22:1, "And he shewed me a **pure river of water of life**, clear as crystal, proceeding out of the throne of God and of the Lamb. 2 In the midst of the street of it, and on either side of the river, [was there] **the tree of life**, which bare twelve [manner of] fruits, [and] yielded her fruit every month: and the leaves of the tree [were] for the healing of the nations."

Curiously, Lehi's dream of the tree of life (1 Ne 8) gives details about a second fountain, which we are told represents the depths of hell (1 Ne 12:16). This corrupted fountain would perhaps be the "opposition in all things" (2 Ne 2:11) to the fountain of living waters. Many years later, Moroni finishes the Book of Mormon with a perfect chiasmus concerning what these two fountains represent. In Moroni chapter 7 we find:

> 11 For behold, a bitter fountain
>   cannot bring forth good water;
>   neither can a good fountain
>   bring forth bitter water;
>   wherefore, a man
>   being a servant of the devil
>   cannot follow Christ;
>   and if he follow Christ he cannot be
>   a servant of the devil.

Notice that the segments "bitter fountain" and "bitter water" are parallel to "servant of the devil", whereas "good water" and "good fountain" are parallel to "Christ". Just as the angel compares the tree of life to the living fountain, it seems obvious that the forbidden tree is the source of the filthy water which Lehi sees. (For a chart on how the fountain of living waters flows through scripture, see Appendix 5.)

In his next parallel, Nephi adds additional insight concerning who the tree of life represents; that it is not only a representation of the *love of God*, but it is the *Son of God*.

22 And I answered him: It (tree) is the **love of God** which **sheds abroad** in the hearts of **the children of men. (seed)**

24 I beheld the **Son of God** (love) **going forth** among **the children of men. (seed)**

Elder Jeffrey R. Holland also taught that the tree of life is a symbol of Jesus Christ. He said: "The images of Christ and the tree [are] inextricably linked. At the very outset of the Book of Mormon, Christ is portrayed as the source of eternal life and joy, the living evidence of divine love, and the means whereby God will fulfill his covenant with the house of Israel and indeed the entire family of man, returning them all to their eternal promises" [74]

Interestingly, if we understand the tree of life to be a representation of Christ, then the emblems of the sacrament (tokens of his flesh and blood) also have parallels to the fruit of that tree, both of which must be eaten in order to have eternal life. Confirming this sacral connection, Alma ties the image of the sacrament emblems (the bread and water) to the tree of life in Alma 5:33-34: "Yea, he (Christ) saith: Come unto me and ye shall partake of the **fruit of the tree of life**; yea, ye shall **eat and drink** of the **bread and the waters** of life freely"!

8 I beheld a tree, and the beauty exceeded all beauty, and the **white**ness thereof did exceed **whiteness** of the **snow**.	31 I beheld the **Lamb** of God going forth healing the sick and afflicted.

Once we understand that the tree represents Christ, it is easier to understand how "the tree" in verse 8 is parallel to the healing Lamb of God in verse 31. Also, verse 8 tells us that the tree is white, which is parallel to the whiteness of the Lamb in verse 31.

Connecting these ideas, Ezekiel 47:9 speaks prophetically of healing waters flowing out from the heavenly temple of God: "And it shall come to pass, *that* every thing that liveth, which moveth, whithersoever the rivers shall come, shall live: and there shall be a very great multitude of fish, because these waters shall come thither: for **they shall be healed**; and **every thing shall live** whither the river cometh." During his life, Christ incarnate was personally that healing fountain of water that flowed out into the world, and through the Holy Ghost he continues to be. Moreover, just as the tree exceeded all beauty, Christ's power to heal wounded, broken, and dying man also exceeds all beauty. By and through him we will not perish, but prosper; we will not die, but live.

16 Knowest thou the condescension of God?	26 Behold the condescension of God!
18 Nephi beholds the **virgin**, the mother of the Son of God who is **carried away in the Spirit**, and then sees the child. The angel says; behold **the Lamb of God**. (Christ's mortal birth)	27 Nephi beholds the baptism of the **Lamb of God**, and the **Holy Ghost** (Spirit) descends and abides in the form of a **dove**. (Christ's figurative rebirth, anointing from on high)

These verses, on either side of Nephi's central thought, are perhaps two of the most stunning in chapter 11. As told in the bible, Nephi witnesses in verse 18 that Jesus was of divine mortal birth, and in verse 27, and that to fulfill all righteousness he was also "born of the water and the Spirit"! These verses represent the two births of all our lives, the natural (18) and that of the Spirit (27)! We should also note that the Holy Ghost is present in the form of a dove, which we know is *yonah* (Jonah) in Hebrew, the only sign that Jesus gives of his messiahship.

It is between these two births where we find what ignites, or is the catalyst for the process of spiritual rebirth Shown below, Nephi uses the word "heart", and the angel uses the word "soul" – to express the level on which God communicates\speaks his joyous love to man.

> 22 And I answered him: It is the **love of God** which **sheds abroad** in the hearts of **the children of men (seed).**

> 23 wherefore, it is **the most desirable** above all things

> And he spake unto me saying,

> 23 yea, and **the most joyous** to the soul

> 24 I beheld the **Son of God** (love) **going forth** among **the children of men (seed);** and I saw many fall down and worship him.

Like Nephi's other chiasmi, in this most-central-of-all apex, we also find the same variety of seed found in his many others. For instance, verses 22 and 24 both contain the phrase, "the children of men", which is the seed of posterity to whom God's love is focused, and in the middle is the seed of the word — that which "he spake unto me." Though it may seem unlikely at this point to turn to Paul for insight concerning the tree of life, there is a verse in Romans which adds astounding clarity to Nephi's center-most experience. In Romans 5:5, Paul tells us (using Nephi's exact expression) how the love of God is spoken to our hearts - "And hope maketh not ashamed; because **the love of God is** shed abroad in our hearts **by the Holy Ghost**, which is given unto us." Clearly, the warmth of God's love is personally revealed in no other way. In fact, even before he sees the tree of life Nephi already knows by what power he will experience it: "I, Nephi, was desirous also that I might see, and hear, and know of these things, **by the power of the Holy Ghost**, which is the gift of God unto all those who diligently seek him (1 Ne 10:17). However, some of our best clarity concerning Nephi's experience at the tree of life is provided by Alma,

119

who also tasted the joy of its fruit: "I have labored without ceasing, that I might bring souls unto repentance; that I might **bring them to taste of the exceeding joy of which I did taste**; that they might also be **born of God,** and be **filled with the Holy Ghost**" (Alma 36:24) Clearly, tasting of the tree of life symbolizes rebirth – being born of the Spirit and coming to Christ.

Nephi has recounted prophets, angels, men dressed in white, and the Spirit or Holy Ghost; all speaking to man.[75] Surely in one of these forms God has also spoken his love to you and me - revealing the covenant plan of salvation and the promised Messiah at the center of that plan. This "word" of loving redemption, ultimately confirmed by the power of the Holy Ghost, is the pivot upon which all of Nephi's thoughts move (as well as the hinge upon which swing the patriarchal stories as related by Steven). Fruitfulness (the *third* phase, the 40 years in the wilderness phase) only starts after God has revealed his love, calling to your heart and mine. The question for each of us, as it ever was for the all the patriarchs, prophets, and Israelites in the wilderness is — do your thoughts hinge on His voice which beckons; do you desire and rejoice in it? If you have been born of this love, then you are truly his covenant seed (Gal 3:29), his spiritual son or daughter, qualifying for eternal life and the fullest promises of his atoning love. (For more on Nephi's joy and the Spirit, see pg 213.)

- **What is Eternal Life – and what we must know (do)?**

Though we don't usually differentiate; whereas the tree of life represents the "love of God" or "fount of living water" (who is Christ), the fruit of the tree of life sometimes has its own particular designation, which is eternal life (see quote from Jeffrey Holland above). Indeed, in Eden the fruit of one tree caused death, whereas eating of the other brought eternal life (Gen 3:22). Alma also identifies this extra designation, explaining that: "if ye will nourish the word, yea, nourish the tree as it beginneth to grow, by your faith with great diligence, and with patience, looking forward to **the fruit thereof**, it shall take root; and behold it shall be a tree springing up unto **everlasting life**" (Alma 32:42). In addition, there are other scriptures which designate the fruit of the tree of life as eternal life. Nephi tells us in 1 Ne 15:36 that the **fruit of the tree** of life is the "greatest of all the gifts of God." There is a footnote in our scriptures for this verse which directs us to D&C 14:7 where we read more about this greatest of all gifts: "And, if you keep my commandments and endure to the end you shall have **eternal life**, which gift is the **greatest of all the gifts** of God." Thus, the fruit of the tree of life is the greatest gift, and the greatest gift is eternal life.

However, eternal life also has some other fascinating relationships. In Jn 17:3 we read Christ's words: "And **this is life eternal**, that they might **know thee** the only true God, and Jesus Christ, whom thou hast sent." Consequently, eternal life is also to "know God". And if that is so, what is it to know God? Fortunately the scriptures are very specific in this regard. In 1 Jn 4:7-8 we read:

"Beloved, let us **love one another**: for love is of God; and **every one that loveth is born of God, and knoweth God**. He that **loveth not knoweth not God**; for God is love.

Clearly, in addition to experiencing the love of God shed abroad in our hearts, to know God is evidenced by loving others. In fact, John tells us that those who do not love others are not born of God; i.e. born again (mighty change of heart - Alma 5). Remarkably, these verses in 1 Jn 4 can also be outlined in wonderful poetic parallel:

A. **Beloved,** let us **love one another:**

    B. for **love is** of **God**;
        and **every one that loveth**
            is born of God,
                and knoweth God.
        He that **loveth not**
            (is not born of God – understood though omitted [ellipsis])
                knoweth not God;
    B. for **God is love.**

    B.' **In this** was manifested the **love** of God toward **us,**
        because that God **sent his** only begotten **Son** into the world,
            that we might live through him.
    B.' **Herein** is **love**, not that we loved God, but that **he loved us,**
        and **sent his Son**
        [to be] the propitiation for our sins.

A'. **Beloved,** if God so loved **us**, we ought also to **love one another.**

Framed on either end by the call to "love one another", John first tells us that to know God is to love others (B), which he then parallels to the way in which God has shown his love to us, by

121

sending his Son (B'). This section also expresses what Nephi saw in the vision of the tree of life – that God loved us so he sent his Son, the Lamb of God. However, John adds what a believer must do with that "knowledge" of Christ's propitiation (Atonement), which is to love others as he loved us. These beautiful verses are like another vision of the tree of life, with a practical application of how its fruits are manifest in our lives. Clearly, if eternal life is to know God and his Son, and to know God is to love one other, then when we love our fellow man (through service, kindness, patience) eternal life in that instant begins. It is not a future event, but of necessity, by commandment, it (eternal life) begins now.

- **To know God is to obey him – How the love of God is perfected**

There is also one other attribute which John tells us is required to "know God" and experience eternal life. In 1 Jn 2:3-5 we read:

> "And hereby we do **know** that we **know him**, if we keep his commandments. He that saith, I **know him**, and keepeth not his commandments, is a liar, and the truth is not in him. But whoso **keepeth his word**, in him verily is the **love of God perfected**: hereby **know we** that we are in him."

In order to have eternal life, which is to know God, only those who obey his commandments or "keep his word" truly know him. In such is "the love of God (which is the tree of life) perfected" – bearing its fruit of eternal life (Alma 32:42). John also clarifies a few verses later (in Jn 2:8-10) what God's encompassing commandment is: "Again, **a new commandment** I write unto you, which thing is true in him and in you: because the darkness is past, and the true light now shineth. He that saith he is in the light, and hateth his brother, is in darkness even until now. **He that loveth his brother abideth in the light**, and there is none occasion of stumbling in him." (Laman and Lemuel, who Lehi tells us wandered away from the tree of life [God's love] into darkness, easily fit John's description here.) All other commandments are circumscribed in this new commandment, which when obeyed testifies that we know God and have entered into eternal life.[76]

Indeed, Christ's perfect love and obedience led him to the cross, produced the Atonement, the fruit of which gives eternal life to all who do likewise. As we follow this great model of atoning love, we come to know God and see his face in those we serve. Eternal life, it seems, is eternal love.

10

1 Nephi 12-14, Revelation on the Sea of Glass

As mentioned in the first chapter of this book, Lehi proclaims in vision, "Great and marvelous are thy works, Lord God Almighty." John later records in Revelation 15 that these are the words expressed by those who are redeemed and stand before the throne of God, upon the sea of glass (Rev 4:2, 15:2). Not surprising, when Lehi and John visit God's temple there are other similarities documented by each record. Significantly, both see the tree of life (although in a subsequent vision for Lehi), the heavenly throne, and both record that only a select group will be allowed to eternally partake of its fruit. Lehi also records that there is an iron rod (the word of God) which one must hold to in order to come to the tree, whereas John records in Rev 22:14 a version of how the tree is accessed in the SAME manner (parenthesis mine)!

> Blessed [are] they that do his commandments (hold to his word), that they may have right to the tree of life, and may enter in through the gates into the city.

When Nephi is allowed access to the tree of life, he also prophesies and records (in chapters 12-14) significant future events which lead up to the restoration of the gospel in the latter days. However, the angel tells Nephi that John, the apostle of the Lamb, has been designated to record the remainder of the things (end time events) which he also saw while at the tree (14:25-27). Because all three of them (Lehi, John, and Nephi) prophecy while at the tree of life, we might wonder, if we were there, would see such visions as well? Thanks to modern revelation, through Joseph Smith we know a little bit more about the place where these men stood and why it had such an affect on them. In D&C 130 we learn about the amazing properties of the sea of glass (found at the throne of God) — that it is a revelatory Urim and Thummim:

> 7 But they reside in the presence of God, on a globe like a sea of glass and fire, **where all things for their glory are manifest, past, present, and future, and are continually before the Lord.** 8 The place where God resides is a great **Urim and Thummim**. 9 This earth, in its sanctified and immortal state, will be made like unto

crystal and will be a **Urim and Thummim** to the inhabitants who dwell thereon, whereby all things pertaining to an inferior kingdom, or all kingdoms of a lower order, will be manifest to those who dwell on it; and this earth will be Christ's.

In the celestial place where John, Lehi, and Nephi stood, all things are manifest, "past, present, and future, and are continually before the Lord." What an amazing concept! All three are guided by an angel in white, and experience an "eternal round" of ever-present revelatory information. By this method they were instructed. In fact, Nephi is specifically told several times to "look" (followed by a description of what he beheld). To where do we suppose he was looking? I would suggest that it was just as D&C 130 tells us; to the sea of glass or Urim and Thummim which is at the "place where God resides."

In a wonderful way, the record preserved by these prophets in scripture is now our access to the Urim and Thummim. As we read their words and "hold to" them, by the power of the Holy Ghost we are likewise "blessed" to partake of the fruit of the tree of life (Rev 12:14). In faith, their recorded visions become our "sea of glass" to past, present, and future events, and through their divinely preserved experience we can come closer to the throne of God and feel the fire of His Spirit testifying of their truth.

- Chiasmus at the Sea of Glass

As previously stated, 1 Nephi has a double parallel center; two grand chiasmi sharing a common thematic climax. We have just looked at the chiasmus found in chapter 11, the first part of Nephi's vision of the tree of life. Its parallel is the additional revelation given to Nephi which consists of chapters 12-14, which is also a tree of life; a song of redeeming love; an historical restoration and rebirth. Below is an outline of Nephi's additional revelation, which has been condensed in order to fit on the page:

A 12:2 Wars and **rumors of war**

12:4-5 Earthquakes, vapor of darkness, fire, great and terrible judgments of the Lord

12:7-10 Robes of twelve **apostles** are **made white** by blood of the Lamb (Beholds 1st coming of Christ)

B 16-18 Beholds fountain of **filthy water** and spacious building – pride and vain imaginations

20 Beholds **multitudes upon face of land**

C 13:4-8 **Great and abominable** church of the devil

D 9 For the praise of the world they **bring them (gentiles) into captivity**

E 12-19 The Spirit of God is wrought upon the **Gentiles** (Columbus vs 12, Pilgrims vs 13, Revolutionary War vs 17)

a 20 Beheld that they did prosper in the land, **out of captivity**

F 20-29 Beheld **a book** from the Jews, goes forth by the **12 apostles**, plain and **precious things taken away**, is book of the Lamb (Bible)

G 30 Gentiles **lifted up by power of God**
upon land that God has covenanted for inheritance

H Chiasmus – 30-32 Will not suffer thy **seed** to be destroyed

H Chiasmus - 33,34 Lamb & Angel **spake unto me**– visit remnant, merciful

H' Chiasmus – 34,35 After **seed** dwindles, Christ to minister to seed

G' 37 Shall have **power of Holy Ghost and be lifted up**, and if they endure shall be saved in the everlasting kingdom of the Lamb

F' 38-41 Beheld **the book** of the Lamb, from the Jews, and other books (Book of Mormon), records of **12 apostles** are true, plain and **precious things taken away**, the last book establishes truth of first

E' 14:1-2 The **Gentiles** shall hearken, and He shall manifest himself unto them in word, power, deed

a 2 They shall be a blessed people upon the promised land forever, **no more brought down into captivity**

D' 3-7 **Gentiles** either delivered by "marvelous work", or **brought into captivity**

C' 9-10 **Great and abominable** church of the devil

B' 11-12 Beholds whore of all earth "upon **many waters**" (Babylon – Jer 51:12-13)

13 Beholds **multitudes upon all the face of the earth**

A' 14:15 Wars and **rumors of war**

14:14-17 Wrath of God poured out upon mother of all harlots

14:18-30 Behold man **in white** robe, John one of the twelve **apostles** of the Lamb. He will write concerning the end of the world. (Beholds 2nd coming of Christ)

At the heart of this vision (H) is a group of *three* smaller chiastic structures. We might expect the middle chiasmus to express something similar to chapter 11's center – "he spake unto me", which it does! Below are the three central chiasmi, which emphasize God's merciful preservation and restoration of the Gentiles and Israel, a parallel to the tree of life:

30 wherefore, **thou seest**
        that the Lord God will not **suffer that the Gentiles**
            will utterly **destroy** the mixture of thy seed, which are among thy brethren.
        31 Neither will he **suffer that the Gentiles**
            shall **destroy** the seed of thy brethren.
        32 Neither will the Lord God **suffer that the Gentiles**
            shall forever remain in that **awful state of blindness,**
which **thou beholdest** they are in

32 **neither will the Lord God suffer that the Gentiles shall forever remain in that awful state** of blindness,
which thou beholdest they are in,
        because of the plain and most precious parts of the gospel of the Lamb which have been kept back
        by that abominable church, whose formation thou hast seen.
            33 Wherefore saith the Lamb of God: I **will be merciful unto the Gentiles,**
                unto the **visiting of the remnant** of the **house of Israel**
                    In great **judgment.** And it came to pass that the
                        34 angel of **the Lord**
                            spake unto me, saying:
                            Behold, saith
                        the **Lamb of God,**
                after I have **visited the remnant** of the **house of Israel**—and this remnant of whom I
                speak is the seed of thy father-
                    wherefore, after I have visited them **in judgment**, and smitten them by the
                    hand of the Gentiles,
        and **after the Gentiles do stumble** exceedingly,
        because of the most plain and precious parts of the gospel of the Lamb which have been kept back
        by that abominable church, which is the mother of harlots,
saith **the Lamb—I will be merciful unto the Gentiles** in that day

34 **saith the Lamb—I will be merciful** unto the Gentiles **in that day,**
    insomuch that I will **bring forth unto** them,
        in mine own **power,**
            much of **my gospel,**
                which **shall be plain** and precious, saith the Lamb.
                    35 For, behold, saith the Lamb: **I will** manifest myself **unto thy seed,**
                        that **they shall** write many things
                            which **I shall** minister unto them,
                      which **shall be** plain and precious;
                and after **thy seed shall be** destroyed, and dwindle in unbelief, and also the **seed of**
                thy brethren,
            behold, these things **shall be hid** up,
    to **come forth unto** the Gentiles,
      by the gift and **power** of the Lamb.
        36 And in them shall be written **my gospel,**
saith **the Lamb,** and my rock and my salvation. 37 And **blessed are they** who shall seek to bring forth my Zion **at that day,**

Let's take a brief look at each structure individually. Below is the first small chiasmus that resides at the center of 1 Nephi 12-14. You will notice that there is a series of *three* similar statements concerning the Gentiles, which again in literary terms is a cycloid.[77] This first formation (vs 30-32) also parallels the third of these center chiasmi (vs 34-37), both of which emphasize Nephi's seed preserved by the Lord - Nephi's ever present theme.

13: 30 wherefore, **thou seest**

> that the Lord God will not **suffer that the Gentiles**
>
> > will utterly **destroy** the mixture of thy seed, which are among thy brethren.
>
> 31 Neither will he **suffer that the Gentiles**
>
> > shall **destroy** the seed of thy brethren.
>
> 32 Neither will the Lord God **suffer that the Gentiles**
>
> > shall forever remain in that **awful state** of blindness,

which **thou beholdest** they are in

Next, the chiasmus which forms the midpoint of 1 Nephi chapters 12-14 has an almost identical center to its chiastic partner in 1 Nephi 11, "he spake unto me"! As in chapter 11, the angel is again speaking, showing to Nephi how God's love is "shed abroad" among the children of men (1Ne 11:22). Centered on events in the New World, we see God's plan of mercy to Lehi's remnant seed as well as the Gentiles; a covenant promise of restoration and rebirth, which, like the fruit of the tree of life, is desirable and joyous (1 Ne 11:23). Notice that this chiasmus starts by re-using part of verse 32, which also served as the last verse of the chiasmus we just discussed.

32 Neither will the Lord God suffer that the Gentiles shall forever remain in that awful state of blindness, which thou beholdest they are in,

> **because of the plain and most precious parts of the gospel of the Lamb which have been kept back by that abominable church,** whose formation thou hast seen.

> 33 Wherefore saith the Lamb of God: **I will be merciful unto the Gentiles,**

>> unto the **visiting of the remnant** of the **house of Israel**
>> in great **judgment.** And it came to pass that

>>> 34 the angel of **the Lord**

>>> **spake unto me,**

>>> **saying**:

>>> **Behold, saith**

>>> the **Lamb of God,**

>> after I have **visited the remnant** of the **house of Israel**—and this remnant of whom I speak is the seed of thy father-
>> wherefore, after I have visited them **in judgment**, and smitten them by the hand of the Gentiles,

> and **after the Gentiles do stumble** exceedingly,

> **because of the most plain and precious parts of the gospel of the Lamb which have been kept back by that abominable church,** which is the mother of harlots,

saith **the Lamb—I will be merciful unto the Gentiles** in that day

Another indication that we are at the center of this part of Nephi's vision is the change in how the angel of the Lord talks to Nephi. All of the teaching up until this time (since 12:1) has been in the 3rd person, however, in verse 13:33 the instructions change to the 1st person, which are the very words of the Lord. In verse 33 we hear for the first time, "thus saith the Lamb of God", followed by the voice of the Lord. In verse 37, exactly where these three middle chiasmi end, the angel finishes using the direct speech of the Lord and returns to the 3rd person until the end of the vision (14:30). This change in tense to 1st person is amazingly exclusive to our chiastic center. The personal words of the Lord heighten the impact of the angel's instructions, accentuating for Nephi that he has arrived at the pinnacle of his vision.[78]

You might also notice that Christ's personal speech is parallel to the center of 1 Nephi 11's chiasmus, the tree of life, Jesus Christ! 1 Nephi 11's center is the **love of God** shed abroad among the children of men, and chapters 12-14 center is **the mercy of God** promised specifically to the Gentiles and Nephi's remnant seed. Both most desirable and joyous.

Below is the third small chiasmus, which, as just indicated, is also presented to Nephi entirely in the 1st voice of the Lord. Notice that it also begins by using the last line of the previous chiasmus, "I will be merciful" (vs 34). This third chiasmus is entirely about the coming forth of the Book of Mormon, and a restoration of the gospel fullness in the latter days!

34 **saith the Lamb—I will be merciful** unto the Gentiles **in that day,**

    insomuch that I will **bring forth unto** them (Gentiles),

        in mine own **power,**

            much of **my gospel,**

                which **shall be plain** and precious, saith the Lamb.

                    35 For, behold, saith the Lamb: I will manifest myself **unto thy seed,**

                        that **they shall** write many things

                            which **I shall** minister unto them,

                        which **shall be** plain and precious;

                        and after **thy seed** shall be destroyed, and dwindle in unbelief, and also the **seed of thy** brethren,

                    behold, these things **shall be hid** up,

  to **come forth unto** the Gentiles,

      by the gift and **power** of the Lamb.

          36 And in them shall be written **my gospel,**

saith the Lamb, and my rock and my salvation. 37 And **blessed are they** (Gentiles) who shall seek to bring forth my Zion **at that day,**

Like the other small chiasmus, at the center of this structure, seed in its variety is again a focus.

Christ's personal visit to the Americas (vs 35) is foretold, as well as a remarkable reference to the coming forth of the Book of Mormon – the precious things "hid up" to come forth to the Gentiles by the power of the Lamb. In that regard, note that Nephi has wonderfully placed "hid up" (vs 34) as an antithetical parallel to "plain and precious" (vs 35)! We might even see a pattern of the resurrection in this, a necessary burying of the record in order that its "resurrection" might restore life to Lehi's remnant seed and the Gentiles. Indeed, as the keystone of the restoration, the Book of Mormon is filled with the healing power of plain and precious truth.

As further evidence that we are at Nephi's chiastic center, these center *three* chiasmi also have a cluster of 17 future tense verbs, all expressing important future events (e.g. shall, will). This is striking because for one and a half chapters a future tense state-of-being verb has been used only once (12:9 he shall judge). In sharp contrast, at almost precisely the center of these three visionary chapters, approximately 50 verses from the beginning and 50 from the end, starting with these three chiasmi, the verb tenses change to a prophetic future tense and remain that way until the end of Nephi's vision! This also happens simultaneously with the switch to 1st person in verse 33 (as previously mentioned)! Thus, along with Nephi's chiasmus, we have two additional unique indicators which help to corroborate the center of Nephi's vision.

Until we see the structure, as we read these chapters there is perhaps a feeling of random repetition by Nephi; i.e. wars and rumors of war, the great and abominable, and multiple references to the gentiles. Nephi repeats to emphasize, however, it is also obvious that this was done in order to preserve a marvelous chiastic structure. Indeed, as Nephi beheld, the Lamb has been merciful to us in our day, and hopefully you experience what I do as I examine what Nephi has done – enormous joy and wonder.

- Centered concentration of "seed" in 1 Nephi

Because seed (of word, of posterity) has been one of Nephi's foci., if we chart its use in 1 Nephi we find another fascinating pattern which is curiously concentrated in the chapters that relate Nephi's vision of the tree of life:

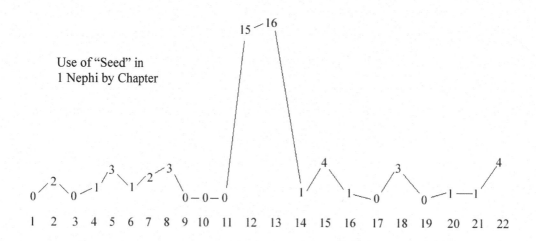

Use of "Seed" in
1 Nephi by Chapter

Visually speaking, this graph (of seed's usage) even resembles a tree of life rising up in the middle of 1 Nephi. Interestingly, the only other chapter in the entire Book of Mormon where we encounter such a concentration of "seed" is in Alma 32, where Alma, preaching to the Zoramites (from the Hebrew *zerah* meaning seed), compares the word to a seed which is planted in the believer's heart and grows into a tree of life! (Alma 32 also uses "seed" 16 times.) Whether or not Nephi does this intentionally (using seed so many times), it seems a natural tribute to find an abundance of seed juxtaposed to his vision of the tree of life. Indeed, the "eternal life" (propagation) of any tree depends its producing much fruit or seed. The more fruit and seed it bears the greater chance it will continue forever.

Using this analogy of fruit bearing from within, in John 15:5 Christ fittingly refers to himself as the true vine, stating, "He that abideth in me, and I in him, the same bringeth forth much fruit." He continues in verses 8-9 telling his disciples how this fruit manifests itself in love: "Herein is **my Father glorified**, that ye **bear much fruit**; so shall ye be my disciples. As the Father hath loved me, so have I loved you: continue ye in my love." These verses are also parallel thought:

> Herein is my Father glorified,
>   that ye bear much fruit;
>   so shall ye be my disciples.
> As the Father hath loved me,
>   so have I loved you:
>   continue ye in my love.

The Father's glory is love. It is also the fruit produced by His spiritual seed. If we look at the various nuances of the verb "to glorify," in the Greek lexicon we find that the word used here by John (*doxazō*) means to honor or to praise. As well, to glorify can mean to beautify with brightness, or splendor, or with luster.[79] In this regard, when Nephi sees the tree of life (God's love), he visually describes its glory: "the beauty thereof was far beyond, yea, exceeding of all beauty; and the whiteness thereof did exceed the whiteness of the driven snow" (1 Ne 11:8). The reason that Nephi sees a gloriously white tree is because it is covered in so much splendid fruit. Nephi's description of a fruited tree illustrates how the fullness of God's perfect love might appear if we could see it, which depiction is simultaneously the brilliant and beautiful glory of God. In this way, with the eyes of our heart, when we feel God's love we behold the splendor of the tree of life!

- **Restoration**

Thus, Nephi's second grand chiasmus (chapters 12-14) is a fruitful witness to the first (Nephi 11), establishing the central feature of God's plan; that he speaks to man, fills us with the joy of his word, and embraces us with his love. It expresses the healing fruits from the tree of life which guide history; fills Columbus with the Spirit so that he comes to America, stirs within the souls of European pilgrims fleeing religious captivity, and buoys the hearts of our patriot fathers; all of which prepares a way for the restoration of plain and precious truths which are brought forth by Joseph Smith.

Though Adam and Eve were prevented from returning to the tree of life, in the book of Revelation we read that to those who overcome the world (the effects of the other tree) God has overturned the earlier prohibition and restored man's access (Rev 2:7, 22:14). Of these verses in Revelation one Bible commentator writes: "Seeing the tree of life again points to a restoration of all things."[80] In a similar way, the tree of life in the Book of Mormon points to a "restoration of all things" preparatory to His coming. God's "love shed abroad" in the first chiasmus (chapter 11) is a figure of the latter-day restoration of his uncompromised gospel truth which is shed abroad in the other (12-14). As Nephi beholds, because God loves his children he has preserved a remnant to hear the word, plant the seed of the Tree of Life (Alma 32), partake of its fruit, and experience its restorative and life-giving power.

11

1 Nephi 16

Three objects - The Bow, Ball, Boat, and Three Locations - Shazer, Nahom, Bountiful

- **An inverse parallel**

By the time we arrive in chapter 16, Nephi has interpreted various objects as symbols and types. For instance; the iron rod is a type of the word, the tree of life represents the love of God, the spacious building is the pride of the world, and the filthy water is the depths of hell. As we proceed we will continue to encounter more objects, as well as people and places that are also types of spiritual things. What about the Liahona, or Nephi's bow and ship, which also test the faith of Lehi's people; or new places such as Shazer, Nahom, and Bountiful? We would be wise to remember that "all things which have been *given of God* from the beginning of the world, unto man, are the typifying of him." (2 Ne 11:4)

Naturally, since we have now passed the center of 1 Nephi, the remaining chapters of this book will examine the chiastic counterparts to the preceding chapters, identifying important points in common between them. 1 Nephi 16 relates the events that occur when Lehi and Ishmael's groups leave the valley of Lemuel and travel to Bountiful, which was a journey was to get Ishmael's daughters. Likewise, there is a chiasmus here that parallels the chiasmus already discussed in 1 Ne 7. Below is the diagram of this relationship:

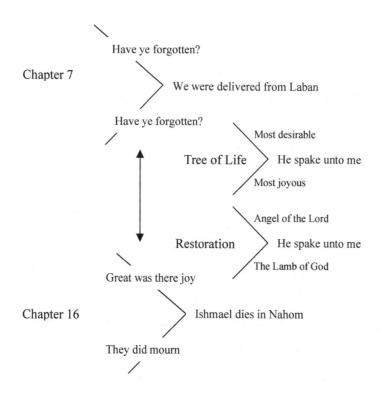

Our discussion of this chapter will profit by a reading of what the prophet Alma, who lived nearly 500 years after Lehi, had to say specifically about the journey detailed in chapter 16. Speaking to his son Benjamin, he explains that Lehi's journey is a shadow or a type. On the morning of their departure Lehi finds the "round ball of curious workmanship" outside his tent. Of this event Alma interprets (I have emboldened some important ideas):

Alma 37:38 And now, my son, I have somewhat to say concerning the thing which our fathers call a ball, or director—or our fathers called it Liahona, which is, being interpreted, a compass; and the Lord prepared it. 39 And behold, there cannot any man work after the manner of so curious a workmanship. And behold, it was prepared to show unto our fathers the course which they should travel in the wilderness. 40 And it did **work for them according to their faith** in God; therefore, if they had faith to believe that God could cause that those spindles should point the way they should go, behold, it was done; therefore they had this miracle, and also many other miracles wrought by the power of God, day by day. 41 Nevertheless, because those miracles were worked by small means it did show unto them marvelous works. They were slothful, and forgot to exercise their faith and diligence and then those marvelous works ceased, and they did not progress in their journey; 42 Therefore, they tarried in the wilderness, or did not travel a direct course, and were afflicted with hunger and thirst, because of their transgressions. 43 And now, my son, I would that **ye should understand that these things are not without** a **shadow;** for as our fathers were slothful to give heed to this compass (now these **things were temporal**) they did not prosper; even so it is with **things which are spiritual.** 44 For behold, it is as easy to give heed to the **word of Christ,** which will point to you a straight course to eternal bliss, as it was for our fathers to give heed to this compass, which would point unto them a straight course to the promised land. 45 And now I say, **is there not a type in this thing**? For just as surely as **this director** did bring our fathers, by following its course, to the promised land, **shall the words of Christ, if we follow their course, carry us beyond this vale of sorrow into a far better land of promise.**

Alma lets us know with certainty that Lehi's journey has elements that are both "temporal and spiritual" (vs 43). The Liahona, for instance, he compares to the "words of Christ." In fact, his final statement, "carry us beyond this vale of sorrow into a far better land of promise" goes well beyond typing only the Liahona as the words of Christ (vs 45), but also reveals his belief that Lehi's wilderness journey is a type of mortality or a "vale of sorrow" that leads to a heavenly land of promise. Of course, any reading that does not consider this spiritual aspect would be missing a good portion of the intended focus, which is meant to lead us to a deeper appreciation of the plan of salvation and Christ's promised atonement. As we will see, there are many more types to examine in chapter 16. Below is Nephi's chapter 16 in its stunning chiastic form. It has been condensed in the interest of conserving space:

A 12 Depart **into wilderness** Cross River Laman
  13 Travel **four** days south south-east
    13 Pitch tent, **call the name Shazer**
      14 Slay **food** for families
        14 Keep in the most **fertile** parts
          14 By Red **Sea**
            We followed the direction of the ball which led us in the **most fertile** parts

              B 17 We did **pitch our tents** that we might rest (nuwach, Noah)
                a 18 I did go forth to **slay food,** 18 I did **break** my bow, made of steel,
                  b 19 We did obtain **no food,** 20 Brothers did murmur because of **sufferings** and **afflictions,**

Rely on their own   c 20 They were exceedingly sorrowful, **did murmur** against the Lord,
strength for food.   d 21 It began to be **exceedingly difficult**, insomuch that we **could not obtain food**
There is murmuring   e 22 They had **hardened their hearts,** 23 Nephi makes wood bow and straight arrow
           f 24 I said unto my father: **Whither shall I go to obtain food?**

                      C 25 **Voice of Lord came** unto my father
Chastened, repent,   25 Father **truly chastened**
Lord points to ball   25 **Brought down into depths of sorrow**
to find food   26 And the voice of the **Lord** said to look upon the ball (word) and behold the things are written

                        D 27 And when my **father** beheld the things on the ball he did **fear and tremble**
                          28 The **pointers (lead)** which were in the ball
                            did work **according to the faith and diligence** and heed given them
                              29 And there was written new writing which was **plain to be read**
By cunning means the   29 Thus we see **by small means (machashaba)**
ball works by faith to   the Lord can bring about **great things**
lead them,   30 I Nephi did go up into **the top of the mountain** (ministered by angel
                                according to directions which were upon **the ball (word)**

                                  E 31 I did **slay wild beasts**
Nephi slays wild   32 how **great was their joy**
beasts. They rejoice   32 **they did humble themselves**
and give thanks   32 **and did give thanks**
                                    33 Take our **journey, traveling** same course (south), pitch
                                      tents
                                        F 34 Came to pass that **Ishmael** died
                                          34 Buried in **Nahom**
                                            F 35 Came to pass that the daughters of **Ishmael**
                                              35 did **mourn** (nacham) exceedingly
                                          35 We **have wandered** much in wilderness
They desire to slay   35 **They did murmur,** we have suffered much affliction,
Nephi. They murmur   hunger
                                          36 they **did murmur** against my father and me
                                            36 Desire to return to Jerusalem (opposite of joy)
                                        E 37 Let us **slay Nephi** who would be our ruler

The brothers accuse   38 Now he says the **Lord has talked to him (word)**,
Nephi of using cunning   and also **Angels have ministered** (on top of the mountain)
arts to mislead them.   38 We know he lies; he **worketh many things**
                                      by his cunning arts (machashaba),
                                        that he may **deceive our eyes**, thinking
                                          38 perhaps that he may **lead us** away into some strange wilderness;
                                            38 he thought to make himself a ruler over us **according to his will and**
                                              pleasure
                                        D 38 And after this manner did **Laman** stir up their hearts to **anger**

Chastened, repent, Lord   C 39 **Voice of Lord came** and did speak many words
blesses with food   39 and did **chasten** them **exceedingly**
                                  39 and they did **turn away their anger** and did **repent of sins**
                                    39 The **Lord** did again **bless us with food** (word) that we did not perish

                  B 17:1 We did **take out journey** and travel eastward (towards God)
                    b 1 Wade through much **affliction,** 1 Our women did **bear** children
                  a 2 **Great were blessings of the Lord upon us**
Rely on the Lord for   d 2 Live on raw meat – (miracle like manna), 2 **Plenty** of suck
food. No murmuring   c 2 Began to bear journey with **no murmurings**
                      e 3 Thus we see that **commandments** must be fulfilled, and if the **children of men keep them**
                        f 3 God does **nourish** them, and **strengthen** them, and **provide means**

138

A 4 Sojourn **in the wilderness** for
  eight years
   5 Come to **land we call Bountifu**l, because of its **much fruit**
    5 and **wild honey**, and these things were prepared (**food**) that we might not perish
     5 we beheld the **sea** Irreantum
      6 Pitch our tents by **sea**shore, 7 Suffered mush difficulty
       7 Called the place Bountiful because of **its much fruit**

As you can see, I have provided a short summation (in italics, to the left) for each parallel grouping, which should help to clarify the similarities in these verses which relate the many ups and downs of Lehi's family. At the heart of this chiasmus is the death of Ishmael in Nahom. As indicated earlier (see chapter 7 of this book), Ishmael's death is a parallel to Laban's, who we have come to understand as a symbol of death and carnal man. In all likelihood, we would never have considered the Ishmael of the Book of Mormon in this light except for the results of our structural analysis of these two parallel chapters, which have yielded Laban and Ishmael at their centers, the only two people in all of 1 Nephi that die. Let's consider for a moment how each of these apexes substantiates a figurative interpretation of the other.

Precious, though perhaps unexpected assistance with regard to Ishmael's figurative significance comes from the apostle Paul who confirms that the events in the lives of the patriarchs are "allegorical", and teach spiritual truths. Speaking of how we become sons of God, worthy of his spiritual birthright\inheritance, in Galatians 4 Paul uses messianic imagery to express how "Christ be formed in you". He then allegorizes how the spiritual new covenant represented by Isaac, differs from the old or carnal man, who is Ishmael (parenthesis and bold print are mine):

Gal 4:22 For it is written, that Abraham had two sons, the one by a bondmaid, the other by a freewoman. 23 **But he *who was* of the bondwoman (Ishmael) was born after the flesh; but he** of **the freewoman *was* by promise.** 24 **Which things are an allegory**: for these **are the two covenants;** the one from the mount Sinai, which gendereth to bondage, which is Agar. 25 For this **Agar is mount Sinai in Arabia,** and answereth to Jerusalem which now is, and is in bondage with her children. 26 But **Jerusalem which is above is free, which is the mother** of us all. 27 For it is written, Rejoice, *thou* barren that bearest not; break forth and cry, thou that travailest not: for the desolate hath many more children than she which hath an husband. 28 **Now we, brethren, as Isaac was, are the children** of **promise.** 29 **But as then he (Ishmael)**

that was born after the flesh persecuted him *that was born* **after the Spirit, even so** *it is* **now.** 30 Nevertheless what saith the scripture? Cast out the bondwoman and her son: for the **son** of **the bondwoman (Ishmael) shall not be heir** with the son of the freewoman.

Applied broadly, these verses lead us to understand that not just Ishmael, but all of the elder sons of the patriarchs, including Lehi's eldest sons, are patterned expressions of the old or carnal man, sons of the bondwoman (death, sin) whom "shall not be heirs" of that which is born of the Spirit (the younger brother). As formulated by one scholar:

"Put it down as an incontrovertible fact of the Bible that the **land of promise and the seed of promise are inseparably linked**. At this point one may be inclined to ask why, then, was Ishmael the firstborn? The Bible **principle is that the natural ever comes first and is superseded by the spiritual**. First it is the natural Adam, then it is the spiritual Last Adam; first Ishmael, then Isaac; first Esau, then Jacob; first the natural birth, then the spiritual birth." [81]

For background, consider Genesis 21 and the story of Ishmael where once again we see the hand of God directing one of his servants, in this case Abraham, to do something seemingly cruel and perhaps avoidable. Like the story of Nephi and Laban, it is an account of life and death. We agonize with Abraham for the severity of the task which the Lord asks him to do, which was to send his eldest and much loved son Ishmael into the desert to face almost certain death.[82] (Abraham's first great test of faith it seems was with Ishmael [the flesh], which prepared him for his later and more difficult test with Isaac [the spiritual].) As modern readers we wonder why Abraham's family can't simply get along and live happily together under one roof, while instead there is perpetual dysfunction within all the patriarchal families – Cain killed his brother Abel, Esau seeks the life of his brother Jacob, Joseph is sold into slavery by his brothers, and Laman and Lemuel seek to kill Nephi. Indeed, at the time of the patriarch Noah, the whole wicked human family (as a type of the eldest brother) was slain so that mankind could be born anew. (Noah is a story that we understand to be "the like figure whereunto [even] baptism doth also now save us", 1 Pet 3:21) The travail of putting off the flesh, followed by spiritual rebirth, is the figurative pattern at the center of Abraham's and all the patriarch's stories, pointing to Christ's Atonement as the great and final sacrifice for carnal sin. Based on what we know of Nephi's scriptural competence, it seems probable that he knew the figurative significance of Ishmael's story in Genesis. Likely, Paul's allegorical interpretation of Ishmael is not original, but is rooted in a more ancient source, one that perhaps Nephi also had access to. Nephi's hope might have been that we would possess the same competency and appreciation of Abraham's story, and be able to compare (parallel) its allegorical similarities to his struggle with Laban.[83]

Though there are more elements that we could discuss from the life of Ishmael which reinforce him as a type of carnal man, let's turn our discussion to several other fascinating parallels in 1 Ne 16. Just as the ancient Israelites remembered their Exodus by the name of the places they encamped, Nephi has done likewise, providing us with the name of the locations his family's encampments. We will organize the next few segments of our discussion based on these parallel places and their symbolic meanings.

- **River Laman – Crossed (1 Ne. 16:12)**

It has been said that the image of crossing a body of water represents a "natural metaphor for the transformative journey arising out of embracing adversity."[84] In the spirit of this symbol, people today cross the Rio Grande to come to America, the land of opportunity. Similarly our Mormon pioneer ancestors first crossed the Missouri River, endured the adversity of a long exodus, and later crossed the Sweetwater River of Wyoming in order to arrive in Zion. For many, like the Willie-Martin group, these crossings were transformative beyond our contemporary experience, especially in the winter extremes when many froze and died. Whether river, lake, or sea; water as the source of life can also be the cruelest of contradictions. Staying in the valley would no doubt be safer, but not life altering. Whether adversity is embraced or endured, a river is a recognized marker of transformation, unto life or death, as the case may be. When Lehi's family, who are a figure of all humanity, cross over, they leave the comfortable and familiar behind, and enter into an unknown future where they will walk by faith. From Alonzo Gaskill we find, "In scripture, water can symbolize two very different concepts: (1) cleansing, sanctification, revelation, and the Holy Spirit and (2) chaos, death, and the grave."[85] Similarly, we know that Lehi's group will also cross the great chasm of water in order to enter a promised land, which crossing, as we will discuss, is likewise a symbolic struggle. Both the Lehites and the Israelites cross water to begin and end their exoduses.

- **Three days or phases – Shazer, Nahom, Bountiful**

For a moment, consider below how Nephi's *three* camps correspond to the *three* phases of Nephi's earliest journey back into Jerusalem (and to Noah's dove):

Journey to Obtain Brass Plates	Lehi's Journey	Noah' Dove
Laman's unsuccessful attempt	Shazer	Sent – returns with nothing
Brothers unsuccessful 2ⁿᵈ time, angel appears and promises success	Nahom	Returns with olive branch
Nephi enters by faith into Jerusalem obtains word of God, will prosper	Bountiful	Does not return, fruit of faith, fruitful in new world

The following discussion, which reveals the Hebrew meanings of these locations, should help to shed light on how Lehi's camps are parallel to these other stories.

- South to Shazer – 1ˢᵗ of Three Locations

In 16:11 Lehi's group *take seed* of every kind and depart into the wilderness. They cross the river Laman, which symbolizes a new beginning. Nephi tells us in verse 12-13:

> 12 And it came to pass that we did take our tents and depart into the wilderness, across the river Laman. 13 And it came to pass that we traveled for the space of **four days**, nearly a south-southeast direction, and we did pitch our tents again; and we did call the name of the place *Shazer*.

Nephi indicates that they travel for four days. Four in the Old Testament is thought to be a number that symbolized earth, creation, or the worldly.[86] For instance, there are four rivers that flow out of Eden into the carnal world, or in Revelation 7:1 there are four angels which stand on the four corners of the world. The 4th seal of the book of Revelation is death:

> Rev 6:7 And when he had opened the fourth seal, I heard the voice of the **fourth beast** say, Come and see. And I looked, and behold a pale horse: and **his name that sat on him was Death**, and Hell followed with him. And power was given unto them over the fourth part of the earth, to kill **with sword**, and **with hunger**, and **with death**, and **with the beasts** of the earth.

Ezekiel by prophecy predicts four kinds of death in Eze.14:18,

> For thus saith the Lord GOD; How much more when I send my **four sore judgments** upon Jerusalem, **the sword**, and **the famine**, and **the noisome beast**, and **the pestilence**, to cut off from it man and beast?

Twice, Jeremiah also uses four as death in Jer. 15:2,

> Thus saith the LORD; Such as are for **death, to death**; and such as are for the sword, to the sword; and such as are for the famine, to the famine; and such as are for the captivity, to the captivity. And **I will appoint over them four kinds**, saith the LORD: the sword to slay, and the dogs to tear, and the fowls of the heaven, and the beasts of the earth, to devour and destroy.

When the Lord makes his covenant with Abraham, he tells him that his seed will spend four generations in captivity:

> But in the fourth generation they shall come hither again: for the iniquity of the Amorites [is] not yet full.

Four is the number of generations required for the Amorites, as well as the Israelites, to be fully corrupted and officially dead. Recall that when Lazarus died he lay 4 days in the tomb. It is believed that Christ waited intentionally until the 4th day so that all would know that He truly had power over death. (The Jewish rabbinical tradition was that a man was officially dead on the fourth day; when the soul departs the body.)[87]

Next, Nephi tells us that the direction that they are traveling is to the south, which is also the direction that Moses travels with the children of Israel upon leaving Egypt. Nephi's family, in fact, follows the same directional pattern of Israel's exodus as they move from camp to camp.[88] On the third stage of Lehi's journey, after the Lord has revealed himself powerfully to them, they will change direction and travel eastward, which is the considered the divine direction, towards God. [89] (Christ will come from the east) Israel also wanders to the East of Canaan before going west into their land of promise. Similarly, Lehi's group travels east in its third period wilderness experience before sailing west to their land of promise.

Finally, Nephi tells us that the first location where they pitched their tents was called Shazer. The Hebrew meaning of this word will give us valuable information concerning the spiritual whereabouts of Lehi's family. Hugh Nibley wrote:

> The first important stop after Lehi's party had left their base camp was at a place they called Shazer. The name is intriguing. The combination shajer is quite common in Palestinian place names; it is a collective meaning "trees," and many Arabs (especially in Egypt) pronounce it shazher. [90]

From another source (Joseph F. McConkie) we find that in scripture "trees are the symbol for man: Trees represent men: green trees are the righteous, dry trees the wicked (Luke 23:31; D&C 135:6)."[91] Coincidently, Moses' first official encampment with Israel was Elim, which in Hebrew also means trees.[92]

Thus, Nephi has given 4 clues to help his readers understand the location of Lehi's group (they cross the river, 4 days, going south, the name Shazer), all of which refer to a place of mortality or carnal man. According to the patriarchal pattern, Shazer is exactly where we would expect Lehi's family to be. Also, Shazer is the place where Nephi breaks his steel bow and Lehi's group faces the prospect of famine, just as Jacob's family in Genesis faced the same prospect before going down into Egypt to seek bread from Joseph. Shazer is a place of hardship where all are humbled, and is preparatory to major revelation, which we would expect to find in the next period of their three part wilderness journey.

- **Nephi's wooden bow of Shazer**

When Nephi's steel bow breaks in Shazer (trees) he faithfully crafts a wooden and seemingly weaker one to replace it. After conferring with his father, Nephi follows the instructions of the Liahona and goes with his wooden bow to the mountain to hunt for food. In 16:29 he reflects that "by small means the Lord brings about great things." (Does Nephi here refer to only the Liahona, or also to his wooden bow?) With faith like steel, and seemingly the weakest of bows, Nephi goes to the mountain according to the directions of the ball (word of God) where he slays animals, and in so doing saves his family from hunger. Consider how something weak, like wood, is used symbolically in scripture, and how the Lord uses it to test our faith and bring about great things:

> Christ carries **wood** for his sacrifice up to the mount, is the Lamb to be slain, saves mankind

> Isaac prepares and carries **wood** up mount, Lord provides ram to be slain, preserves Abraham's seed

> Nephi prepares and carries **wooden** bow up mount, Lord directs Nephi to animals to be slain, saves family from famine

> Moses receives instructions on mount to craft timbers of **wood** for tabernacle and ark, a place to sacrifice in similitude

> Nephi receives instructions on the mount for crafting timbers of **wood** for a ship (ark), so "great a work" done in faith, and he will be bound, like Isaac, on the wooden craft he has prepared

> Noah receives instructions for building a **wooden** ark with *three* levels. (The ark is covered in *kophar* or pitch, which generally means ransom in Hebrew [e.g. Ex 3:20]; from the root *kaphar*, the word for Atonement). Thereby life is preserved and reborn

Wooden rod of Moses is "least of means", yet it is used to part the Red Sea, to cleave the rock of living water, and to lead Israel out of bondage and death.

Christ, the carpenter who worked with **wood,** invites all men to take his yoke (of wood) upon them, for by such means the great work of the Atonement lightens their burdens

The small seed, planted in faith, grows the great tree (**wood**) of life (Alma 32). Christ is nailed to that tree

Conversely, the steel bow of Shazer seems to be another symbol for the spacious building, a representation of our pride. It is a symbol of the world's power to provide what the natural man craves, which must therefore ALWAYS be broken before we can truly make Christ the center of our lives. If we checked, everyone in the spacious building of Lehi's dream would likely have a steel bow. Those at the tree of life, however, don't need a steel bow in order to "obtain food", which is provided freely because of their faith, and is better than any steel bow. You might want to read 1 Ne 16:18 again where Nephi says, "I did break my bow". Nephi offers no excuse or explanation about how it came to be broken. Is it unreasonable to suggest that Nephi perhaps broke it on purpose? We know that as they traveled Nephi "looked upon the ball and beheld the things that were written" (vs 26-27). Could the writing of the Lord have instructed Nephi to break his bow in an act of faith? Has the Lord ever been known to ask such an unlikely and difficult sacrifice, knowing all the while the growth it will bring?

Counterpoints to Nephi's abiding faith, Laman and Lemuel never truly plant the seed of the word in their hearts, they forever cling to a bow of steel or the arm of flesh, which by the sight of it (faith is not seeing) is a far superior bow, not trusting that the Lord can and will provide. May I suggest that if the steel bow in our life has not already been broken then we must do all in our power to see that it is! If we want to make it to the land of promise, its breaking seems to be a requisite. Only then can we be led as Nephi, by the Spirit and not by our personal desires and direction. The breaking of the steel bow is a necessary prelude in a sequence of events that culminates at the center of chapter 16, the death of Ishmael at Nahom, which as we have seen, is a symbol of putting off the carnal man (even as covenant Abraham cast out Ishmael).

- **South to Nahom – 2nd of Three**

In 1 Nephi 16:33 Lehi leaves Shazer:

33 And it came to pass that we did again take our journey, traveling nearly the same course as in the beginning; and after we had traveled for the space of many days we did pitch our tents again, that we might tarry for the space of a time. 34 And it came to pass that Ishmael died, and was buried in the place which was called **Nahom**.

The footnotes of the Book of Mormon tell us what Nahom in Hebrew probably means: "consolation," from the verb *naham*, "be sorry, console oneself" (often transliterated as *nacham*). In the Hebrew lexicon we can read a fuller meaning of this word:

NIPHAL נָחַם—(1) *to lament, to grieve* (as to the use of passive and middle forms in verbs of emotion, compare נֶאֱנַח, ὀδύρομαι, *contristari*, etc.)—(*a*) because of the misery of others; whence, *to pity*. Constr. absol. Jer. 15:6, נִלְאֵיתִי הִנָּחֵם "I am weary of pity-ing;" followed by עַל Psal. 90:13; אֶל Jud. 21:6; לְ verse 15; מִן Jud. 2:18.—(*b*) because of one's own actions; whence, *to repent* (compare Germ. reuen, which formerly and still in Switzerland is *to grieve*, Engl. *to rue*), Exod. 13:17; Gen. 6:6, 7; const. followed by עַל Ex. 32:12, 14; Jer. 8:6; 18:8, 10; אֶל 2 Sa. 24: 16; Jer. 26:3.

(2) reflex. of Piel *to comfort* oneself, [*to be comforted*], Gen. 38:12; followed by עַל on account of any thing, 2 Sa. 13:39; and אַחֲרֵי i. e. for any one's loss, Gen. 24:67. From the idea of being consoled it becomes — 93

Thus, *naham* can mean either to mourn, to repent (meaning grieved "by one's own actions"), or to comfort. The events at Nahom seem to indicate that all three meanings are apropos; Ishmael dies and they grieve, they repent for their rebellion, and they also are comforted by the voice (words) of the Lord! For related scriptural context, *naham* is used in Psalms 23:4,

> Yea, though I walk through the valley of the shadow of death, I will fear no evil: for thou [art] with me; thy rod and thy staff they **comfort** (*naham)* me.

Speaking of the Messiah, Isaiah uses *naham* in 52:9-10,

> Break forth into joy, sing together, ye waste places of Jerusalem: for the LORD hath **comforted** (*naham*) his people, he hath redeemed Jerusalem. The LORD hath made bare his holy arm in the eyes of all the nations; and all the ends of the earth shall see the salvation of our God.

The word "repent" (*naham*) is often used for the change of heart and the grief man experiences for what he has done, as in the case of Job 42:5-6,

> I have heard of thee by the hearing of the ear: but now mine eye seeth thee. Wherefore I abhor [myself], and **repent** (*naham*) in dust and ashes.

Certainly in these meanings for the word *naham* we also see the workings of the Holy Ghost (Jonah) who was send by the Father to comfort those who grieve, to witness of a promised Savior (Isa 52:9-10), and to sanctify those who repent. And, since Nahom is the second of our three patterned encampments, it is the period in which the Lord should reveal himself and his promises. What happens in Nahom is therefore very similar to what happened to Nephi when he was grieved by his brothers on their second attempt to get the plates. At that time an angel arrived with promises of deliverance and comfort (1 Ne 3). Similarly, 1 Nephi 17: 39 relates:

> 39 And it came to pass that the Lord was with us, yea, **even the voice of the Lord came and did speak many words (seed) unto them**, and did chasten them exceedingly; and after **they were chastened by the voice of the Lord** they did turn

away their anger, and did repent of their sins, insomuch that the Lord did bless us again with food, that we did not perish.

Here is the revelation we expected. In Nahom the voice of the Lord speaks to all, even those who are rebelling. We aren't given details concerning how or in what form they heard the Lord's voice, but we know that Laman and Lemuel will not murmur again for eight years after this transforming incident (eight is a number in scripture which often symbolizes rebirth[94]). Suitably, the result of this experience is captured in the Hebrew name that Lehi's group gives to the place where Ishmael dies – a place where they are chastened, repent, and are comforted.   Though this was a very significant experience, sadly the seeds that the Lord plants do not take permanent root in Laman and Lemuel's carnal hearts, and like so many who initially come to the tree of life, over time Laman and Lemuel's faith wanes, and eventually they "wandered off and were lost" (1 Ne 8:23).

- **East to Bountiful – Third of Three**

Chapter 17:1-6 is the beginning of the *third* period of Lehi's journey in the wilderness (mortality). The chiasmus which began in 1 Nephi 16, actually ends in the first verses of chapter 17 (initially the book of Mormon had no chapters or verses). In verses 1-6 we read:

1 And it came to pass that we did again take our journey in the wilderness; and we did travel nearly **eastward from that time forth**. And we did travel and wade through much affliction in the wilderness; and our women did **bear children** in the wilderness. 2 And so **great were the blessings** of the Lord upon us, that while we did live upon raw meat in the wilderness, our women did give **plenty** of suck for their children, and were strong, yea, even like unto the men; and they began to bear their journeyings without murmurings. 3 And thus we see that the commandments of God must be fulfilled. And if it so be that the children of men keep the commandments of God he doth nourish them, and strengthen them, and provide means whereby they can accomplish the thing which he has commanded them; wherefore, he did provide means

for us while we did sojourn in the wilderness. 4 And we did sojourn for the space of many years, yea, even eight years in the wilderness. 5 And we did come to the land which **we called Bountiful, because of its much fruit (seed).** 6 And it came to pass that we did pitch our tents by the seashore; and notwithstanding we had suffered many afflictions and much difficulty, yea, even so much that we cannot write them all, we were exceedingly rejoiced when we came to the seashore; and we called the place **Bountiful, because of its much fruit.**

Whatever the Lord said to Laman and Lemuel, and how ever he said it, it must have made quite an impression, for at last they bear "their journeyings without murmurings." Like Moses and the Israelites, Lehi's family is also provided with a version of manna (seed); their meat is sweetened while they journey and does not need to be cooked (17:12). Nephi affirms that because of their faithfulness they are fruitful on their journey; bearing children, being nourished, arriving in Bountiful - a fruitful place. Curiously there is a verse in the Old Testament which speaks of such fruitful places in the wilderness, which seems to also refer to Lehi's remnant group. In Isaiah 32:15-16, 19-20, Isaiah prophecies (parenthesis mine):

> Because the palaces shall be forsaken; **the multitude of the city shall be left**; the forts and towers shall be for dens for ever, a joy of wild asses, a pasture of flocks; **Until the spirit be poured upon us** from on high, and the **wilderness be a fruitful field**, and the **fruitful field** be counted for a forest (people). Then judgment shall dwell in the wilderness, and righteousness remain in the **fruitful field.** When it shall hail, coming down on the forest (people of Jerusalem); and the city shall be low in a low place. **Blessed [are] ye that sow beside all waters**, that send forth [thither] the feet of the ox and the ass.

In fact, Lehi's family has left the palaces and multitudes of Jerusalem, the Spirit has poured out upon them at Nahom, and fruitful in the wilderness, Lehi's group is "sowing beside all waters" as they pitch their tents by the sea in Bountiful! It is worth noting that the third period Lehi's family's sojourn is called Bountiful, "because of its much fruit" (1 Ne 17:5). As a type of our mortal sojourn, it is a season of grace, when the seed planted by the word of the Lord, and watered by the Spirit, comes to fruition in our lives, preparing us for our return to the Land of Promise. Because old things (carnal man) are passing away, it is a time of renewal when the tree of life can mature and prolifically bear the fruits of the Spirit (Gal 5:22).

- **The Liahona – small means or cunning art?**

As previously mentioned, for each encampment there emerges within Nephi's story a related object. The chart below illustrates the relationship between Lehi's three encampments, and the three objects.

Shazer	Steel Bow	Dove w/ nothing
Nahom - Lord speaks	Liahona - word of Christ	Dove w/ promise
Bountiful	Ship	Dove is fruitful

It shouldn't be too surprising that each object represents a new test in a progressing story. The steel bow represented pride and self-reliance which needed to be broken in order to ready Lehi's family to receive instruction from the Lord provided through the Liahona. Since the Liahona is the second of three, it isn't surprising that it is also a type for the word of God (as Alma tells us in Alma 37:45). In the next chapter Lehi's family builds a ship, which represents, among other things, faith and obedience to the instruction they have received.

Nephi makes the comment in verse 16:29, "thus we see by small means the Lord can bring about great things". Alma later uses this same term (small means) to describe the many miracles of faith that occurred "day by day" during Lehi's journey (Alma 37:41). And though we considered earlier how this phrase might refer to Nephi's wooden bow of faith, there is a parallel in chapter 16's chiasmus which equates the phrase "small means" specifically to "cunning arts". Let's look at an extract of just these verses (C through D). There are some insights to consider which makes the parallels between these verses fascinating:

C 25 **Voice of Lord came** unto my father

> D 27 And when my father beheld the things on the ball he did **fear and tremble**
> 28 The **pointers (lead)** which were in the ball
> > did work **according to the faith and diligence** and heed given them
> > 29 And there was written new writing which was **plain to be read**

> > 29 Thus we see **by small means (machashaba)**

> > > the Lord can bring about **great things**
> > > > 30 I Nephi did go up into **the top of the mountain** (ministered by angels**)**
> > > > according to the **directions** (words) which were upon the ball

E and F, Apex - Nahom

> > > 38 Now he says the **Lord has talked to him,**
> > > and also **Angels have ministered** (on top of the mountain)
> > > 38 We know he lies; he worketh **many things**

by his cunning arts (machashaba),

> > > that he may **deceive our eyes**, thinking
> > 38 perhaps that he may **lead us** away into some strange wilderness;
> > > 38 he thought to make himself a ruler over us **according to his will and pleasure**
> D' 38 And after this manner did Laman stir up their hearts to **anger**

C' 39 **Voice of Lord came** and did speak many words

Notice how the "voice of the Lord" wonderfully frames these center-most parallels (C,C'). Also, take note of the word that is in parenthesis – **machashaba**. This Hebrew word is used in a variety of ways, and could easily be the source for "means" in verse 28-29, as well as the Hebrew source for the parallel "cunning arts", "thinking", or "thought" in verse 38. In the Old Testament, *machashaba* is rendered as — thought, device, purpose, work, imaginations, cunning, devised, invented, and "means"[95]. For instance, it is used to describe the cunning work that went into building Israel's tabernacle:

> Ex 31:3 And I have filled him with the spirit of God, in wisdom, and in understanding, and in knowledge, and in all manner of **workmanship**, 4 To **devise cunning works** *(machashaba)*, to work in gold, and in silver, and **in brass.**

Interestingly we see that Moses also had divinely inspired works made in brass which were *machashaba*! Nephi's brothers use this word in almost the same way - "he worketh many things by his cunning arts" to describe the way in which they think they have been deceived by Nephi's use of the Liahona (small means).

For an example of how *machashaba* is also rendered as "means", in 2 Samuel 14:14 we read:

> For we will surely die and become like water spilled on the ground, which cannot be gathered up again. Yet God does not take away a life; but He devises **means** *(machashaba)*, so that His banished ones are not expelled from Him.

Just like Lehi's group, where the "small means" was provided by the Lord, in this Old Testament example the Lord is again the one who devises means to preserve his people.

Along these lines, consider what new understanding ("new writing") we find in Nephi's very next parallel verses. Verse 30 relates that Nephi "did go to the mount according to the directions on the ball." However, he doesn't mention angels ministering to him. Yet, when we compare the parallel, verse 38, we find his brothers complaining that Nephi has spoken about angels ministering to him, and also that he has talked with the Lord.

30 And it came to pass that I, Nephi, did go forth up into the top of the mountain, according to the directions which were given upon the ball.	38 Now, he says that the Lord has talked with him, and also that angels have ministered unto him.

Though we may have guessed this, these chiastic parallels wonderfully confirm that the place where Nephi was ministered to by angels and did talk to the Lord was on the mount!

- **Some other interesting parallels found in this chapter's chiasmus**

In verses 31-33, which lead up to the apex of Ishmael's death, we find that they had great joy, they humbled themselves, and gave thanks. Antithetical to this, in verses 35-36, they murmur and desire to return to Jerusalem – spiritual darkness. We might again be reminded of Paul's words in Galatians: "Even so we, when we were children, were in bondage under the elements of the world: … But now, after that ye have known God, or rather are known of God, **how turn ye again to the weak and beggarly elements**, whereunto ye desire again to be in bondage? . . . But as then he that was born after the flesh persecuted him [that was born] after the Spirit, even so [it is] now. . . Nevertheless what saith the scripture? Cast out the bondwoman and her son (Ishmael): for the son of the bondwoman shall not be heir with the son of the freewoman." (Gal 4:3, 9, 29, 30) Paul is describing the people of his time who had the same problem as Lehi and Ishmael's group, some who had "known God" and experienced its joy, yet were turned again to "weak and beggarly elements" of the world and of the flesh, which was represented by Ishmael.

Another intriguing parallel is verse 16:31 to verse 16:37. In verse 31 Nephi has slain the "wild beasts" as directed by the Lord, and in verse 37 his brethren now desire to slay him. If you remember, in 1 Ne 7 when they went to get Ishmael's family they also wanted to kill Nephi by giving him to the "wild beasts". As mentioned earlier, the phrase "wild beast" is used only 2 times in the Book of Mormon, and coincidently in the parallel chiasmi of 1Nephi 7 and 1Nephi 16. Also, though Jerusalem is often mentioned in Nephi's writing, the phrase "desire to return" to Jerusalem is a unique element found in chapter 16's center, and also at the center of chapter 7. Both chapters are about the internal struggles of Lehi's group (travailing as in birth).

12

Joseph's Famine (Chapter 5) = Moses' Thirst (Chapter 17)

Chapter 17 is Nephi's account of events that happen in Bountiful before they leave on their ocean crossing to the Promised Land. Eight years have now passed and the Lord once again speaks to Nephi, telling him to go to a high mountain, where he is he is taught how to build a ship. Laman and Lemuel once more begin to be a source of dissention, claiming (yet again) that the people of Jerusalem were righteous, and that father Lehi has deceived them by his words. Nephi refutes them by recounting for his brothers how their journey, like the ancient Israelite Exodus, has been divinely guided. Whereas chapter 5 (this chapter's parallel), centered on Jacob and Joseph going *into Egypt*, chapter 17 is a narration about Moses *leaving Egypt*. Below is a diagram of this relationship:

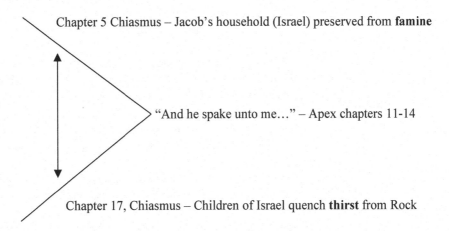

Chapter 5 Chiasmus – Jacob's household (Israel) preserved from **famine**

"And he spake unto me…" – Apex chapters 11-14

Chapter 17, Chiasmus – Children of Israel quench **thirst** from Rock

1 Ne 5 illustrates the remedy for the famine that existed in Joseph's day – which was bread, and 1 Ne 17 has the remedy for the thirst of Moses' exodus – the waters of life! Together they represent the most basic elements to sustain life, which were chosen by Christ to represent the eternal life that comes through Him alone - He is the bread of life, and the fount of living water. To those who know His love, they are the emblems of the sacrament and tokens of his Atoning sacrifice. As they did anciently for Israel, these elements still have the power to save all those who worthily partake of them.

Let's look at this chiasmus in chapter 17, whose center is living water. As mentioned, Nephi likens Israel's exodus to his family's journey, curiously centering their success on the rock which Moses smote in Horeb (Ex 17:6), and not Mt Sinai as many might presume.

A 17-19 Ship to **cross** the great waters
Did **complain against** me
Desired **not to labor** on ship
Sorrowful over the **hardness of their hearts**
Thou canst not accomplish **so great** a work

  B 20 Like unto our **father**, wandered in wilderness, women have born children, toiled, suffered, afflictions, came **out of Jerusalem**

    C 21 We might have enjoyed our **possessions** and our **land**

      D 22 We know that the people in the land of Jerusalem are **a righteous people** for **they kept the statutes and judgments of the Lord**

        E 23 **Do ye believe our fathers** would have been led away if not hearkened?

          F 24 **Do ye suppose** that had the Lord not commanded Moses that he would **lead** them **(fathers)** out of bondage?

            G 25 The children of Israel were in **bondage**, they were **brought out** of bondage

              H 26 ye know that **by his word the waters of the Red Sea were divided**

                I 27 Egyptians were **drowned** in the Red Sea, the armies of Pharaoh

                  J 28 They were **fed manna** in the wilderness

                    29 Yea, And we know that Moses, **by his word** according to the **power of God** which was in him, smote the rock, and there came forth **water**, that the children of Israel might quench their **thirst**.

                  J 30 They being led … **leading them by day, giving light unto them by night**

                I 31 And it came to pass that according to his word he led and he did **destroy** them. (Israelites)

              H 31-32 Not anything done save **by his word**. And after **they crossed the river Jordan**

            G 32 he did make them **mighty** unto the **driving out** of the children of the land, scattering them to destruction

          F 33 **Do ye suppose** that the children of this land who were **driven** out by our **fathers** were righteous?

        E 34 **Do ye suppose our fathers** more choice if not righteous?

      D 35 He that is **righteous** is favored of God, but **this people has rejected every word of God.**

    C 36 God created **the earth** and his children that they should **possess** it

  B 40 Loved our **fathers**, Abraham, Isaac, Jacob, remembered covenants made. Did bring them **out of Egypt**

Because of the **simpleness or the easiness** of it, perished
Did **harden their hearts**
Labor which they had to perform was to look upon Serpent
Did **revile against** Moses
A 41-42 They were **led forth** by his matchless power into the land of promise

In his account, Nephi completely skips Mt. Sinai where God's word was also given to Israel, while still accounting for it (the word) several times at the center of this chiastic thought – "by his word the waters of the Red Sea were divided" (vs 26), "by his word . . . he smote the rock and there came forth water" (vs 29), "not anything done save by his word" (vs31). In regard to Mt Sinai, it may be that he conflates the two events (much as Stephen conflates Mt Zion and Mt Sinai in Acts 7:7). Certainly Mt Sinai (the Ten Commandments) is prefigured by the events at Horeb, also a rock that brought forth the living water of the word. The place-name Horeb is not only used in the Old Testament for the rock which Moses struck (Ex 17:6), but is used many times in place of Mt Sinai. In the Lexicon we read that Horeb is "a lower summit of Mt Sinai, from which one ascends Mt Sinai", or that "Horeb seems to have been a general name for a mountain, of which Sinai was a particular summit".[96] In any event, Nephi has gone out of his way to create a structure which is harmonious to its parallel in chapter 5, even when a more traditional center (the law given on Mt Sinai) is perhaps expected!

- **Serpent = Ship**

Let's look for a moment at the endpoints of Nephi's chiasmus (A,A'). Verses 17-19, Nephi's instructions to build a ship, reflect verses 41-42, the story of Moses' brass serpent. I have paraphrased and aligned them below for closer inspection:

Ship verses 17-19	Brass Serpent verses 41-42
Ship to cross great waters (to Promised Land)	Led forth by His matchless power into the land of promise
Did complain against me	Did revile against Moses
Desired not to labor	Task (labor) was to look upon Serpent
Harden their hearts	Harden their hearts
It was **too "great** a work"	It was **too simple** or easy

The children of Israel thought that God's command to look upon the serpent was too simple, and hardened their hearts, whereas Nephi's brethren thought that the task of building a ship too difficult. (Certainly our lack of faith, and disobedience to God's word, falls somewhere in this range.) Because the brass serpent symbolizes Jesus Christ (Jn 3:14), Nephi's ship is its equivalent, also a symbol of Christ (by whose "matchless power" the worlds were created, and the Atonement was accomplished)! Indeed, Nephi's ship will keep his family safe as they cross the perilous waters as surely as looking to the Brass Serpent saved ancient Israel!

- **"Not anything done save by his word"**

Between the two symbols for Christ (the serpent and the ship), the rest of this chiasmus in chapter 17 is mostly a discussion of the word's power in the lives of Moses' Israel and the covenant fathers. Below is a list of some of these structured parallels, several of which are also antithetical. (Also, notice how precisely the questions of verses 23 and 24 parallel the only other questions in this chiasmus, verses 33 and 34):

20 Our father led out of Jerusalem	40 Loved fathers, because of Abraham's covenant fathers brought out of Egypt
22 Brothers think those in Jerusalem are righteous, keep the statutes (word)	35 People of Canaan were not righteous and had rejected every word
23 Fathers led away if had not hearkened (to word)?	34 Our fathers more choice if not righteous?
24 Would Moses lead fathers without God's commandment (word)?	33 Were people driven out by fathers more righteous?
26 By word Red Sea divided	32 By word Jordan divided
27 Egyptians were drowned, (by his word)	31 Israelites were destroyed, according to word
28 Fed with manna	30 Led by day, given light by night

29 Moses, by his word according to the
power of God which was in him, smote the rock,
and there came forth water

You might observe that Nephi directs our attention to the "word" (directly or implied) in these parallels, and also at the apex (vs 29). Particularly beautiful is Nephi's assurance in verse 31 that, "according to his word He did do all things for them; and there *was not anything done save it were by his word*". Why the Lord did all of this for Israel, is explained in verse 40 - to preserve His covenant with the fathers (a covenant given by his word and preserved by its power). Parallel to verse 40 is verse 20, where Nephi parallels his own father to the ancient fathers, affirming the Lord's continued covenant blessing in Lehi. All of which leads to the center of these verses (vs 29), a miracle that preserved God's covenant, which prefigures the enduring covenant emblems and life saving miracle of Jesus Christ.

- **Covenant Emblems**

Let's look at a comparison of the apexes from chapter 5 and chapter 17, water at the center of one (thirst), and bread at the center of the other (famine).

24 **Do ye suppose** that had the Lord not commanded Moses that he would **lead** them **(fathers)** out of bondage?

26 ye know that **by his word the waters of the red sea were divided**
27 Egyptians were **drowned** in the red Sea, the armies of Pharaoh
28 They were **fed manna** in the wilderness (miracle)

1 Nephi 17
Apex

29 Yea, And we know that Moses, **by his word** according to the power of God which was in him, smote the rock, and there came forth **water**, the children of Israel (seed) might quench their **thirst**.

30 They being led … **giving light unto them by night** (miracle)
31 And it came to pass that according to his word he led and he did **destroy** them.
31-32 Not anything done save **by his word**. And after **they crossed the river Jordan** he did make them mighty

33 **Do ye suppose** that the children of this land who were **driven out** by our **fathers** were righteous?

Vs 13 And also the **prophecies** of the holy prophets to Zedekiah; and also many prophecies spoken by **Jeremiah**

Lehi also found a **genealogy** (record) of his **fathers**,
    descendent of Joseph,
        son of **Jacob**
        sold into Egypt (death), who was
        preserved
            by hand of Lord that he might
            preserve his father Jacob

1 Nephi 5
Apex

Vs 14 and all his **household** (seed) from perishing with **famine** (seed of the word)

They were led **out of captivity**
out of the Land of Egypt (death)
    by that same God who had
    preserved them.
And **Laban** was a
descendent of Joseph, wherefore
he and his **fathers** had kept the **records**

Vs 17 **My father** was filled with the spirit and began **to prophecy** concerning his seed

If you look at the chiasmus for chapter 5 above, you will see that it also has several variations of the "word"; i.e. prophecies, records, genealogy, and an allusion to the famine of the word. In addition, like chapter 17, chapter 5 also has verses which focus multiple times on "the fathers," celebrating the miraculous events which preserved God's promises (covenant). Also, as you look at these centers you might get a sense of the pattern proposed by Stephen in Acts 7 (pgs 224, 227, 229), which positioned life in the middle and figures of death or destruction on either side. (Chapter 17 has the destruction of pharaoh's army and Israel's death in the wilderness on both sides, and chapter 5 has Egypt as a symbol of bondage or death on either side.)

160

Also, in the event that you question water as a true sacrament emblem, please note the confirming words of Paul in 1 Cor 10:3-4, where he compares his contemporary "partakers at the Lord's table" to ancient Israel at Horeb (parenthesis mine):

3 And did all eat the same spiritual meat (manna); 4 And did all drink the same spiritual drink: for they **drank of that spiritual Rock** that followed them: and that Rock was Christ.

The water at Horeb was a spiritual drink which prefigured the sacrament. The "Rock was Christ" and the water which flowed from it is a figure of the blood which flowed from Christ - whose death brings life, even as life came forth out of a lifeless rock.

- Implications – His Emblems, The Sermon on the Mount

As we contemplate Nephi's unique composition, especially the parallel centers of chapters 5 and 17, which allude to the sacrament elements, we should realize that Nephi's ideas can enhance our understanding of other scriptures. For instance, where else in scripture do we read about famine and thirst, or "hungering and thirsting"? An obvious example is from the Sermon on the Mount when Christ teaches, "Blessed are those that hunger and thirst after righteousness, for they shall be filled." (Mat 5:6) When Christ comes to America he will deliver the same sermon, but with an important addition at the end of this beatitude, "Blessed are all they who do hunger and thirst after righteousness, for they shall be filled with the Holy Ghost." (3 Ne 11:6) Upon examination, this beatitude is using the imagery of the sacrament prayer and teaching the same lesson, that as we partake of the bread (preserving us from hunger) and water (preserving us from thirst), which are the designated tokens to help us remember Him, we will "always have his Spirit" to be with us (filled with the Holy Ghost). The bread which saved Joseph's family, and the water from the rock which saved Moses' Israel, are the tokens which can also save us and bring us the righteousness (through Christ) that we seek.

- **Nephi's boat – Living Timbers of Faith**

As we have discussed, the *third* major item of this *three* part journey, Nephi's boat, is compared chiastically to the brass serpent of Moses, which also represents Christ. It is the vessel that will carry Lehi's seed of every kind across the sea to the land of promise. It is built by following the Lord's direction and not "after the manner of men." Appropriately, it is constructed during the *third* stage (Bountiful), in which we journey in faith according to the Lord's promise. Like a ship, Christ is the only safe purveyor of men through life, as well as across death's stormy sea. He will safely ferry the seed of posterity, the brass plates (word-seed), and all other good seed acquired in mortality.

In a spiritual sense, the "timbers of the ship" (18:1) are symbolically cut from the tree of life that we have planted in our hearts from a single seed of the word and nurtured in faith within us to a mature tree, which is a figure of Christ in us (Alma 32:41-42). "But if ye will nourish the word, yea, nourish the tree as it beginneth to grow, by your faith with great diligence, and with patience, looking forward to the fruit thereof, it shall take root; and behold it shall be **a tree springing up unto everlasting life**. And because of your diligence and your faith and your patience with the word in nourishing it, **that it may take root in you**, behold, by and by ye shall pluck the fruit thereof, which is most precious, which is sweet above all that is sweet, and which is white above all that is white, yea, and pure above all that is pure; and ye shall feast upon this fruit even until ye are filled, that ye **hunger** not, neither shall ye **thirst**". (Isn't it interesting how Alma also emphasizes the tree's ability to alleviate hunger and thirst, which is Nephi's chiastic thrust in chapters 5 and 17 - an allusion to the sacrament's bread and water.) Its timbers are living timbers which provide for all our needs, and ultimately, the land of promise can only be reached in a craft constructed of this personally grown spiritual material. Like the oil of the ten virgins which could not be borrowed, no one else can build it for us.

Nephi tells us that his ship was "not built after the manner of men." The language that he uses in 18:1-4 to describe its construction, "work timbers of curious workmanship", also alludes to the building of the Israelite tabernacle in Ex 31:5, "carving **of timber, to work** in all **manner of workmanship**." The Book of Hebrews later confirms that the tabernacle's construction and its contents (including the Ark) were patterned after "heavenly things", which were given to Moses while on the mount (where Nephi also received his instruction). In Ex 25:8-22 we find the ark's divine specifications, and that from above its mercy seat the Lord would commune with and guide Israel. Concerning the ark's meaning, the bible scholar Andrew Jukes says, "If there is a type in the Bible, the ark is surely a type—of Christ without doubt—but of Christ viewed dispensationally. Christ is the Ark, taking the chosen family from the world of judgment to the new heavens and the new earth."[97]

Others have noted that Nephi's ship, like the Ark of the Covenant, as well as Noah's ark, is also a symbol for Christ. The writer L. H. Read compares Nephi's ship to these arks:

> "the arks fulfilled God's covenant. They were the instruments of the "pass over." In every case, their true pattern, "the pattern shewed to thee in the mount" (Heb 8:5), was Jesus Christ, the Savior and Redeemer of the world, the *true ark of the covenant."* [98]

Even as Noah's ark carried the seeds of life to establish a new and better world, so the Ark of the Covenant contained several items which could be considered seeds essential for life and salvation. Hebrews 9:4 reminds us that the Ark of the Covenant contained *three* items:

> …and the ark of the covenant overlaid round about with gold, wherein [was] the golden pot that had **manna**, and Aaron's **rod** that budded, and the **tables** of the covenant;

All of these items represent the miraculous means by which God brought life to Israel. Moreover, Christ is found (personified) in all of them - the Manna represented the bread of life (seed) come down that literally and symbolically sustained spiritually famished Israel in the wilderness; the tablets are the word (seed), which if followed returns us to God.; and the "budded rod" was originally Moses' rod, which is a symbol of death bursting forth into new life (see Num 17:8 where it is left in the tabernacle and overnight newly buds). In the hands of Moses, the rod led Israel out of bondage (death) after performing many miracles in Egypt. Filled with these symbols, the ark led the camp of Israel (God's seed) through the desert (Num 10:33), and across the divided Jordan into the land of promise. Significantly, the ark was the only place where Israel could receive atonement for her sins (at the mercy seat). In a similar way the Lord wants to direct our journey, cleanse us of sin, and mercifully navigate us (help us "pass over") to the promised land.

Like our Savior, we are also compared in scripture to vessels to be filled with a variety of fruit-bearing seed. However, if our hearts are full of what the natural man has filled it with, there is no room for the things (seed) of God. In 2 Timothy 2 we read (parenthesis mine):

21 If a man therefore purge himself from these, he shall be a vessel unto honour, sanctified, and meet for the master's use, [and] prepared unto every good work. 22 Flee also youthful lusts (bad seed): but follow righteousness, faith, charity, peace, (good seed) with them that call on the Lord out of a pure heart (prepared vessel).

There is a song by Doug Walker that beautifully expresses how we can only bear the fruit of the seeds our vessels hold:

My life is made of seeds

Every one I plant becomes part of me

Good or bad ones, I must choose

And I should think about the future when I do

'Cause when the harvest finally comes

I will reap what I've become [99]

The last verse in this song ends with the question – "will the seeds that I have sown make me more like Him?" For that to happen we must allow Christ to form and ultimately be the master of our vessels in this life, our hearts filled with a most precious possession; the power of his word. Begotten of incorruptible seed, as his spiritual offspring, He will carry us through mortality and into eternity, forever bountiful.

- **My Soul is Rent with Aguish - Bountiful not fruitful for some**

After showing Laman and Lemuel how their journey has been a similitude of the patriarch fathers, Nephi in summation (not part of the chiasmus) compares the wicked and hardened hearts of the Israelites to Laman and Lemuel's. In verses 45-47 Nephi tells them, more than any other reason, the cause of the anguish which rends his soul:

> 45 Ye are swift to do iniquity but slow to remember the Lord your God. Ye have seen an angel, and **he spake unto you**; yea, ye have **heard his voice** from time to time; and he hath **spoken unto you in a still small voice**, but ye were past feeling, that ye could not **feel his words**; wherefore, he has **spoken unto you like unto the voice of thunder**, which did cause the earth to shake as if it were to divide asunder. 46 And ye also know that by **the power of his almighty word** he can cause the earth that it shall pass away; yea, and ye know that **by his word** he can cause the rough places to be made smooth, and smooth places shall be broken up. O, then, why is it, that ye can be so hard in your hearts? 47 Behold, my soul is rent with anguish because of you, and my heart is pained; I fear lest ye shall be cast off forever. Behold, I am full of the Spirit of God, insomuch that my frame has no strength.

Nephi powerfully describes the many ways in which his brother's have heard "the word" of the Lord. Indeed, few have ever experienced so much divine revelation in its many forms as his brothers Laman and Lemuel. Their rejection cuts deeply to the heart of Nephi's thoughts and many chiasmi, and to the innermost focus of his entire book - that which is "most desirable above all things and the most joyous to the soul." It is the cause for which Nephi entered into Jerusalem, the heart of the patriarchal pattern, the sign of Jonah, the resurrection and the life of all mankind, and the love of God spoken to man through the Holy Ghost. By rejecting God's command (word) to build the "ship", Laman and Lemuel reject Christ, who the ship represents (as do we all through our faithlessness). Perhaps our souls are rent with anguish not just for Nephi's brothers, but also for ourselves as we ponder what we have done with the Lord's sacred word spoken to us. Has it caused the hard places of our hearts to be broken up; has it been planted, taken root and grown to a tree bearing fruit in our lives? Has it filled us with the power of the Lord unto the consuming of our flesh? (17:48) Nephi invites us to come to Bountiful, to bring our timber born of good seed, leave spiritually dead Jerusalem behind and build our ship (shape our vessel) by divine instruction, not after the manner of man, but of Christ!

13

1 Nephi 18 – Death is Swallowed up in Victory

Because the entire book of 1 Nephi is a chiastic structure, if the reader understands one leg of the structure, but is unsure of the meaning of the corresponding leg, then he/she can combine both legs to better understand the entirety of the author's intent. Such is the case with Nephi's voyage to the Promised Land. In chapter 4 Laban threatened to kill Nephi and his brothers, as well as take all they possessed. In chapter 18, the depths of the sea threaten to swallow up Nephi's family in a "watery grave." Just as Laban was a type for death and sin which Nephi overcame, the menacing depths of the sea (along with Laman and Lemuel) represent the same thing – destruction and death. The events of chapter 18 go a long way towards confirming the initial interpretation of Nephi as a type of Christ and Laban as death in chapter 4, each chiasmus serving as a witness of the atoning message of the other. Indeed, without Nephi and his ship, all would have perished and not prospered. Below is a graphic of this parallel structure which by now has become familiar:

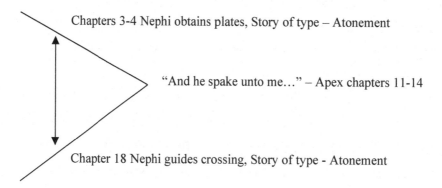

Chapters 3-4 Nephi obtains plates, Story of type – Atonement

"And he spake unto me…" – Apex chapters 11-14

Chapter 18 Nephi guides crossing, Story of type - Atonement

- **Poetic and chiastic structure in 1 Nephi 18**

The chiastic structure in 1 Nephi 18, which spans most of the chapter, uniquely references several events from the Old Testament. Nephi once again weaves these allusions into his story, creating a collage of messianic and gospel imagery which ultimately focuses on several "euphemisms of death" (verses 17-18). As in chapter 4, Nephi through obedience once again prevails against overwhelming deadly odds.

A 8 We did put forth **into the sea** and were driven towards **the promised land**

  B 9 **After we had** driven forth before the wind **for the space of many days**

    C 10 **I Nephi** began to speak to them, they didn't want brother **to rule (guide)** over them

      D 11 They **bound me**,
       E 12 the **compass did cease to work**,
        F 13 there **arose a great storm**
         G 14 the tempest began to be **exceedingly sore**

          H 15 a We were **about to be swallowed up in the depths of sea.**
           b **They began to see** that the
            c **judgments of God** were **upon them**, and that
             d must **perish**,
              e save **they repent**,
               f wherefore they **loosed the bands**

         I 16 I did not murmur because **of mine afflictions**
          J 17 **My Father** Lehi said many things unto them, and also unto the **Sons of Ishmael, they did breathe out threatenings**

           K and my parents **being stricken in years**, and having **suffered much grief**
            L **because** of **their children**,

              M 17 **they** were **brought down**, yea, even upon their *sick-beds.*
               18 **they** were brought **near** even **to be carried** *out of this time to meet their God;*

              M yea, **their grey hairs** were **about to be brought** *down to lie low in the dust;*
               yea, even **they** were **near to** *be* cast *with sorrow into a watery grave.*

           K 19 And Jacob and Joseph **also being young**, having need of nourishment, were **grieved**
            L **because of** the afflictions of **their mother**

         I And also of **my wife** with **her tears and prayers** (afflictions),
          J and also **my children**, did not **soften their hearts of my brethren.**

          H 20 a Nothing but **power of God** that **threatened them**
           c with **destruction** could soften their hearts
           b **They saw**
            d they were **about to be swallowed up in depths of sea.**
             e **They repented** of the thing they had done
              f and **loosed me**

      D 21 After they **loosed me**
       E 21 the **compass did work**,
        F 21 I prayed and **the storm ceased**
         G 21 and there was **a great calm**

    C 22 **I Nephi** did **guide** the ship

  B 23 **After we had** sailed **for the space of many days**

A 23 We did arrive at **the promised land** and went forth **upon the land.**

Since Nephi uses several scriptural elements of type to develop this chiastic story, let's review a few of them in order to deepen our understanding and appreciation of the Savior's Atonement through Nephi's eyes.

- **1 Nephi 18 – Crossing the Sea (the great gulf) – Suffer it**

Nephi, who built the vessel by going "into the mount oft," wherefore the Lord showed him "great things," is God's primary instrument to prepare for the ocean crossing. By way of comparison, we know that Christ also went to the mount often. In Luke 22:29 we read, "And he came out, and went, as he *was wont*, to the mount of Olives; and his disciples also followed him." The phrase "as it *was wont*" means "as it was his custom", and we can well imagine that Christ was often instructed and "showed many great things" (18:3) in the mount before the final night he prayed, atoned, and journeyed to the cross. Following a similar pattern of waiting for instruction, the Israelites at Sinai do not leave until Moses has received instruction on the mount and the tabernacle and Ark of the Covenant are built. Equally, Lehi's family cannot leave Bountiful without the ship's proper completion. Faithfulness to the divine instruction learned on the mount concerning how to build these vessels is prerequisite to departure. Likening ourselves to Nephi, Moses, and Christ, we cannot hope to successfully cross the everlasting gulf, which we are told is death and misery (Alma 26:20), without having first received instruction and practiced consistent faith, making a Christ-like vessel of ourselves.

Having "gone down into the ship" (18:9), his brothers begin to make merry, dancing and singing, demonstrating a "forgetfulness of the power" which brought them thither. (Conversely, it was Nephi's "remembering" while in Jerusalem that helped him to obediently comply with the constraints of the Spirit and slay Laban [death]). As a marker that 1 Ne 4 and 1 Ne 18 are reflecting stories, both begin with Nephi's brethren not wishing their brother to "rule over them", which is comparable to Moses and Joseph (types of Christ), whose brethren also did not wish them to be a judge over them (Ex 2:14). Laman and Lemuel bind Nephi with cords about the wrists and feet, and in verse 11 Nephi tells us:

11 Nevertheless, the Lord *did suffer it* that he might show forth his power, unto the fulfilling of his word (seed) *which he had spoken concerning the wicked.*

Nephi's ambiguous language here stimulates a few questions. Consider for a moment, to what or to whom "suffer it" refers. It is sufficiently ambiguous that we are not quite sure if it refers to Nephi's suffering or to the Lord's. We might also ask, what is the "fulfilling of his word concerning the wicked", or to what it alludes, and also, when was it "spoken", or where do we specifically find what "he had spoken concerning the wicked" in scripture? Nephi, who loves the plainness of Isaiah, might have referred us to that prophet for clarification. In Isaiah 53:7-8 we read:

5 But he [was] wounded for our transgressions, [he was] bruised for our iniquities: the chastisement of our peace [was] upon him; and with his stripes we are healed. All we like sheep have gone astray; we have turned every one to his own way; and the LORD **hath laid on him the iniquity of us all**.

Who are the wicked then? It seems that the wicked are those that dance, make merry, and sing on the ship, as well as those that murmur as the Jews in Jerusalem, and also those that would not have Christ, Moses, Joseph, or Nephi to rule over them. Is this not also a picture of ourselves as we forget the power that has brought us thither (18:9), likewise struggling to submit fully to the Master's rule? Sadly, the wicked of whom Nephi speaks is "us all", and it is our iniquity that "the Lord hath laid on him". Nephi's meaning therefore is possibly two-fold when he writes that the "Lord did suffer it", referring to Nephi's suffering as a type of Christ, and to the very Savior in Gethsemane - who came "unto the fulfilling of his word which he had spoken concerning the wicked", that he would suffer on their behalf and atone for their sins.

As it turns out, "suffer it" is a very unique phrase, used only one other time in the Book of Mormon, in chapter 19 where Nephi completely explains to whom the phrase "suffer it" refers. Let's go there briefly.

- **"Suffer it"**

Upon arriving in the Promised Land, in chapter 19 Nephi speaks of making the small plates. The first information that he inscribes concerns the coming of Christ six hundred years from that time. Nephi quotes the words of the *three* unknown prophets, Zenock, Neum, and Zenos, who each shed light on the origins of the ambiguous statement in 18:11, that "the Lord did **suffer it** that he might show forth his power, unto the fulfilling of his word which he had spoken concerning the wicked." In 19:9-10, speaking of Christ, Nephi uses the phrase in question:

9 And the world, because of their iniquity, shall judge him to be a thing of naught; wherefore they scourge him, and he **suffereth it**; and they smite him, and he **suffereth it**. Yea, they spit upon him, and he **suffereth it**, because of his loving kindness and his long-**suffering** towards the children of men. 10 And the God of our fathers, who were led out of Egypt, out of bondage, and also were preserved in the wilderness by him, yea, the God of Abraham, and of Isaac, and the God of Jacob, yieldeth himself, **according to the words** of the angel, as a man, into the hands of wicked men, to be lifted up, **according to the words** of Zenock, and to be crucified, **according to the words** of Neum, and to be buried in a sepulchre, **according to the words** of Zenos, which he spake concerning the three days of darkness, which should be a sign given of his death unto those who should inhabit the isles of the sea, more especially given unto those who are of the house of Israel.

Nephi repeats the phrase "suffereth it" (or "long-suffering") four times in verse 9, which run parallel to the four uses of "according to the words" in verse 10, spoken by the three prophets and the angel. These verses can also be easily arranged in a wonderful chiasmus with a familiar lesson at the apex - preservation from bondage (binding):

9 they scourge him, and he *suffereth it*

    9 they smite him, and he *suffereth it*

        9 they spit on him, and he *suffereth it*

            9 because of loving kindness and long-*suffering* toward men

                10 The **God** of our **fathers**

                    who were led out of Egypt

                      out of bondage

                      were preserved

                  in the wilderness

                10 by the **God** of **Abraham, Isaac, and Jacob**

              10 yieldeth himself, *according to* the words of the angel

            10 into the hands of wicked men, to be lifted up, *according to* words of Zenock

        10 to be crucified, *according to* the words of Neum

10 to be buried in a sepulcher, *according to* the words of Zenos

* See Chapter 2 (pg 35) for a discussion of the entire chiasmus in 1 Ne 19 and its parallel, 1 Ne 3.

Applying what we learn here to Nephi's binding in 18:11, the phrase, "nevertheless the Lord did **suffer it**", seems to directly apply to Christ. Further, the phrase "concerning the wicked" in 1 Ne 18:11 is also clarified by the words of these three prophets (vs 10), who prophecy that "the God of their fathers" will be "lifted up" and "crucified" by the "**hands of wicked men**".[100] Nephi's ambiguous use in 1 Ne 18 therefore seems purposed to allow his readers to think that this phrase also applies to his suffering at the hands of his wicked brethren, casting himself as a type of Christ.

- **Nephi's imagery - binding, the storm, swallowed**

Let's return again to 1 Ne 18 and consider some of the additional Atonement imagery found there. In the Old and New Testament binding was a scriptural motif which anticipated the Messiah who would be sacrificially bound.[101] Indeed, the binding of Christ is mentioned in all of the Gospels. Other figures of Christ, who "did suffer it" by being bound, would be Joseph of Egypt who was "bound" and thrown in prison, Isaac who was "bound" and placed on the altar on Mt. Moriah, the same mound where Christ was "bound" and taken before Pilate; as well as John the

Baptist, Paul, Samson, Meshach, Shadrach and Abednego, Daniel, Lazarus, Peter, Abraham, Abinadi, Ammon, Alma and Amulek, Lehi and Nephi III. Concerning the meaning of binding in scripture, one author reflects, "In like manner, the Lord, being slain, saved us; being bound, He loosed us; being sacrificed, He redeemed us…"[102] While bound, Nephi does not murmur, just as Christ is silent before his accusers. From Isaiah we read:

> Isa 53:7 He was oppressed, and he was afflicted, yet he opened not his mouth: he is brought as a lamb to the slaughter, and as a sheep before her shearers is dumb, so he openeth not his mouth.

After Nephi is "treated harshly" and bound, the ship is "driven back upon the waters for the space of *three* days" in a "great storm, yea, a great and terrible tempest" (18:13). The footnotes of our LDS scriptures fittingly refer us to Jonah 1:4 in this verse, upon whom a great storm and tempest also arose as a sign of God's judgment - "But the LORD sent out a great wind into the sea, and there was a mighty tempest in the sea, so that the ship was like to be broken." (Jonah's storm is perhaps also a figure of the *three* hours of darkness and the great storm which accompanied the death of Christ.) Also reminiscent of Jonah, Nephi *three* times uses the phrase "swallowed up in the depths" (verses 10, 15, 20). An expression of death, there are several examples in the Old Testament where the phrase "swallow up" is used:

> Psa 21:9 Thou shalt make them as a fiery oven in the time of thine anger: the LORD shall **swallow them up** in his wrath, and the fire shall devour them.
>
> Psa 69: Let not the waterflood overflow me, neither let the deep **swallow me up**, and let not the pit shut her mouth upon me.
>
> Prov 1:12 Let us **swallow them up** alive as the grave; and whole, as those that go down into the pit:
>
> Jonah 1: 17 Now the LORD had prepared a great fish to **swallow up** Jonah. And Jonah was in the belly of the fish three days and three nights.

In Christ, however, the tables are turned as death is "swallowed up in victory". Isaiah, foretelling the Messiah, writes:

Isa 25:8 He will **swallow up death in victory**; and the Lord GOD **will wipe away tears** from off all faces; and the rebuke of his people shall he take away from off all the earth: for the LORD hath spoken [it].

The Prophet Abinadi, 450 years later, also seizes upon this language using both elements of being bound and "being swallowed up" to wonderfully describe Christ's atonement and its consequences:

Mos 15:7 Yea, even so he shall be **led, crucified, and slain, the flesh becoming subject even unto death,** the **will of the Son** being **swallowed up in the will of the Father**. 8 And thus God **breaketh the bands** of death, having gained the victory over death; [103]

While contending with the sea, Nephi here in 1 Ne 18 also performs a miracle which prefigures an event from Christ's ministry. Nephi prays and the storm is calmed, even as Christ calmed the storm on Galilee (Mat 8:26). Precedence for this wonder, however, comes from the Old Testament where the Lord several times "calms the sea" (Psalm 89:9, 65:7, 107:29) demonstrating his preeminence and kingship over the earth and the sea. When Christ in mortality calms the storm and quiets the waves, it witnesses that he is the Lord, with the same power over water's chaos (death). In Psalms 107 we can read some of these Messianic verses, and how they also closely mirror the situation of Lehi's family (parenthesis mine):

23 They that go **down to the sea in ships**, that do business (works) in great waters;
24 These see the works of the LORD, and his wonders in **the deep.**
25 For he commandeth, and raiseth the stormy wind, which lifteth up the waves thereof.
26 They mount up to the heaven, they go **down again to the depths: their soul is melted because of trouble.**

27 They reel to and fro, and stagger like a drunken man, and **are at their wits' end**.

28 Then **they cry** unto the LORD **in their trouble**, and he bringeth them **out of their distresses.**

29 **He maketh the storm a calm, so that the waves thereof are still**.

30 Then are they glad because they be quiet; **so he bringeth them unto their desired haven** (the Promised Land).

Unaware of this scripture, we might think that Nephi is borrowing Jesus' calming of the storm directly from the New Testament, but clearly that is not the case. Because Nephi had the brass plates which contained the Psalms, it seems very likely that he was aware of this Psalm and the similarity of his actions to those described in these verses. We might also marvel that he viewed this prophecy as messianic, to be fulfilled in Christ. That he had studied the Psalms is attested in his second book, where upon arriving in the promised land Nephi composes his own inspired and poetic psalm (2 Nephi 4:16-35).

- **The Apex of chapter 18 – Three euphemisms of death, parallel to three constraints of the Spirit**

Adding to the threatening images that we just examined, at the apex of this chiasmus there is a triplicate poetic parallelism. Scholar Donald Parry describes this unique construction:

they were brought near even to be *carried out of this time to meet their God;*

yea, their grey hairs were about to be *brought down to lie low in the dust;*

yea, even they were near to *be cast with sorrow into a watery grave.* (1 Nephi 18:18)

Parry tells us that these three phrases are "united with **three different euphemistic expressions of death**— *to meet their God, to lie low in the dust,* and *into a watery grave*—to make up a remarkable extended synonymous parallelism."[104]

Using dark and foreboding language, Nephi takes us to a place of peril where death seems inevitable. His brothers, the sea, and all the forces of nature are determined to destroy him and his family. Here in the depths of Nephi's desperation is also the heart of his chiasmus. It is also here, with death and destruction looming, that we may recall Nephi's first life-and-death situation, which was in Jerusalem deciding whether or not to slay Laban. In fact, the heart of that conflict, as we know, is the complimentary chiastic center to Nephi's dilemma here in chapter 18. Death, whether euphemistically expressed as in chapter 18, or detailed in the events of Nephi slaying Laban (chapter 4 of this book), is clearly the subject matter at the core of these reflective and parallel stories. Wonderfully, each apex is characterized by a unique literary feature or "triplicate poetic parallelism" - three constraints to slay Laban in 1 Ne 4, and three expressions of death in 1 Ne 18.

- **Judah and Joseph**

If you recall, at the center of 1 Ne 4 is the angel's explanation to Nephi that it is better for "one man to perish than that a nation should dwindle and perish." Clearly here in 1 Ne 18, Lehi's family is again redeemed by the actions of one who would perish (Nephi) so that a nation might not. To completely understand the center of 1 Ne 18 we should consider how Nephi has been using the things which "were written in the books of Moses" to "fully persuade his brethren of their Lord and Redeemer" (1 Ne 19:23). Up to this point Nephi has predominantly used the story of Moses leaving Egypt and the story of Joseph going into Egypt with which to encourage his family. Repeating this approach, at the center of 1 Ne 18, Nephi has left us a scriptural trail of allusion which leads to the most sublime of moments in the story of Joseph, where again the Lord speaks his covenant promise of preservation and prosperity to his children through the selfless actions of one man.

As mentioned earlier, both 1 Ne 3-4 and 1 Ne 18 begin with Nephi's brethren not wishing their brother to "rule over" them. In the Nephi and Laban story (1 Ne 4), our LDS scriptural footnotes direct us to Moses and Exodus 2:14. In 18:10, however, our LDS scripture footnotes astutely cite the other instance, directing us to Gen 37:8-11. Here we also find elder brothers who want to kill a younger brother, as well as parents who "suffered much grief because of their children." As you may recall Joseph has dreamed that his brothers' sheaves will bow to his, which causes them to envy him and eventually to cast him in a pit. In Gen 37:28 they sell him to Ishmaelites (think of the carnal sense of Ishmael), which foreshadows Christ who will be sold as a ransom for carnal man's sin.

As the scripture tells us, when Joseph's brothers later come to Egypt during the famine, they do not recognize their brother Joseph who they *sold for a price,* and who will paradoxically be their *savior* from the famine. If you recall, upon their arrival Joseph accuses the brothers of being spies, and in order to prove that they are not, he requires them to return with Benjamin, the youngest brother and their father's favorite (Gen 42:19). They leave and return to Canaan with grain, but are unaware of its true source (Joseph). When their father Jacob hears that Benjamin is required to go with his brothers, he refuses and uses the phrase found at the center of Nephi's chiasmus, "bring down my grey hairs with sorrow to the grave". Jacob in fact uses it *three* times. Our LDS scriptures footnote this reference in 1Ne 18:18, recognizing that is a highly unique allusion to the story of Joseph!

> Gen 42:38 And he said, My son (Benjamin) shall not go down with you; for his brother
> is dead, and he is left alone: if mischief befall him by the way in the which ye go, then
> shall ye *bring down my gray hairs with sorrow to the grave.*

At the center of his chiasmus, using this phrase, Nephi shifts our attention to the story of his ancestor, whose story was preserved on the brass plates. It is here, in this parallel story, that Nephi intends for the reader to find supplementary insight. So let's continue with Joseph's story.

When the family runs out of grain, Jacob again addresses the need to return to Egypt. You may recall that it was Judah's idea to sell Joseph rather than kill him (Gen 37:27). Now, as they contemplate their family's dire situation, it is one man, a repentant Judah, who again steps forward with a plan. Thinking not of himself but the others, Judah graciously proposes in Gen 43:

> 8 And Judah said unto Israel his father, Send the lad with me, and we will arise and go;
> that we may live, and not die, both we, and thou, [and] also our little ones.
> 9 I will be **surety** for him; of my hand shalt thou require him: if I bring him not unto
> thee, and set him before thee, then let me bear the **blame** for ever:

In the Hebrew, the word for "surety" primarily means "in exchange for"[105], and the word "blame" is *chata,* which almost exclusively is rendered in the Old Testament as "sin".[106] Judah offers himself as a substitutional sacrifice, willing to bear the sin (blame) if Benjamin is lost; perhaps even thinking to amend or atone for his sin and ill treatment of his father's other favorite son, Joseph. In Judah's promise also resonates the constraint of the Spirit to Nephi in Jerusalem, "Better that one man (Judah) should perish than a whole nation dwindle in unbelief", which they surely would have without Judah's plan. In some way, mercy and justice are balanced by his actions; the justice that he deserved in exchange for his merciful promise. An aged Jacob, who has been reticent, is assured by Judah's promise of selfless redemption and allows Benjamin to go down to Egypt. Surely we see the tender similarities to another famous story, that of Christ's substitution for us. Judah is the first example in the Old Testament (with the possible exception of Adam) to offer his own life as a substitute for the life for another, which could certainly be considered one of the highlights of the entire book of Genesis.

The brothers return to Egypt and are welcomed by Joseph who weeps to see Benjamin. As a final test of his brothers' repentance, Joseph fills their grain sacks but secretly places his silver cup in the sack of Benjamin. The silver cup we are told was used by Joseph for "divining", which is exactly what he is doing as he determines the true nature of his brothers' hearts. When Joseph's servants are sent to search the bags, and the supposed stolen cup is discovered, Joseph insists that Benjamin be punished (drink the cup) for his crime. It is at this point we read one of the most beautiful speeches in all of scripture as Judah, a figure of Christ, asks that the cup be "passed from" Benjamin (a symbol of us) to himself (Mat 26:39). He expresses his reasons for doing so; reasons which focus extensively on his love for the father he once grieved by his selfish actions. Gen 44:

27 And thy servant my father (Jacob) said unto us, Ye know that my wife bare me two *sons:* 28 And the one went out from me, and I said, Surely he is torn in pieces; and I saw him not since: 29 And if ye take this also from me, and mischief befall him (Benjamin), **ye shall bring down my gray hairs with sorrow to the grave.** 30 Now therefore when I come to thy servant my father, and the lad *be* not with us; seeing that his life is bound up in the lad's life;

31 It shall come to pass, when he seeth that the lad *is* not *with us,* that **he will die**: and thy servants **shall bring down the gray hairs of thy servant our father with sorrow to the grave.** 32 For thy servant (Judah) became **surety** for the lad unto my father,

saying, If I bring him not unto thee, then I shall bear the blame to my father for ever. 33 **Now therefore, I pray thee, let thy servant abide instead of the lad a bondman to my lord; and let the lad go up with his brethren.** 34 For how shall I go up to my father, and the lad *be* not with me? lest peradventure I see the evil that shall come on my father.

Judah remembers and twice uses the exact phrase that his father Jacob used in Genesis 42, "bring down my gray hairs with sorrow to the grave." If there was doubt that Judah would be true to his promise it is set aside in these verses. Judah becomes a savior for his brother, and since Joseph is a type of Christ all along, perhaps we can imagine that in this moment Judah reflects that very same image (2 Cor 3:18)! Joseph is moved by Judah's enduring and selfless offering, once himself given as a sacrifice (even as Judah, even by Judah). Able no longer to contain his love and forgiveness, he reveals himself to his brothers whom he will save from the deadly famine. Joseph's revelation of his true identity is equally moving:

> Gen 45:1 THEN Joseph could not refrain himself before all them that stood by him; and he cried, Cause every man to go out from me. And **there stood no man with him**, while **Joseph made himself known** unto his brethren.
>
> 2 **And he wept** aloud: and the Egyptians and the house of Pharaoh heard.
>
> 3 And Joseph said unto his brethren, **I** *am* Joseph; doth my father yet live? And his brethren could not answer him; for they were troubled (trembled) at his presence.
>
> 4 And Joseph said unto his brethren, **Come near to me**, I pray you. And they came near. And he said, **I** *am* Joseph your brother, whom ye sold into Egypt.
>
> 5 Now therefore **be not grieved, nor angry with yourselves, that ye sold me hither: for God did send me before you to preserve life.**

As he weeps, Joseph reveals that the one with the power to give them life is their brother, who once was dead. We also read the promise of forgiveness that I believe Nephi wants us to find – "be not grieved . . . for God did send me before you to preserve life." In these words we easily hear Christ's mission, who was sold for the price of our sins, and was sent by God "before us to preserve life." Joseph's words to a repentant Judah perhaps also remind us of the Song of Moses

178

sung before the throne, that "because thou art merciful thou wilt not suffer those that come unto thee that they should perish!" (1 Ne 1:14) And again, in terms of Nephi's structure, Joseph's words are a reflection of the Spirit's constraint to Nephi in Jerusalem - it is better for one man (Joseph) to perish so as to preserve life for a whole nation (Jacob's covenant family).

We also notice that this revelation is very personal and reserved for only Joseph and his repentant brothers (vs 1), not the idolatrous Egyptians (the carnal world). As his kindred spiritual seed and readers of His divine word, we are also given access to this tender and intimate moment, when the brothers' bitter guilt is changed to "joyous" and "delicious" celebration by Joseph's gracious words. Indeed, we might reflect upon the experience of a repentant Alma, who upon thinking of his "surety", the promise of Christ, exclaims:

> Alma 36:16 And now, for *three* days and for *three* nights was I racked, even with the pains of a damned soul.
>
> 17 And it came to pass that as I was thus racked with torment, while I was harrowed up by the memory of my many sins, behold, I remembered also to have heard my father prophesy unto the people concerning the coming of one Jesus Christ, a Son of God, to atone for the sins of the world.
>
> 18 Now, as my mind caught hold upon this thought, I cried within my heart: O Jesus, thou Son of God, have mercy on me, who am in the gall of bitterness, and am encircled about by the everlasting chains of death.
>
> 19 And now, behold, when I thought this, I could remember my pains no more; yea, I was harrowed up by the memory of my sins no more.
>
> 20 And oh, what joy, and what marvelous light I did behold; yea, my soul was filled with joy as exceeding as was my pain!
>
> 21 Yea, I say unto you, my son, that there could be nothing so exquisite and so bitter as were my pains. Yea, and again I say unto you, my son, that on the other hand, there can be nothing so exquisite and sweet as was my joy.

Judah's and Alma's stories are similar in many ways; both made serious errors in judgment, led others to destruction, struggled under guilt, and ultimately have their lives transformed through a powerful revelation of forgiveness. Though it does not mention that Alma wept, it is easy to imagine that he did, both because of his anguish and also for his transcendent joy.

The genius of Nephi! In the most Hebrew of ways, where a single phrase can initiate a cascade of related scriptural stories in the mind of the reader[107], Nephi has transported us to the heart of this wonderful drama in Genesis, adding texture and profound meaning to his own story. We might also contemplate the conditionality of this story, for if Judah's heart had not changed, it is certain that Joseph would not have revealed himself as their savior. This is because God's plan of salvation is a plan which never varies. One must lose his life to save his life, or in other words, a sacrificial lamb is always required. But because Judah allowed his will to be swallowed up in the will of his grieving father, Abraham's ancient covenant promises were preserved. These events are a marvelous examination of the way hearts become broken, tried, "chastened", and ultimately moved to do the Father's will - offering one's self as surety.

- **Meaning of Judah's name - And I did *praise* Him**

There is another fascinating clue which Nephi gives us, hinting through Hebraic word play, that we have interpreted his intended scriptural allusion correctly. It relates to the meaning of Judah's name. Immediately before the apex of Nephi's words in chapter 18, prefacing his "three euphemisms of death", we read in verse 16:

> 16 Nevertheless, I did look unto my God, and I **did praise him** all the day long; and I did not murmur against the Lord because of mine afflictions.

Nephi appears to be using the same play-on-words that Judah's mother Leah and Jacob each used in Genesis. In Genesis 29 Judah receives his name:

> 35 And she conceived again, and bare a son: and she said, Now ***will I praise*** the LORD: therefore she called his name **Judah**; and left bearing.

The name Judah (*Yehudah*) comes from the Hebrew root verb *yadah,* which means "to praise" and *Yadah* comes from the noun *yad,* which is the word for hand. Anciently when one praised, he extended or cast forth his hands.[108] By using a form of Judah's name at the beginning of his allusion, Nephi confirms his intended reference to the story of Judah and Joseph.

In Genesis an elderly Jacob also plays on the meaning of Judah's name. Before Jacob dies he calls his sons together while in the Spirit, to bless them and to prophecy concerning their posterities. Joseph and Judah receive the greatest blessings. To Joseph will go the double portion of the birthright, and to Judah will go the promise of the scepter, representing the kingly lineage through which the Messiah would come. Jacob introduces Judah's blessing, remembering his wife Leah's words from when his son was born, as well as his tender and enduring sacrifice in Egypt:

> Gen 49:8 **Judah, thou [art he] whom thy brethren *shall praise*: thy hand** [shall be] in the neck of thine enemies; thy father's children shall bow down before thee.
> 9 Judah [is] a lion's whelp: from the prey, my son, thou art gone up: he stooped down, he couched as a lion, and as an old lion; who shall rouse him up?
> 10 The sceptre shall not depart from Judah, nor a lawgiver from between his feet, until Shiloh come; and unto him [shall] the gathering of the people [be].
> 11 Binding his foal unto the vine, and his ass's colt unto the choice vine; he washed his garments in wine, and his clothes in the blood of grapes:
> 12 His eyes [shall be] red with wine, and his teeth white with milk.

Here Jacob foretells Judah's lineage until Shiloh, who is Christ, who is the supreme lawgiver; the lion and the choice vine, who will tread the wine press, and whose garments will be washed in blood. Jacob's blessing is understood to be thoroughly a prophecy concerning the Messiah, with whom Judah's name for his selfless act, is forever recognized![109] Indeed, Christ is ultimately the one Jacob prophetically "praises", to whom all the "Father's children will bow down."

- **Conclusion – two sticks**

Transported by Nephi's allusion to Joseph's story in Egypt, in an extraordinary way we are led to Christ.[110] At the apex of his parallel chiasmus, Nephi brings the "two sticks" together, that of Judah and Joseph, connecting the stories and fulfilling Ezekiel's prophecy (Eze 36) as well as fulfilling his own words in 2 Ne 2:12, "and that which shall be written by the fruit of thy loins, and also that which shall be written by the fruit of the loins of Judah, shall grow together unto the confounding of false doctrines and the laying down of contentions". Through allusion, the stories of the Bible are joined seamlessly with the Book of Mormon, both testifying of Christ and his glorious mission through the typifying lives of old and new world patriarchs. Along the way, Nephi also seems to require progressively more involvement by his readers in his later chapters, elevating the device of scriptural allusion to a fascinating level.

Like the principle of faith, I believe that Nephi wants us to see what is not seen, or at first not easily seen, attuning our spiritual eyes so that the Lord can speak to us through the lives of his ancient servants, whose stories he has carefully preserved for just this purpose. As we follow his guideposts to Judah's story, nourished by its power and incomparable climax, the Spirit reveals the Savior's promise to us, even as Joseph reveals himself to his brothers, and I experience a rush of emotion and love; their reunion becomes ours, their fullness of joy becomes our joy, and we weep with them all.

- **Definition of "grey" – a parallel to Laban, "white"**

Curiously, the word in Hebrew for grey (in the Genesis 42-45 passages cited by Nephi) is *seybah*, which is also rendered as "hoary" (e.g. 2 Ki 2:6,9). Hoar frost, as we know, is the white frost that forms on the surface of objects in the winter. And, if we look in the King James Bible Dictionary we find an interesting definition: "HOARY, *n. See Hoar. White or whitish; as the hoary willows.* 1. White or gray with age; as hoary hairs; a hoary head."[111] This is interesting because the Hebrew meaning for Laban is also white; and, if you remember, Laban was also a euphemism for death and sin. Thus, at the center of these parallel stories of the Atonement we find the "white" of 1 Ne 4 reflecting the "white" of 1 Ne 18!

14

Sign of Jonah - Helaman and III Nephi

Thus far we have examined the writings of Nephi, his many chiasmi, and his use of the sign of Jonah - patterns of three (see Appendix 1, pg 219, for important information on the sign of Jonah). We might ponder if later Book of Mormon writers were also aware of the significance of this sign (three days in the earth) and did they also weave it into the fabric of their writings. This chapter is dedicated to examining some of these later stories in the Book of Mormon to see if we can identify its use there as well. We will not be disappointed.

- **The voice of the Lord three times, Encircled about as if by fire**

About 30 BC, over 500 years since Lehi left Jerusalem, we find the namesake posterity of Nephi and Lehi, though obviously several generations later, serving a mission to the Lamanites. At first they are successful, teaching with power and baptizing many Lamanites in the land of Zarahemla. However, as they head northward toward the land of their first inheritance, they are intercepted by a Lamanite army and cast into prison (Helaman 5:14-22). When their captors return, after several days, to take them from the prison and slay them, Nephi and Lehi are "encircled about as if by fire" (vs 23). Not burned, "their hearts take courage" (vs 24) and they speak to their captors (vs 26), at which time the earth shakes and the prison walls tremble (vs 27). Starting in Helaman 5: 28 we read how the Lamanites are then overshadowed with a cloud of darkness, and hear a voice:

28 And it came to pass that they were overshadowed with a cloud of darkness, and an awful solemn fear came upon them.

29 And it came to pass that **there came a voice** as if it were above the cloud of darkness, saying: **Repent ye, repent ye**, and seek no more to destroy my servants whom I have sent unto you to declare good tidings.

30 And it came to pass when they heard this voice, and beheld that it was not a voice of thunder, neither was it a voice of a great tumultuous noise, but behold, **it was a still voice of perfect mildness, as if it had been a whisper, and it did pierce even to the very soul** --

31 And notwithstanding the mildness of the voice, behold the earth shook exceedingly, and the walls of the prison trembled again, as if it were about to tumble to the earth; and behold the cloud of darkness, which had overshadowed them, did not disperse --

32 And **behold the voice came again**, saying: **Repent ye, repent ye**, for the kingdom of heaven is at hand; and seek no more to destroy my servants. And it came to pass that the earth shook again, and the walls trembled.

Like Elijah's still small voice in the darkened cave on Mount Horeb (1 Kings 19:11-12), God's voice to Nephi and Lehi was not of thunder or of fire, but rather it was one of "perfect mildness, as if it had been a whisper, and it did pierce even to the very soul --" In the verses we are about to read, the voice from heaven comes a *third* time (verse 33), which as we have seen is a sign\marker that testifies of Christ. In verse 45, the Holy Spirit of God comes down from heaven and "enters into their hearts", but before this can happen, the Lamanites must do as the voice has three times instructed; they must "Repent". This process is presented to us in the form of a chiasmus whose center is best appreciated by applying the Hebrew meaning to the name found there. In fact, because Hebrew must be used to fully understand this chiasmus, it is another wonderful testament of the Book of Mormon's antiquity and ancient origins. Before looking at the chiasmus, let's first read the verses themselves:

33 And also again **the third time** the voice came, and did speak unto them marvelous words which cannot be uttered by man; and the walls did tremble again, and the earth shook as if it were about to divide asunder.

34 And it came to pass that the Lamanites could not flee because of the cloud of darkness which did overshadow them; yea, and also they were immovable because of the fear which did come upon them.

35 Now there was one among them who was a Nephite by birth, who had once belonged to the church of God but had dissented from them.

36 And it came to pass that he turned him about, and behold, he saw through the cloud of darkness the faces of Nephi and Lehi; and behold, they did shine exceedingly, even as the faces of angels. And he beheld that they did lift their eyes to heaven; and they were in the attitude as if talking or lifting their voices to some being whom they beheld.

37 And it came to pass that this man did cry unto the multitude, that they might turn and look. And behold, there was power given unto them that they did turn and look; and they did behold the faces of Nephi and Lehi.

38 And they said unto the man: Behold, what do all these things mean, and who is it with whom these men do converse?

39 Now the man's name was Aminadab. And Aminadab said unto them: They do converse with the angels of God.

40 And it came to pass that the Lamanites said unto him: What shall we do, that this cloud of darkness may be removed from overshadowing us?

41 And Aminadab said unto them: You must repent, and cry unto the voice, even until ye shall have faith in Christ, who was taught unto you by Alma, and Amulek, and Zeezrom; and when ye shall do this, the cloud of darkness shall be removed from overshadowing you.

42 And it came to pass that they all did begin to cry unto the voice of him who had shaken the earth; yea, they did cry even until the cloud of darkness was dispersed.

43 And it came to pass that when they cast their eyes about, and saw that the cloud of darkness was dispersed from overshadowing them, behold, they saw that they were encircled about, yea every soul, by a pillar of fire.

44 And Nephi and Lehi were in the midst of them; yea, they were encircled about; yea, they were as if in the midst of a flaming fire, yet it did harm them not, neither did it take hold upon the walls of the prison; and they were filled with that joy which is unspeakable and full of glory.

45 And behold, the Holy Spirit of God did come down from heaven, and did enter into their hearts, and they were filled as if with fire, and they could speak forth marvelous words.

Below is the chiasmus concealed in these verses, which when revealed, provides us with some marvelous parallels and a one-of-a-kind center.

Helaman 5 – Aminadab

A 33 And also again the third time **the voice came** (from heaven)
and **did speak unto them**
marvelous words

    B 34 And **the Lamanites** could not flee because of the **cloud of darkness** which over shadowed them;
    C and they were immovable because **of the fear** which did come upon them

        D 36 And he **turned him about** and saw through the cloud of darkness
        E the faces of **Nephi and Lehi**

            F 36 and **behold** they did **shine exceedingly**
            G and they did **lift their eyes** to heaven;

                H 37 And it came to pass that **this man did cry unto the multitude**

                    I 37and behold there was **power** given unto them that they did **turn and look**; and they did behold the faces of
                    J **Nephi and Lehi**

                      K 38 And **they (Lamanites) said unto the man**:
                      L Behold **what do** all these things mean**?**

                          M and who is it with whom these men **do converse**?
                          N 39 Now the mans name was **Aminadab**

                          N' and **Aminadab** said unto them:
                          M' They **do converse** with the angels of God.

                      K' 40 And it came to pass that **the Lamanites said unto him:**
                      L' **What** shall we **do** that this cloud of darkness may be removed from overshadowing us**?**

                    I' 41 And Aminadab said unto them: You must **repent and cry** unto the voice until ye have **faith** in Christ, who was taught unto you by
                  J' **Alma, and Amulek, and Zeezrom**

                H' 42And it came to pass that **they all did begin to cry unto the voice** of him who had shaken the earth

            G' 43 And it came to pass that when they **cast their eyes** about
            F' **Behold** they saw that they were encircled about, by **a pillar of fire**

        E' and **Nephi and Lehi**
        D' 44 were in the midst of them; yea they were **encircled about**;

    B' 44 Yea, **they (Lamanites)** were as if in **the midst of a flaming fire**
    C and they were **filled with that joy** which is unspeakable and full of glory

A' 45 And the **Holy Ghost did come** down from heaven and enter into their hearts
and they were filled as with fire and **they could speak** forth
marvelous words

First of all, though not written by Nephi we should notice that at the apex of this chiasmus is Nephi's constant theme - God desires to speak to us. (In verse 39, we are told that Nephi and Lehi "do converse with the angels of God.") Surprisingly, the center-most thought also focuses on the newly introduced man Aminadab. He is the first person to "turn" and see through the cloud of darkness. There is significance in this because the Hebrew word for "turn" (*shuwb)* is often used to describe turning from sin.[112] Such meaning is born out in parallels I and I' where "**turn** and look" (I) is parallel to "**repent** and cry" (I'). (Also, notice that in these same verses the "power given unto them that they did turn", is paralleled to "faith in Christ".)

When Aminadab turns and is able to see the light which illuminates Nephi and Lehi, he is incited to "cry unto the multitude" (H). They ask him what they must do to also have the cloud of darkness removed, and Aminadab tells them that they must also "cry" to the source of the heavenly voice as he did. Aminadab's new found willingness and desire to impel the others to cry to the voice is especially remarkable in light of the Hebrew meaning of Aminadab's name. Aminadab is a compound word. The first part, *ami,* means my people, nation, or kinsmen. The second part, *nadab,* is found in many other names in the Old Testament (e.g. Jonadab, Abinadab, Ahinadab, Jehonadab). Below is from the Lexicon for *nadab:*

נָדַב—(1) i. q. Arab. ندب TO IMPEL, TO URGE, TO INCITE to any thing (kindred to נָדַף). It only occurs in this expression, Exod. 25:2, כָּל־אִישׁ אֲשֶׁר יִדְּבֶנּוּ לִבּוֹ "whomsoever his heart impelled;" i. e. who did it willingly, spontaneously, Ex. 35:21, 29.

(2) intrans. like the Arab. ندب to impel oneself; hence to be willing, liberal, generous; see נָדִיב and Hithpael.

> HITHPAEL.—(1) *to impel oneself, to shew one-self willing, to offer oneself freely;* followed by a gerund, Neh. 11:2; specially of volunteer soldiers (compare as to the same usage in Arabic, Alb. Schult. ad Ham. p. 310, Epist. ad Menken. p. 40), Jud. 5:2, 9; compare Psalm 110:3; used of those who offered themselves willingly for sacred military service, 2 Ch. 17:16.
>
> 113

This explanation certainly seems to capture the essence of Aminadab; that his heart has become willing, and that he spontaneously incites\urges\compels the people to cry to the Lord![114] In response, the people also offer themselves "willingly". And, if we put the first compound *ami*, together with *nadab*, we would have the meaning "my people are willing", or perhaps "my people are urged\impelled". For further context we might consider how *nadab* is consistently used in various Old Testament verses:

> Ex 25:2 Speak unto the children of Israel, that they bring me an offering: of every man that giveth it willingly (*nadab*) with his heart ye shall take my offering.

> Ex 35:29 The children of Israel brought a willing offering (*nadabah*) unto the LORD, every man and woman, whose heart made them willing (*nadab)* to bring for all manner of work, which the LORD had commanded to be made by the hand of Moses.

> 1 Ch 29: 17 I know also, my God, that thou triest the heart, and hast pleasure in uprightness. As for me, in the uprightness of mine heart I have willingly offered (*nadab*) all these things: and now have I seen with joy thy people, which are present here, to offer willingly (*nadab*) unto thee.

Notice how all of the verses refer to a willing offering of the heart, capturing the very hinge upon which Aminadab's story swings. And in the end (vs 44), the Holy Ghost illuminates and fills the people (*ami*) with joy because of their willingness (*nadab*) exercise faith in Christ, and turn (*shuwb*) to the light.

Without evaluating the meaning of Aminadab in the Hebrew it is difficult to arrive at the richest appreciation of what the author Alma has written. However, with knowledge of his structure and his play on the meaning of Aminadab's name, Alma's center becomes another compelling witness to the Book of Mormon's antiquity. Also, consider the further genius of this story – Alma knows that those who discover his chiasmus will subsequently be compelled\incited\urged to further investigate its apex – likely examining the meaning of Aminadab's name. When this happens, his message more powerfully reaches out from 2000 years ago, coming right off the page into the present, causing us to ponder more deeply – are we willing to be as turned as Aminadab in the here and now, is our heart eager? No doubt Alma would be excited by our efforts to understand his structure and his inspired use of the word.

I hesitate to move on from this uniquely fashioned chapter in Helaman. I long to remain for awhile longer soaking in the richness of these words and thoughts preserved by the hand of God for us to feast upon in our day. When I ponder what the marvelous words might have been that the heavenly voice spoke to those present that day (vs 45), which they would later speak themselves, I realize that they could not be any greater than the marvelous words we have just now spiritually savored, which have entered into my heart and filled me with he same "unspeakable joy"! Like Alma, I hope the same is true for you.

- **Short catalogue of other stories which utilize "three" – from 1 Nephi through Helaman**

The story of Aminadab in many ways prefigures the events that will happen in the land Bountiful at the time of destruction during the crucifixion of Christ, when his voice is heard three times from heaven while the people are immersed in thick darkness (3 Ne. 9-10). Below is a list of other places in the Book of Mormon where *three* in woven into the story:

Zenos, Zenock and Neum – 3 unknown prophets only in the Book of Mormon prophecy the 3 days of darkness at the time of Christ's death – 1 Ne 19:10

Prophecy that three witness shall behold shall behold the Book of Mormon – 2 Ne 27:12

Abinadai is cast in prison 3 days and then executed – Mosiah 1:2

Alma and Amulek travel 3 days to come to the wicked city Ammonihah – Alma 8:6

Alma and Amulek are cast into prison, after 3 days they are questioned - Alma 14:18

Ammonihah is destroyed by Lamanites, after which there is peace for 3 years – Alma 16:12

After being in the service of the King Lamoni 3 days, Ammon goes to the waters of Sebus (from sabah in the Hebrew is to make sacrifice) – Alma: 17:26

On the 3ʳᵈ day king Lamoni is raised from the "dark veil of unbelief" - Alma 19:12

Korihor asks 3 times for a sign, and is struck dumb, dies – Alma 30:49-49

Alma spends 3 days and nights "racked with pain" and "eternal torment" – Alma 36:10

After 3 years of famine the earth "did bring forth her fruit", followed by another 3 years of peace – Hel 11: 5-22

Samuel the prophet prophesies of 3 days of darkness as a sign for death of Savior – Hel 14:27

Samuel prophecies "a day, a night, and a day" (3 periods) as a sign of Christ's birth. – Hel 14:4

Three Nephites chosen, two possibly named Jonah (3 Ne 19:4) – 3 Ne 28

In the Book of Mormon, "three" might also be a marker\indicator that a chiasmus is nearby (as in the story of Aminadab). Thus, the preceding verses may have hidden chiasmi as yet undocumented. Some instances in 3rd Nephi have been left off of this list and will be discussed in the next section. As we shall see, 3ʳᵈ Nephi is a book rich with chiasmi and the sign of Jonah.

- **Christ's first day in America – many signs of Jonah and a chiasmus**

After the destruction that occurred in the America's, we read in 3 Nephi that the storms, tempests, and quakings (**three** events) lasted for **three hours** (8:19), whereupon the voice of Christ is heard **three times** before he is understood. After which there was darkness for the space of **three days** (8:23). The people then hear the voice of the Father **three times**. On the **third day** it must also be heard **three times** before the people understand. (11:6). Initially the words they hear and understand are, "Wo, wo, wo", a cycloid **of three**. We also know that while the Savior is present, they were asked to pray **three** times, and that the Savior also prays **three times**, even as he prayed **three times** in Gethsemane. Likewise, the Savior spends **three days** with the Nephites before ascending to heaven.

On the first day of his visit Christ will baptize Nephi, call 12 disciples (apostles), deliver anew the Sermon on the Mount, institute the sacrament, and bless the children. (3 Nephi 11-18). Also, Christ speaks exclusively to his chosen 12 about the identity of his other sheep of the house of Israel (of which he spoke in John 10:16). This he does in the following chiasmus from 3 Nephi 15:12-24 (parenthesis mine):

12 **Ye are my disciples**;
    and **ye are a light unto this people**
        who are a **remnant of the house** of Joseph.

        14 And **not at any time** hath the Father given me a command
           that I **should tell it** (hear my voice) unto
              your brethren in Jerusalem (as opposed to the Gentiles).

            15 **Neither** at any time hath the Father given me commandment that I should tell them concerning the **other tribes of the house of Israel**

                17 Other **sheep** I have
                of this **fold**
                  Them also must I bring
                  And **they** shall hear my voice
                and there shall be **one fold**
              and one **shepherd**

                  18 And now **because of stiffneckedness** and unbelief they **understood not** my word

                    19 But verily I say unto you that **the Father** hath commanded me and I tell it unto you, that ye were **separated from among them**

                      19 **because of their iniquity**;
                        (ellipsis)
                      19 therefore it is **because of their iniquity**
                        that they know not of you.

                    20 And verily, I say unto you again that the other tribes hath **the Father separated from them;**

                  20 and it is **because of their iniquity** that they **know not** of them

                21 Other **sheep** I have
                which are not of this **fold**
                  Them also I must bring
                  And **they** shall hear my voice
                and there shall be one **fold**
              and one **shepherd**

            22 And they understood me **not** for they supposed it had been the Gentiles for they understood not that **the Gentiles** should be converted through their preaching

        23 and they understood me not that **the Gentiles**
    should **not at any time**
      hear my voice – save it were by the Holy Ghost

24 Ye have both **heard my voice**, and seen me;
    and **ye are my sheep**,
        Ye are **numbered among those** whom the Father hath given me

Notes:

- The first verse, 12, states that "ye are my disciples, a light unto my people." I like how the Savior in verse 24 then reprises that sentiment in the form of, "ye are my sheep, ye are numbered among those whom the Father hath given me." Disciples are sheep, and those with light are numbered among those remembered by the Father and given to the Son.

- While the rest of the parallels in this chiasmus are fairly self evident, verse 14 and verse 23 require a little closer examination. The phrase "not at any time" is slightly out of order, appearing first in verse 14, but second in verse 23. Also, because the Lord is contrasting the two groups, notice that the "brethren in Jerusalem" (vs 14) is antithetical to "the Gentiles" (vs 23). The ensuing parallel verses, 15 and 22, continue to contrast what the Lord had said about the Gentiles and the remnants of the house of Israel.

- Verse 17 which parallels verse 21, an exact repetition of chiastic thought, removes any doubt about the Lord's parallelistic intent. Notice that his "voice" is the center of these short chiasmi, which is also found in John 10:16 of the New Testament.

It is very interesting that Christ would feel the need to address a statement from the record of the New Testament, which perhaps he knew could cause misunderstanding or speculation. His clarification, which takes up the entirety of chapter 3 Nephi 15, makes it clear that Christ's remarks in John 10 referred to a personal visit, which the Gentiles, to our knowledge, never received. Clearly, this information was meant not just for the Nephites, but just as much for our time when the Book of Mormon would come forth.

- **2nd Day – a grand chiasmus**

On the second day, after renewing the sacramental covenant for the second time, only this time without preexisting bread or wine (a similitude of the miraculous feeding of the 5,000 from

John 6), Christ discourses quoting many of the words of Isaiah and Micah as source. Significantly, his wonderful words are a spiritual breaking of the bread and renewing of covenant, filling and nourishing those who heard with Spirit and life (Jn 6:63).

Again, we might not be too surprised to find that this discourse is a spectacular chiasmus. It covers the better part of three chapters, from 3 Nephi 20:11 to 23:1! In the original 1830 version of the Book of Mormon there were no breaks between chapters 20, 21, and 22; it was a continuous text, accommodating the length of the chiasmus whose content largely concerns the scattering and gathering of Israel, and the gathering of Lehi's remnant in fulfillment of covenant promises. The apex of the chiasmus, and the hinge upon which the gospel will go to Lehi's remnant, is the promise to the gentiles – "that they should be established in this land and set up a free people."

A 20: 11 The **words of Isaiah** should be fulfilled, therefore **search them**

  B 15 If Gentiles do not repent after s**cattering** my people – **16 Micah 5:8, 17 Micah 5:9, 18 Micah 4:12, 19 Micah 4:13**

    C 22 And **this people** will I establish in this land, fulfilling the covenant with Jacob, shall be **a New Jerusalem** (verses 23-26 Acts 3: 23-26)

      D 28 When they (Gentiles) have fullness, **if they harden hearts** I will **return iniquities** upon their heads

        E 31 And when the time cometh gospel preached to gathered remnants of House of Israel - **32 Isaiah 52:8, 33 Jerusalem given unto them, 34 Isaiah 52:9, 35 Isaiah 52:10, 36 Isaiah 52:1, 37 Isaiah 52:2, 38 Isaiah 52:3, 39 Know that I am he, 40 Isaiah 52:7, 41 Isaiah 52:11, 42 Isaiah 52:12, 43 Isaiah 52:13**

          F 44 Isa 52:14 They were astonished at thee – **his visage was so marred**, more than any **man** (Christ)

           G 45 Isa 52:15 Kings shall see, and that which they have not heard **they shall consider**

            H 46 Then shall **this covenant of the Father be fulfilled**, Jerusalem be inhabited again with **my people**

              I 21:1 **give unto you a sign that ye may know** – I shall **gather in and establish Zion**

                J 2 I shall declare herafter myself by the power of **the Holy Ghost**

                  K 2 which shall be given you of the Father, shall **be made know unto the Gentiles**

                    L 2 concerning this my people who **shall be scattered** by them

                      M 3 When **these things** shall be made known of the Father and **shall come forth** of the Father

                        N 4 For it is **wisdom in the Father** that they should be
                        O **established** in this land
                        O and be **set up** as a free people
                        N by the **power of the Father,**

                      M 4 that **these things** might **come forth** from them unto a remnant

                    L 5 unto your seed which **shall dwindle** in unbelief because of iniquity

                  K 6 For it behooveth the Father … that **he may show forth his power unto the Gentiles**

                J 6 that they may **repent** and come unto me and **be baptized** and know the true points of my doctrine

              I 7 And **when these things come to pass** thy seed shall begin to know these things, **it shall be a sign** unto them

            H 7 that ye may know the Father hath already commenced unto **the fulfilling of the covenant** unto **the people**

          G 8 Isa 52:15 Kings shall see, and that which they have not heard **they shall consider**

        F 9-10 Isa 29:14 and Isa 52:14 A marvelous work to come forth, and though **a man** declares it, some will not believe. But behold the life of my servant shall be in my hand; they shall not hurt him, although **he shall be marred**. Yet I will heal him. (Joseph Smith)

      E 11 Shall come to pass that whosoever will not believe … they shall be cut off from among my people **12 Mic 5:8, 13 Mic 5:9, 14 Mic 5:10,15 Mic 5:11, 16 Mic 5:12, 17 Mic 5:13, 18 Mic 5:14, 21 Mic 5:15**

    D 22 But if they will repent and hearken unto my words, and **harden not their hearts**, I will **establish my church** among them

  C 23 And they shall assist **my people**, that they may build a city, which shall be called **the New Jerusalem**

  B 24-29 Then shall they (Gentiles) assist my people that they may **be gathered** in, the power of heaven will come down, gospel preached among remnant and ten tribes, and dispersed, and all nations prepared and his people gathered home - **Chapter 22:1-17 which is Isaiah 54**

A 23: 1 Yea, a commandment I give unto you that ye **search these things** diligently; for great are the **words of Isaiah**.

Below are some thoughts concerning the remarkable features of the Lord's 2nd day chiasmus shown above:

- (A, A') The book-ends, or opening and ending statements by the Savior for this structure (20:11 and 23:1), are that the words of Isaiah are great (20:11) and we should search them (23:1), with the latter parallel given extra emphasis, termed as a commandment!

- (B, B') Christ uses blocks of scripture from Micah and Isaiah, which are positioned in parallel, one group to the other. 20:16-19 contains verses from Micah, which parallel chapter 22:1-17, the entire text of Isaiah 54. Notice that the verses from Micah are antithetical to those of Isaiah, the former telling of what will happen to the gentiles if they don't repent after scattering the Lord's people, and the latter (chapter 22) telling how Israel will "inherit the Gentiles" and how God will again extend everlasting kindness and mercy to his bride Israel.

- (C,C') 20:22 speaks of a "people" that shall be a New Jerusalem, which alludes to a spiritual process and precedes the parallel in 21:23, which asserts that they will build a "city" called the New Jerusalem. We know that Zion is presently being gathered and that it is a spiritual gathering. Zion we are told is a synonym for the New Jerusalem, which means that even now the spiritual city is being built within the saints. The first saints that came to Jackson County had not built Zion in their hearts, and consequently failed in building a physical New Jerusalem.

- Verse 20:28 is antithetical to 21:22; hardening their hearts vs. not hardening their hearts.

- (E,E') The long blocks of Old Testament scripture that next parallel each other are also antithetical (20:31-43 parallel to 21:11-21). Instead of Isaiah 54 and Micah 4, the texts which Christ uses are Isaiah 52 and Micah 5. However, Christ has reversed the order from the previous blocks, making the first block 20:31-43 positive, and the latter parallel, 21:11-21 negative. Chapter 20:31-43 sings of the redemption of Israel - when she is gathered and redeemed (with bridegroom imagery; e.g. put on thy beautiful garment), whereas 21:11-21 tell us of what will come to pass to the Gentiles who will not believe (phrases such as "cut off", "plucked out", "treadeth down", "done away", or "execute vengeance" are used in every verse). Indeed, these Isaiah-Micah parallels bring to its ultimate conclusion the oft repeated prophetic pattern of the Book of Mormon, that we will prosper or perish (be redeemed or cut off) based on our turning to our Heavenly Father and his son Jesus Christ.

- (F, F') 20:44 is another quote by Christ from Isaiah 52:14. It is a verse that is widely recognized to prefigure Christ and his suffering – "his visage was so marred, more than any man". Its parallel, 21:9-10, quotes the beginning of Isaiah 29:14, which comes from a grouping of verses concerning the coming forth of the Book of Mormon ("And the book is delivered to him that is not learned, saying, Read this, I pray thee: and he saith, I am not learned." [Isa 29:12]) Whereas 20:44 references Christ, its parallel in 21:9-10, "he shall be marred because of them", is a prophecy of Joseph Smith!

- (G, G') 20:45 is an exact quote of Isaiah 52:15. Its parallel, 21:8, also from Isa 52:15, has a modified first line, perhaps stressing that it refers not to Christ but to Joseph Smith as a variant\figure of Christ.

- At the apex (N, N' and O, O') found in verse 4, Christ tells us\them that it is wisdom of the Father, and by the power of the Father that they should be "established" in the land and "be set up" as a free people. In the Hebrew the word that would most often be used for "established" or "set up" would be *quwm*. The contextual significance of this word can be understood by reading about God's covenant with Abraham in Gen 17:7, "And I will establish (*quwm*) my covenant between me and thee and thy seed after thee in their generations for an everlasting covenant..." In the same way, here in 3 Nephi the Savior's discourse has been about the scattering and subsequent gathering of Israel in the last days, the fulfillment of which centers around God's covenant promises to mankind through Abraham! The Hebrew context of the words at the apex helps us to better experience\feel that emphasis.

Also, what does "wisdom in the father" mean, and does it have extra significance here at the center of Christ's chiasmus? Proverbs 3:18 tells us that wisdom is, "**a tree of life** to them that lay hold upon her: and happy [is every one] that retaineth her." Moreover, we know that the tree of life is a representation of the love of God (1 Ne 11). Thus, God's wisdom is a tree of life, which is his love. Notice that the parallel to "wisdom in the Father" is "power of the Father", which also tells us that the Father's power is love. That we should find a connection to the tree of life at the center of Christ's message is truly wonderful, poetic, and even expected!

- Joseph Smith plays a significant role in this structure, even compared\parallel to Christ as one who will help kings to see, hear, and "consider" (*biyn*\understand); assisting in the gathering of God's scattered seed. As we have discussed, the meaning of Joseph's name is prophetic:

"The name *Joseph* is itself a prophecy of events of the last days. The etymology of the name is usually given as "the Lord addeth" or "increases." Though appropriate, such renderings have veiled a richer meaning. In the Bible account wherein Rachel names her infant son Joseph the Hebrew text reads *Asaph,* which means "he who gathers," "he who causes to return," or perhaps most appropriately "God gathereth" (Genesis 30:24). No more appropriate name could be given to the prophet of the restoration or to the tribe destined to do the work of the gathering than the name of their ancient father who gathered his family in Egypt."[115]

Indeed, like ancient Joseph of Egypt, Joseph of Palmyra was an instrument in the Lord's hand, used to gather the seed of adopted Israel from the Gentile nations in the latter days!

- **III Nephi 26 – An hundredth Part**

After the extended chiasmus of the second day is finished, Christ continues to be keenly aware and interested in recorded scripture, personally inspecting their records, and commanding them to include events about his coming that had been left out (23:13). We are told in 3 Nephi 23:14 that he then "**expounded** all scripture in one, which they had written." Christ commands them to record the words of Malachi, giving them Malachi 3 and 4, which **he also expounds**. And finally, for the *third* time, Christ **expounds** in chapter 26: 3, "all things, even from the beginning until the time that he should come in his glory – yea, even all things which should come upon the face of the earth, even until the elements should melt with fervent heat, and the earth should be wrapped together as a scroll, and the heavens and earth should pass away" (Isa 34:4).

We are then given a glimpse of how the Savior expounds scripture, using a word that is used just once in all of scripture! In verses 4-6 of chapter 26 we find:

> 4 And even unto the great and last day, when all people, and all kindreds, and all nations and tongues shall stand before God, to be judged of their works, whether they be good or whether they be evil --

> 5 If they be good, to the resurrection of everlasting life; and if they be evil, to the resurrection of damnation; being **on a parallel**, the one on the one hand and the other on the other hand, according to the mercy, and the justice, and the holiness which is in Christ, who was before the world began.

> 6 And now there cannot be written in this book even a hundredth part of the things which Jesus did truly teach unto the people;

In these verses Christ is explaining to the people the "parallels" that exist in scripture! I reflect, is this not exactly the driving force of this book, which is the examination of these "parallels" in their varied and wonderful forms, revealed by the Spirit to us even as Christ expounded them personally many years ago. Perhaps we can even feel a bit of what it would was like to be there that day in person. Also, consider the parallels that we find "hidden" within the Saviors words, revealed in chiasmus:

A And even unto the **great and last day**,

  B when all people, and all kindreds, and all nations and tongues shall stand before **God**,

    C to be judged of **their works**,

      D whether they be **good**

        E or whether **they be evil** --

          F If they be **good,** to the **resurrection of everlasting life**;

            G and if they be **evil,** to the **resurrection of damnation;**

              H **being on a parallel,**

            G the **one** on **the one hand**

          F and the **other** on **the other hand,**

      D according to **the mercy,**

        E and the **justice,**

    C and the **holiness**

  B which is in **Christ**,

A who was **before the world began**.

Like Aminadab's chiasmus, I marvel at the ingenuity of what has been done. Think of it – in a scripture recorded by command of Christ, in which he tells us how he teaches the scripture\word, we find the very literary method which he expounds – parallelism. In the most exemplary of ways, perfectly Christ-like, he explains by doing, giving this scripture new dimension. Like the book ends of this exhilarating chiasmus (A.A'), he was before the world began, even unto that last great day, the beginning and the end, Alpha on the one hand and Omega on the other, a parallel!

Note that we are left with only "a hundredth" of what the Lord expounded. Nephi tells us in the next few verses:

8 And these things have I written, which are a lesser part of the things which he taught the people; and I have written them to the intent that they may be brought again unto this people, from the Gentiles, according to the words which Jesus hath spoken.

9 And when they shall have received this, which **is expedient that they should have first, to try their faith,** and if it shall so be that they shall believe these things then shall the greater things be made manifest unto them.

10 And if **it so be that they will not believe these things, then shall the greater things be withheld from them**, unto their condemnation.

11 Behold, I was about to write them, all which were engraven upon the plates of Nephi, but the Lord forbade it, saying: **I will try the faith of my people.**

Clearly, we need to first utilize the scriptures that we have selectively been given, and if I might be so bold as to suggest, it seems apparent that our hope of receiving greater things (words\seed) is "parallel" to our interest\participation in this initial trial of faith. Since Christ has given us a key to better understand the scriptures, which is to examine them for parallels, could it be that part of the test is our "willingness" (Aminadab) to actively seek poetic parallels in our gospel study, anticipating the Spirit of revelation which accompanies their discovery as we contemplate their divine grandeur? Are they a preparation, or perhaps even a part of the "greater things" to be "made manifest"?

- **III Nephi 27 – The third day, a final chiasmus**

Again, hesitating to move on, hoping to enjoy for just a moment longer the radiance of the last instruction from the Lord, we will not be disappointed to find in the next chapter something equally splendid. On the beginning of the *third* day, the 12 disciples come together uniting in mighty prayer and fasting, when Christ again appears (vs2). The discussion quickly turns to what they are to call the church. Christ explains that the church should be called after his name (vs7), built upon his gospel and works (vs10-11). The Savior, using the parallel method of teaching that he just described in chapter 26, then unfolds the meaning of His gospel, structuring his words in another breathtaking chiasmus. It has been captured and presented to us entirely in first person voice; and because it is the voice of the Savior, we might expect it to be the most brilliant of chiasmi. As you will see, its structure is composed of *three* chiasmi, one at the center or apex (D-F), and two others on either end, each paralleling the other (C,C'). At the apex the Savior repeats the same word *three* times. I suspect that you will not be too surprised by the idea that is repeated *three* times at the apex, which is – the word!

Christ's Chiasmus – This is my Gospel

A 13 **This is my gospel** which I have given unto you.

  B14 That **I might be lifted up** on the cross;

    C that **I might draw all men unto me**
        that as **I have been lifted** up by men
           men should **be lifted up by the father**, to be judged
        for this cause **have I been lifted up**
      therefore, **I will draw all men unto me**, that they may be judged

        D 16 whoso **repenteth and is baptized in my name**
          shall **be filled**
            if he endureth to the end him **will I hold guiltless** before my father

           E 17 **he that endureth not** is also hewn down and cast into the fire
          from whence they can no more return
            because of the justice of the Father

             F 18 This is the **word**
                which he has given unto men
                  For this cause he **fulfilleth the words**
                Which he hath given,
             F' and he lieth not, but fulfilleth all his **words**

           E' 19 And **no unclean thing** can enter into his kingdom, save it be those
          who have washed their garments in my blood
             because of their faith and repentance of all their sins

        D' 20 **Repent,** ye ends of the earth, and come unto me **and be baptized in my name**
          that ye may **be sanctified** by the Holy Ghost
          that ye may **stand spotless** before me at the last day.

A' 21 Verily, verily, I say unto you, **this is my gospel**

    C' and ye know the things that **ye must do** in my church;
      for the works ye have **seen me do**
        that ye **shall also do**;
      for that which ye have **seen me do**
    even that **shall ye do**

  B' 22 Therefore, if you do these things blessed are ye, for **ye shall be lifted up** at the last day.

Consider the sequence of events leading up to this chiasmus; we are told that Christ expounds all things in parallels (vs 4-6), then we are told that before we get additional scripture our faith would be tried with the scripture we have (vs 8-11), and then Christ gives a perfect example of parallelism, discoursing on "this is my gospel" (vs 13-22). It is as though Christ is testing our willingness to "expound" these verses as he just taught – using "a parallel".

As mentioned earlier, "the word" at the center is the hinge for this chiasmus, with the surrounding verses explaining the sanctifying process (standing spotless as in verse 20, or guiltless as in verse 16) made possible by the Atonement. Christ makes the point that the Father's word, which is the gospel plan, must be fulfilled, and that those who **do** His will (obey his word, repent, are baptized), even as Christ did the father's will, shall be those that will **be lifted up** and judged spotless by His blood, prospered according to his promised plan\word (C, C').

Amidst all of the other instances of three that swirl around Christ's visit to his people, which swell to a beautiful crescendo in this final expounding of the gospel, it is hard to consider it (the use of three) unimportant. It is, after all, the number of His sign, the one He gives to all generations, which is the sign of Jonah. By it, the Savior has set his personal seal of the Holy Spirit upon the Book of Mormon for a lasting testimony to bear and lift us up, a lamp unto our feet as we journey through the mists of darkness and temptation back to His shining presence.

In 1791 John Hagerty, a Methodist minister, published this print depicting the Tree of Life. "Under the redemptive rays of God as Father, Spirit and Word, the Tree of Life brings forth twelve fruits of salvation (fruits of the Spirit) for those seeking entry into the New Jerusalem. A large crowd strolls by the narrow gate of salvation along the Broad Way while the Devil and "babylon Mother of Harlots" beckon. The secure sinners are stigmatized with labels indicating: pride, chambering (lewdness) & wantonness, quack, usury, and extortion."[116] Notice that Christ is the tree of life, bringing life and rebirth.

Conclusion

"The manifestation of aesthetic phenomena in Scripture cannot be brushed aside as an unnecessary luxury. The aesthetic exposure is broad and extensive, involving vast swaths of narratives and poetry. God used a complex of aesthetic patterns as He revealed Himself in Scripture."
Jo Ann Davidson, "Toward a Theology of Beauty – A Biblical Perspective"[117]

In this book we have examined the rich fabric of Nephi's writing using a multiplicity of analytical ideas. We have looked for and recognized "vast swaths" of parallel thought, and have repeatedly identified the apexes of surprisingly large chiasmi. We have also examined several Hebrew words in an effort to discover how a fuller sense of their meanings might add shades of understanding to Nephi's message. In our study we have also found the sign of Jonah and rebirth gently pulsating within the pages of the Book of Mormon. Because Nephi often likened his family's story to scripture, we have also examined several instances of allusion which have led us to significant episodes in the lives of the patriarchal fathers, whose patterned lives have enriched our understanding of Nephi's spiritual message. Our souls have stirred with a sense of awe and wonder as we have gazed upon the majesty of Nephi's literary vision.

One of the lasting impressions from 1 Nephi is found at its center, chapter 11, where Nephi describes the breathtaking beauty of the tree of life; "the beauty thereof was far beyond, yea, exceeding of all beauty." As Nephi's vision progresses several elements are paralleled to the beautiful tree. We learn that the tree of life is a representation of God's love, inferring that God's love must also exceed all beauty. We also learn that the tree of life represents Jesus Christ, which therefore implies that Jesus Christ exceeds all beauty. Below are these reciprocal relationships:

Like-kind elements	Like-kind attribute
Tree of life (vs 8)	exceeds all beauty
Tree of life represents God's love (vs 22)	exceeds all beauty
Jesus Christ is God's love shed abroad (vs 24)	exceeds all beauty

Most people recognize the power of beauty to stir their emotions. In this regard, Leo Tolstoy wrote, "Its love that makes us see beauty,"[118] We might consider that the opposite is also true, that beauty helps us to see love. Describing God as beauty, John Muir adds, "No synonym for God is so perfect as Beauty. Whether as seen carving the lines of the mountains with glaciers, or gathering matter into stars, or planning the movements of water, or gardening - still all is Beauty!"[119] It is interesting that Nephi's vision begins with a series of beautiful and inspiring vistas; from an "exceedingly" high mountain he sees the beautiful tree, the great city of Jerusalem, a "beautiful and fair" virgin who conceives by the Spirit, and the Christ child in her arms who is the perfect "Son of the Eternal Father." Nephi is then asked to answer his own question, "Knowest thou the meaning of the tree?" Without hesitation he replies, "Yea, it is the Love of God, which sheddeth itself abroad in the hearts of the children of men, wherefore it is the most desirable above all things." We might ask, how does Nephi know this? Certainly there is no way that he could have intellectualized that the tree of life symbolizes the love of God. Rather, we must assume that he answers using only what has been "shed abroad" in his heart at that very moment, a feeling that he has undoubtedly experienced before – the beauty of God's love, revealed by the Spirit. (Rom 5:5 – "the love of God is shed abroad in our hearts by the Holy Ghost") Not only is Nephi able to correctly identify the tree's symbolism, but because of the joy which fills his heart, he also knows that it is the "most desirable of all things."

Nephi's vision thus climaxes, defined by what he feels in his soul. And wonderfully, if you are like me, it is hard to read his account and not feel what he is feeling - God's very love shed abroad in our hearts, right along with Nephi and the angel! In this way, as our hearts stir we also "see" the beautiful tree - a tree whose beauty is not experienced outwardly, but one which is felt within. This is clearly what the prophet Alma later teaches the Zoramites about the tree of life, which is, that it is grown within one's own heart. Alma's implication is that if we are filled with His love, the tree of life becomes a part of our nature and who we are - we become beautiful, filled with the heart and mind of Christ.

As Nephi completes his vision of the tree, in verse 33 we become aware that there is one other parallel which the tree of life represents, which is the cross. (This parallel was first discussed on pages 118-119.) Adding this element to our list, we see paradoxically that the cross is also beautiful and "precious above all":

Like-kind elements	Like-kind attribute
Tree of life (vs 8)	exceeds all beauty
Tree of life represents God's love (vs 22)	exceeds all beauty
Jesus Christ is God's love shed abroad (vs 24)	exceeds all beauty
Christ lifted up on cross (vs 33)	**exceeds all beauty**

That one should die so that many can live is the great spiritual pattern of truth and salvation. Though it seems counter-intuitive that life comes by way of death, it is the spiritual key which unlocks the door to becoming as our Savior - taking his name upon us and emulating his selfless love.[120] In this way, like absolute truth, the tree of life represents the ideal of supreme beauty. Nephi's description, "beauty exceeding all beauty," certainly implies that there is nothing else which can surpass the beauty of Jesus Christ and his sacrifice for man.

- **Death and Resurrection – Lifted up**

If you recall, in the third chapter of this book we contemplated the Spirit's involvement in the creation story – that the Spirit moved upon the waters. The beauty of God's creation begins with this gentle stirring. We examined how Jonah is a Hebrew word for dove, God's chosen symbol for the Spirit. We studied how Noah's dove (Jonah) went out over the waters *three* times; once without result, then returning with an olive branch, and then abiding fruitfully in a new land. Jonah the prophet would also move over the water to create a spiritual heart in Nineveh. To those that sought a sign of his messiahship, Christ would later announce that the only sign he would give was the testimony or sign of Jonah, the dove moving within their hearts. When Christ is baptized it is the dove (Jonah) which alights upon his shoulder to anoint him with the Father's fullness. Besides being a sign for the Spirit which whispers Jesus is Christ, Jonah's three days in the belly of the whale foreshadow Christ's three days in the tomb and resurrection, pointing to the major hallmark of God's love (the tree of life), the promise of rebirth and life eternal. As Christ contemplated his death in Jn 12:24, he taught, "Except a corn of wheat fall into the ground and die, it abideth alone: but if it die, it bringeth forth **much fruit**. He that loveth his life shall lose it; and he that hateth his life in this world shall keep it unto **life eternal**." This pattern of dying in order to produce living fruit is the grand and beautiful pattern of salvation by which all men are saved, loving others and God at the sacrifice of self.

Marion G. Romney wonderfully reconciles and gives simple application to this principle, relating its atoning pattern to our lives: "In the one who is wholly converted, desire for things [contrary] to the gospel of Jesus Christ has actually died, and substituted therefore is a love of God with a fixed and controlling determination to keep his commandments."[121] Consider for a moment the following illustrations:

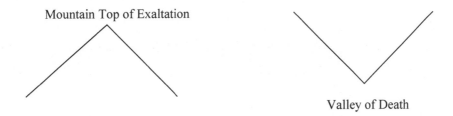

When God asked Abraham to take his son Isaac to the mountain top it was more heart wrenching than heart warming. Indeed, in spiritual terms the mountain's heights are transcendent only because of Abraham's faithful and willing obedience. Surprisingly, his difficult valley and mountain top are the same place; he can go no higher than he is willing to descend, swallowed up in God's will. In this same way, as Nephi's chiastic parallel indicates, the tree of life is only as beautiful as the depths of Christ's suffering and obedience, lifted up on the cross. One writer uniquely personalizes the heights of love as it relates to the valley's obedience (parenthesis mine): "Many erroneously construe the hour of strong feeling to be their spiritual apogee and the hour bereft of such feeling as their spiritual perigee. They are unaware of the fact that one's true life is lived by *his Spirit through the will*. The position (height) to which his volition attains in the hour of barren sensation represents the reality of the Christian's attainment. The way he dwells amid drought is his *authentic* life."[122] By this measure the genuine character of Nephi, who at first "shrunk" when challenged by the Spirit, is ultimately revealed as he obeys. And in this same regard, Christ's drinking of the bitter cup to perform the crowning work of the Atonement parallels the valleys of our trials and temptations, the test of our will to love and obey, which reveals who we truly are. Mountain tops, such as the temple, are only available to those who are daily overcoming in the valley, living "by his Spirit through the will."

- **Meaning of "saint" – a tree of life**

As saints in the church of Jesus Christ, who are we, or who should we be? Do we simply know the story of Nephi's vision, or is it practiced in our lives? Has the word of Christ been planted in our hearts and are we nourishing it with our faith, obedience, and love? Is it bearing desirable and joyous fruit? In our LDS Bible dictionary we read:

> **Saint.** The word *saint* is a translation of a Greek word also rendered "holy," the fundamental idea being that of consecration or separation for a sacred purpose; but since what was set apart for God must be without blemish, the word came to mean "free from blemish," whether physical or moral. In the N.T. the saints are all those who by baptism have entered into the Christian covenant.

This definition should cause us to reflect on our "Christian covenant" or baptismal covenant, wherein we take the name of Christ upon us and promise to "be" as he is. However, there is a companion definition to the word saint which is also valuable. There are two Hebrew words for saint. One, *qadowsh*, is relatively close to its Greek counterpart, meaning holy, but the other, *chasiyd*, stems from the word for loving kindness or mercy:

> חֶסֶד [" in pause חָסֶד"], with suff. חַסְדִּי pl. חֲסָדִים, const. חַסְדֵּי prop. *desire, ardour* (see the root), whence—
> (1) in a good sense, *zeal* towards any one, *love, kindness,* specially —(*a*) of men amongst themselves, *benignity, benevolence,* as shown in mutual benefits; *mercy, pity,* when referring to those in misfortune, Gen. 21:23; 2 Sam. 10:2 (LXX. often ἔλεος); Job 6:14. The expression often occurs, עָשָׂה חֶסֶד עִם to act kindly towards, Gen. loc. cit.; 2 Sa. 3:8; 9: 1, 7; also followed by אֶת Zec. 7:9; עַל 1 Sa. 20:8; more fully, עָשָׂה חֶסֶד וֶאֱמֶת עָם Gen. 24:49; 47:29; Josh. 2:14; 2 Sa. 9:3, אֶעֱשֶׂה עִמּוֹ חֶסֶד אֱלֹהִים"I will act kindly towards him like unto God." נָטָה חֶסֶד לְ to turn, or incline, kindness upon any one, Gen. 39:21; [123]

This definition touches on what the tree of life is all about – God's love. You might even notice that the very first part of this definition is "desire", the exact word that Nephi uses to describe how his soul felt as he contemplated the Lamb of God and his love ("the most desirable above all things"). If we were able to see Nephi's original engraving for this verse, no doubt we would see some variation of this word *chesed*. Saints, according to this definition, are those who are merciful, loving, and kind. Though *chaciyd* is most often rendered "saint", consider for a moment how it is other times rendered as "the merciful" (parenthesis mine)[124]:

> 2 Sam 22:26 With the **merciful** (saints) thou wilt shew thyself merciful, [and] with the upright man thou wilt shew thyself upright. 27 With the pure thou wilt **shew thyself pure**;

Written by David, these exact verses are also found in Psalm 18:25-26. In them we find allusions to two of the last beatitudes from the Lord's Sermon on the Mount: Blessed are the merciful for they shall receive mercy, and blessed are the **pure in heart for they shall see God** (Mat 5). From these Old and New Testament teachings, we understand that purity, the quality whereby one can see God, is founded on mercy (a second name for love[125]). In fact, when John tells us that "God **is** love" (1 Jn 4:8), he describes God's state of being, which infers that if we are to see him, then we must also "be" in the same state of pure love and mercy (1 Jn 3:2-3). By this same reasoning, Alma tells us that the tree of life is within us, a state of being – continually bearing fruit; an eternal reflection of God's love, purified in his image and possessing a beauty which reflects his. Consequently, a saint in the Church of Jesus Christ "is" also a tree of life, a representation of God's love.

- **What is perfection? Is it possible?**

One of the most well known verses in the Bible is Mat 5:48, "**Be ye therefore perfect, even as your father which is in heaven is perfect**." It is the last verse in Mat 5 and is meant to sum up a series of earlier verses given by Christ while teaching on the mount. For its proper context, consider the verses which immediately precede it:

43 Ye have heard that it hath been said, Thou shalt love thy neighbour, and hate thine enemy. 44 But I say unto you, Love your enemies, bless them that curse you, do good to them that hate you, and pray for them which despitefully use you, and persecute you; 45 **That ye may be the children of your Father** which is in heaven: for he maketh his sun to rise on the evil and on the good, and sendeth rain on the just and on the unjust. 46 For if ye love them which love you, what reward have ye? do not even the publicans the same? 47 And if ye salute your brethren only, what do ye more [than others]? do not even the publicans so?

Here Christ tells us how we become "children of the Father", which is to love others, even our enemies. It is important to notice that he is not talking about any other commandments when he directs us to be perfect. Indeed, he is asking us to be perfect in how we love, which should emulate the Father's perfect and selfless love. In other words, Christ invites us to come to the tree of life, and experience God's love shed abroad in our hearts, that which is joyous and desirous above all things, as we love and serve others. For verification that this is the proper interpretation, consider how Luke records the same teachings in Luke 6:35-36, "But love ye your enemies, and do good, and lend, hoping for nothing again; and your reward shall be great, and ye shall be the **children of the Highest**: for he is kind unto the unthankful and [to] the evil. 36 **Be ye therefore merciful**, as your Father also is merciful." If you compare the parallels of what each gospel author (Luke and Matthew) has recorded, you have the following equations:

children of the Father = children of the Highest
BE YE PERFECT = BE YE MERCIFUL.

Isn't scripture marvelous! As Moroni concludes the Book of Mormon he reiterates this formula of perfection, recapitulating for us how we become "sons of God" ("children of the Highest"):

Moroni 7:47 But charity is the pure love of Christ, and it endureth forever; and whoso is found possessed of it at the last day, it shall be well with him. 48 Wherefore, my beloved brethren, pray unto the Father with all the energy of heart, that ye **may be filled with this love**, which he hath bestowed upon all who are true followers of his Son, Jesus Christ; that ye may become **the sons of God**; that when he shall appear we shall be like him, for we shall seehim as he is; that we may have this hope; that **we may be purified even as he is pure**. Amen.

Moroni wonderfully tells us that if we are filled with His love, that we "shall be like him", and that we will "be purified even as he is pure." Notice how this love is "bestowed upon all who are true followers of the Son, Jesus Christ". If we add Moroni's parallels to those of Luke and Mathew, we get the following equations:

children of the Father		children of the Highest		sons of God
BE YE PERFECT	=	BE YE MERCIFUL	=	FILLED WITH HIS LOVE
(Mat 5:43-48)		(Lk 6:35-36)		(Moroni 7:47-48)

In D&C 88:125 we find the same definition of perfection, which is also an unmistakable parallelism:

And above all things, clothe yourselves
        with the bond of charity
as with a mantle
        which is the bond of perfection and peace

Note the parallel: bond of charity (love) = bond of perfection

- **Imagery of the tree of life – the Doctrine of Christ**

It wouldn't be too surprising if during his life Nephi looked back on his vision of the tree of life many times. And, if elements of that vision found their way into his later writing, that also wouldn't be too unexpected. In 2 Ne 31, Nephi preaches the Doctrine of Christ and what we must do in order to have eternal life, which is also what happens when we partake of the tree of life:

211

> Wherefore, ye must press forward
>> with a steadfastness in Christ,
>>> having a perfect brightness of hope,
>>>> and a love of God and of all men.
> Wherefore, if ye shall press forward,
>> feasting upon the word of Christ,
>>> and endure to the end, behold,
>>>> thus saith the Father: Ye shall have eternal life.

Notice how these two sentences are parallel, and, though we may not have considered it before, a lot of the phrases and images in these verses come from the vision of the tree of life. Below is a comparison:

1 Ne 8 and 11	2 Ne 31:20
Press forward	Press forward
Partaking	Feasting
Iron Rod – word	Word of Christ
Tree represents – Love of God	Love of God and all mankind
Tree of life is symbol of Christ	Steadfastness in Christ
Tree is white to exceed all white	Perfect brightness
Many came to tree but were ashamed, fell away, were lost (don't endure)	Endure to the end
Fruit of tree is Eternal Life	Ye shall have Eternal Life

Where does Nephi get the phrase "press forward"? Undoubtedly it finds its origins in Lehi's vision (the only other place in Nephi's writing where the phrase is found). In 1 Ne 8:24 we read, "And it came to pass that I beheld others **pressing forward**, and they came forth and caught hold of the end of the rod of iron; and they did **press forward** through the mist of darkness, **clinging to the rod of iron**, even until they did come forth and partake of the fruit of the tree." Notice that pressing forward is done by holding to the iron rod. Thus, if the Rod of Iron is the word of God, then "feasting on the words of Christ" is another way of clinging to the Iron Rod. Expressed either way, both lead to the tree of life.

In Nephi's Doctrine of Christ, also notice that "ye shall have eternal life" is parallel to "love of God and of all mankind". If you recall, in our discussion of the tree of life (pg 122) we defined what eternal life is. Jn 17:3 tells us that life eternal is to "know" God and his son Jesus Christ. And in 1 Jn 4:7-8 we find the best definition of what it is to "know" God; "Beloved, let us love one another: for love is of God; and **every one that loveth** is born of God, and **knoweth God**. He that loveth not knoweth not God; for God is love." Thus, Nephi's parallel (eternal life = love of God and man) is perfect. [126]

- **Filled with Joy - Filled with the Spirit - The Tree of Life**

When Lehi partakes of the fruit of the tree of life he says, "And as I partook of the fruit thereof it filled my soul with exceeding **joy** . . . for I know that it was **desirable** above all other fruit." (1 Ne 8:12) Surprisingly, in Nephi's vision of the tree, he never actually tells us that he partakes of the fruit! Yet, by his account, which closely matches Lehi's, we know he is describing what it is to partake. In 1 Ne 11:22 Nephi relates, (using words similar to Lehi's) "Yea, it is the love of God, which sheddeth itself abroad in the hearts of the children of men; wherefore, it is the most **desirable** above all things. And he spake unto me, saying: Yea, and the most **joyous** to the soul." The sense of this experience is also captured by several later Book of Mormon prophets who continued to use Lehi and Nephi's expression of "joy" to communicate a transforming spiritual experience. Each of the following examples is a story of coming to the tree of life and rebirth, and each adds a little more to our understanding of what Lehi and Nephi deeply felt. Most important, you will notice that in every instance the Spirit, which fills their souls, is the cause of their transcendent joy!

King Benjamin's people are converted

Mosiah 4:2 O have mercy, and apply the atoning blood of Christ that we may receive forgiveness of our sins, and our hearts may be purified; for we believe in Jesus Christ, the Son of God, who created heaven and earth, and all things; who shall come down among the children of men. 3 And it came to pass that after they had spoken these **words the Spirit of the Lord came upon them, and they were filled with joy**

Mosiah 4:11 And again I say unto you as I have said before, that as ye have come to the knowledge of the glory of God, or if ye have known of his goodness and **have tasted of his love**, and have received a remission of your sins, **which causeth such exceedingly great joy in your souls**, even so I would that ye should remember, and always retain in remembrance, the greatness of God

Mosiah 4:20 And behold, even at this time, ye have been calling on his name, and begging for a remission of your sins. And has he suffered that ye have begged in vain? Nay**; he has poured out his Spirit upon you**, and has **caused that your hearts should be filled with joy**

King Lamoni is reborn

Alma 19:6 Now, this was what Ammon desired, for he knew that king Lamoni was under the power of God; he knew that the dark veil of unbelief was being cast away from his mind, and the **light which did light up his mind**, which was **the light of the glory of God, which was a marvelous light of his goodness—yea, this light had infused such joy into his soul**, the cloud of darkness having been dispelled, and that the **light of everlasting life was lit up in his soul**

King Lamoni's Father

Alma 22:15 And it came to pass that after Aaron had expounded these things unto him, the king said: What shall I do that I may have this eternal life of which thou hast spoken? Yea, what shall I do that I may be **born of God**, having this wicked spirit rooted out of my breast, and **receive his Spirit, that I may be filled with joy**, that I may not be cast off at the last day? Behold, said he, I will give up all that I possess, yea, **I will forsake my kingdom, that I may receive this great joy**

Zoramites are newly created – become as trees of life

Alma 31:36 Now it came to pass that when Alma had said these words, that he clapped his hands upon all them who were with him. And behold, as he clapped his hands upon them, **they were filled with the Holy Spirit**. 38 And the Lord provided for them that they should hunger not, neither should they thirst; yea, and he also gave them strength, that they should suffer no manner of afflictions, **save it were swallowed up in the joy of Christ**

Alma 33:23 And now, my brethren, I desire that ye shall **plant this word in your hearts**, and as it beginneth to swell even so nourish it by your faith. And behold, **it will become a tree, springing up in you unto everlasting life**. And then may God grant unto you that your burdens may be light, **through the joy of his Son**. And even all this can ye do if ye will. Amen

Alma recounts his mighty change

Alma 36:20 And oh, what joy, and **what marvelous light I did behold; yea, my soul was filled with joy** as exceeding as was my pain! 21 Yea, I say unto you, my son, that there could be nothing so exquisite and so bitter as were my pains. Yea, and again I say unto you, my son, that on the other hand, **there can be nothing so exquisite and sweet as was my joy**

Alma 36:24 Yea, and from that time even until now, I have labored without ceasing, that I might bring souls unto repentance; that I might **bring them to taste of the exceeding joy of which I did taste**; that they **might also be born of God**, and be **filled with the Holy Ghost**

Helaman's people become saints

Helaman 3:35 Nevertheless they did fast and pray oft, and did wax stronger and stronger in their humility, and firmer and **firmer in the faith of Christ, unto the filling their souls with joy** and consolation, yea, even to the purifying and the sanctification of their hearts, **which sanctification cometh because of their yielding their hearts unto God**

People of the Land of Nephi are born again

Helaman 5:44 And Nephi and Lehi were in the midst of them; yea, they were encircled about; yea, they were as if in the midst of a flaming fire, yet it did harm them not, neither did it take hold upon the walls of the prison; **and they were filled with that joy which is unspeakable** and full of glory. 45 And behold, **the Holy Spirit of God did come down from heaven, and did enter into their hearts**, and they were **filled as if with fire,** and they could speak forth marvelous words

Jesus Christ (the tree of life), prays for the people in Bountiful

3 Nephi 17:17 And no tongue can speak, neither can there be written by any man, neither can the hearts of men conceive so great and marvelous things as we both saw and heard Jesus speak; and **no one can conceive of the joy which filled our souls at the time we heard him pray** for us unto the Father 18 And it came to pass that when Jesus had made an end of praying unto the Father, he arose; but **so great was the joy of the multitude that they were overcome**

Though each story expresses it slightly different, the common thread is the same, which is that true and great joy is experienced through the Holy Ghost. We might reconsider Nephi's famous quote from 2 Nephi 2:25. "Adam fell that men might be; and men are, that they might have joy." The kind of joy that Nephi is talking about is this highest form, which is to taste the love of God, communicated by the Holy Ghost. In so doing, man returns to the tree of life and divine presence of God, from which Adam fell.

Appendix 1

Steven's Defense – A Patriarchal Pattern

In chapter 3 of this book (Nephi and Laban) we examined one of Stephen's three patriarchal stories (the story of Joseph), which was valuable background information for interpreting Nephi and Laban's story as a presentation of Christ's (and our) mortal journey. If you recall, we read the thoughts of the apostle Bruce R. McConkie regarding the words of Malachi 4:5-6:

> "He shall plant in the hearts of the children the promises made to the fathers." That immediately raises the questions: Who are the *children,* who are the *fathers,* and what are the *promises?* If we can catch a vision from the doctrinal standpoint that answers those questions—who the fathers are, who the children are, and what the promises were—**we can have our understanding of the gospel and our comprehension of the plan of salvation expanded infinitely**. We shall then catch a vision of what the whole system of salvation is all about. Until we do that, really, we never catch that vision.[127]

Indeed, the histories of the patriarchal fathers, largely recorded in Genesis, contain a foundation for understanding all subsequent scripture. For this reason it is important for us to get better acquainted with these sacred histories. Let's explore a few events in the Bible which provide us with more needed background, and which will help us immensely anytime we study scripture. Couched in these verses is a common prophetic or patriarchal pattern which testifies of the plan of salvation, which we will identify and examine. We will start with the creation, and then Noah's dove, the story of Jonah, and finish with more of Stephen's patriarchal stories in the New Testament.

- **Genesis 1 – Spirit Moves**

Genesis 1 tells of the Spirit's participation in the creation. Before any life was formed, and simultaneous to the creation of light, we are told that:

> 2 And the earth was without form, and void; and darkness [was] upon the face of the deep. And the **Spirit of God moved** upon the face of the waters. 3 And God said, Let there be light: and there was light.[128]

If we look closer at the Hebrew for the word "moved" (*rachaph*) we find an interesting definition:

רָחַף [" pr. TO BE SOFT"], TO BE MOVED, AF-FECTED (cogn. to רָחַם), specially — (*a*) with the feeling of tender love, hence *to cherish*, see Piel.— PIEL, *to brood over* young ones, *to cherish* young (as an eagle), Deut. 32:11; figuratively used of the Spirit of God, who brooded over the shapeless mass of the earth, cherishing and vivifying. Of far more frequent use is the Syr. ܪܚܦ, which is used of birds brooding over their young, Ephr. ii. p. 552; of parents who cherish their children, Ephr. ii. p. 419; [129]

It seems reasonable to suggest that the Christian phrase, "a move of the Spirit", originates (has its genesis) in this verse. Wonderfully, it expresses not just motion, but loving or tender movement, as a bird which broods over her young. In fact, in Deut 32:11 *rachaph* is used in that context. Speaking of his love for Israel the Lord says, "As an eagle stirreth up her nest, **fluttereth** (*rachaph*) over her young, spreadeth abroad her wings, taketh them, beareth them on her wings." Indeed, this earliest image of the Spirit gently moving or fluttering still superbly expresses how we feel the soft stirring of the Spirit within our hearts.

In another memorable "act of creation", when Christ is baptized a fluttering bird again stirs over the water as the Spirit descends in the form of a dove: "And straightway coming up out of the water, he saw the heavens opened, and the Spirit like a dove descending upon him" (Mark 1:10). Christ's baptism in water with the anointing of the Holy Ghost is curiously traceable all the way back to the creation in Genesis 1, which is a pattern for all those who are newly created in the waters of baptism.

- **Noah's Dove**

Another story from the Old Testament where the fluttering dove is again a symbol of rebirth is that of Noah. Noah in the Hebrew comes from the Hebrew *nuach,* meaning rest, which is apropos since by the flood the world is given rest for a season from mankind's iniquity. (This is also prophetic of the future when the earth will permanently rest from iniquity.) There is a pivotal moment in Noah's story when a bird, coincidently a dove, again softly moves over the water as a symbol of another creation process. Forty days after the rain stops, Noah sends out the dove for the first time:

Genesis 8:8 Also he sent forth a dove from him, to see if the waters were abated from off the face of the ground;

9 But **the dove found no rest for the sole of her foot**, and she returned unto him into the ark, for the waters [were] on the face of the whole earth: then he put forth his hand, and took her, and pulled her in unto him into the ark.

Because there is found no "rest for the sole of her foot", Noah will wait seven days and then send out the dove a second time:

10 And he stayed yet other seven days; and again he sent forth the dove out of the ark;

11And the dove came in to him in the evening; and, lo, **in her mouth [was] an olive leaf** pluckt off: so Noah knew that the waters were abated from off the earth.

This time the dove returns with an olive leaf as a sign to Noah that there would be land for inheritance and a place to raise seed. It is noteworthy that the token of the promise is a *living* **olive** branch, newly created from the receding waters of the flood. We might also consider the significance of the olive, which prefigures an even greater promise, that of the Savior's Atonement in the Garden of Gethsemane, which means the place of the **olive** press[130], where Christ was crushed and bruised for man. Indeed, the resurrected Lord has promised upon his return to stand upon the Mount of Olives as a peaceful new millennial world begins (Acts 1). We might also contemplate, that like the waters of the creation (Gen 1) or the waters of Noah (Gen 8), as we emerge from the waters of baptism, the same dove of the Spirit "moves" upon us with the promise of rebirth. Could the dove have brought a greater symbol of promise, life, or peace to Noah, or mankind? Noah will send the dove out a third time in verse 12:

12 And he stayed yet other seven days; and sent forth the dove; which returned not again unto him any more.

This time the dove returns no more to the ark, and we might guess that it now sojourns in the land. If we have faith we might also believe that the dove is being fruitful and multiplying in this newly born world. In fact, at this point the story requires us to actually exercise faith in order to "see" that which hasn't necessarily been written, which is coincidently also how God's promises of fruitfulness are fulfilled (according to our faith). To be sure, without faith we never grasp the end of the story or the eternal lesson it teaches. Noah's dove also sets a symbolic pattern by the *three* times that it is sent out, which will be repeated often in scripture. Below is a simple chiastic diagram of this event:

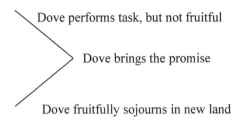

Dove performs task, but not fruitful

Dove brings the promise

Dove fruitfully sojourns in new land

Generally speaking, these *three* stages represent a process whereby fruitLESSness becomes fruitfulness, hinged on a divine promise of new life. Hopefully you can see that this is a pattern of our spiritual lives as well; our spiritual fruitfulness hinges on the bright promise of our Savior's Atonement, the reality of which is revealed to us by the Spirit (dove).

- **Number (sign) of Jonah – the Dove**

In Matthew's gospel, Christ is asked for a sign that he was the messiah, to which he replies: "An evil and adulterous generation seeketh after a sign; and there shall no sign be given to it, but the sign of the prophet Jonas: For as Jonas was three days and three nights in the whale's belly; so shall the Son of man be three days and three nights in the heart of the earth" (Mat 12:39-40). Because Christ identifies Jonah as a type of himself and his resurrection, he also connects himself to several other aspects of Jonah's story; e.g. the symbolic number *three*, the status of prophet (Mat 12:41), and the underlying meaning of Jonah in Hebrew.

In comparative terms, even as Jonah came forth after three days in a watery grave to save Nineveh, so Christ after three days emerged from the grave to save mankind. And symbolically, our baptism is patterned after both of these events, wherein we enter the water and resurrect to new life. If we take a closer look at Jonah's story we will see that there are many other parallels that resonate with tones of the Savior's life and Atonement:

- Jonah from Gaththepher (the wine press) in Galilee, and Jesus from Galilee will tread the winepress alone (Isa 63:3)
- Jonah swallowed by whale for three days, and Christ in the heart of the earth for three days. Both result in impossible and miraculous re-births.
- Jonah pays a price to "go down" into the ship on the chaotic sea, Christ pays a price to go down into a chaotic mortality
- Jonah freely offers himself as sacrifice to bring peace to the chaotic sea, Christ freely offers himself to bring peace to a chaotic world

- Lots are cast at the time of Jonah's sacrifice; lots are cast when Jesus was sacrificed
- Jonah prayed for "salvation" while in the depths of the sea, Jesus (whose name means salvation) secures salvation for all men while in the heart of the earth.
- Jonah preached repentance to Nineveh, as did Jesus to Judea and mankind
- All Nineveh turns to the Lord; all mankind will confess that Jesus is Lord.

Strikingly, to this day the story of Jonah is read on Yom Kippur, the Jewish Day of Atonement.[131] By taking Jonah as his sign, Christ closely binds himself to the Jewish understanding of the Atonement and the slaying of the sacrificial lamb. In the Encyclopedia Judaica we read about Jonah:

> The book is to be understood as a lesson in Divine forgiveness and mercy --- to Jonah as well as to the people of Nineveh --- and as a lesson in obedience to God's will. As a symbol of the effectiveness of repentance it is read as the haftarah at the afternoon service of the Day of Atonement.[132]

Certainly, Jonah's obedience to God's will is a foreshadow of Christ's supreme obedience to the Father, by which forgiveness and mercy is provided to all men, not just Nineveh. However, the full meaning of Christ's sign becomes especially clear when we consider Jonah's remarkable connection to Noah's dove (which was used to "seek a sign" of renewal) or to the Spirit which flutters in creation, because in Hebrew, Jonah (*yonah*) means the "dove"! From Joseph Smith we learn that this sign was not chosen haphazardly, but was given special significance from before the foundation of the world. He said, "The sign of the dove was instituted before the creation of the world, a witness for the Holy Ghost, and the devil cannot come in the sign of a dove."[133] Indeed, the story of Jonah (the dove) is another revelation of the Spirit's involvement in creation, for when Jonah (the dove) moves out over the waters from Joppa, creation and rebirth happens in Nineveh.

If we apply this meaning figuratively, then it was *yonah* (the dove) who descended upon Jesus while at the waters of baptism, **a sign** from the Father that he was the "anointed one." In fact, Messiah in Hebrew and Christos in Greek, mean "anointed one." And moreover, we understand that Christ was anointed with a fullness of the Spirit (*yonah*) - "For he whom God hath sent speaketh the words of God: for God **giveth not the Spirit by measure** [unto him]" (Jn 3:34). Truly, when Christ says that the sign that he gives is the sign of Jonah (Mat 12:39), he is referring not just to the three days he will be in the earth before resurrection, but as important, he is referring to the Spirit (dove) which "signals" to the heart of man that He is the Christ. There is indeed no grander sign of his divinity that you or I could hope to experience, for our creation and rebirth begins when the Holy Ghost moves upon the spiritual waters of our lives. (Coincidently, humans are composed of mostly water.[134])

When we read the story of Jonah we marvel that this entire city, so big that it took *three* days to cross, "believed God, and proclaimed a fast, and put on sackcloth, from the greatest of them to the least of them" (Jonah 3:5). Miraculous repentance on this scale, 120,000 people, is unequaled in scripture (only rivaled by its parallel – Christ who saves all repentant mankind). Why did the people of Nineveh repent? There could only ever be one reason for their "change" of heart, which is because the Holy Ghost revealed to them that Jonah's words were true. When Jonah (the dove) alights upon us to speak divine truth, it can have the same effect, which is to "overthrow" (the word that Jonah used to prophesy against Nineveh) our selfish lives. Expressed another way, the sign that Christ gives is inward, the whisper of the still small voice, the burning in the bosom, without which no one receives a witness of His love ("no man can say that Jesus is Lord except by the Holy Ghost" [1 Cor 12:3]). The heart must be stirred if faith is to grow, and a "mighty change of heart" begins to take root with Jonah.

Ultimately, though we may not connect the two, when Moroni promises that "by the power of the Holy Ghost" we can know if the Book of Mormon is true, he is confirming that by the sign of Jonah we can know it is true. Indeed, by the sign of Jonah we can "know the truth of all things" (Mor 10:4-5).

- **Nicodemus and the gentle wind**

Finally, consider how Christ personally describes this gentle moving of the Spirit (dove) which precedes creation and rebirth. During Christ's ministry there was a man named Nicodemus who was seeking a witness (testimony) that Jesus was the Messiah. Jesus tells him how the Holy Ghost works, comparing it to the way we softly hear or **feel** the wind, but don't see it (parenthesis mine).

> John 3:8 "The wind bloweth where it listeth, and thou hearest the sound thereof, but canst not tell whence it cometh, and whither it goeth: so is every one that is born of the Spirit."

The meaning of this verse is often unappreciated because of the ambiguous phrase "canst not tell". However, what the Lord wants Nicodemus, and us, to learn is that the Spirit and the wind are very similar in that neither is seen, but both are **felt.**

Important as well, the Greek word for "wind" in this verse is *pneuma*, which also serves as the primary word used in Greek for Spirit! (In Genesis 1:2 the word for Spirit is also the Hebrew for wind, *ruach!*) When we look at the principal entry in the lexicon for "pneuma" (wind or Spirit), we find something remarkably consistent with how the Spirit has been described in the other scriptures we just examined:

πνεῦμα, -τος, τό, (πνέω), Grk. writ. fr. Aeschyl. and Hdt. down; Hebr. רוּחַ, Lat. *spiritus*; i. e.
    1. *a movement of air,* (gentle) *blast*;   **a.** of the **wind**: ἀνέμων πνεύματα, Hdt. 7, 16, 1; Paus. 5, 25; hence the *wind* itself, Jn. iii. 8; plur. Heb. i. 7, (1 K. xviii. 45; [135]

Notice that the Spirit is compared to "a movement of air" or "gentle" blast of air, which is a striking allusion to the way the "Spirit moved" in Genesis 1:2. The image of a dove's wings softly moving the air as it hovers certainly comes to mind. In just this way, the popular children's song suggests to us how we **feel** the presence of the Holy Ghost:

> We do not have to see
> To know the wind is here;
> We do not have to see
> To know God's love is near [136]

In our hearts then, the voice of the Holy Ghost, like a gentle breeze, tells us; Christ is real, that Joseph Smith saw God the Father and his Son, and that the Book of Mormon is true (Mor 10:5). Alma uniquely teaches this same principle in Alma 32 when talking about the small seed, which when planted begins to "swell within your breast". He describes this subtle movement of the seed in verse 28, "when you **feel** these **swelling motions**, ye will begin to say within yourselves - It must needs be that this is a good seed, or that the word is good, for it beginneth to enlarge my soul; yea, it beginneth to enlighten my understanding, yea, it beginneth to be delicious to me." Similarly, in 1 Ne 17:45 Nephi compares the still small voice of the Spirit to "feeling" his words in our heart – "and he hath spoken unto you in a still small voice, but ye were past **feeling**, that ye could not **feel his words**."

When a member of the church bears his testimony and states that he "knows" a divine principle is true, the process by which he arrives at his "knowledge" is first and foremost through the subtle swelling, fluttering, or gentle motion of the Holy Ghost. Indeed what he really knows is what he has **felt**. By placing our faith in the seemingly least of sensations, Elijah's still small voice or Nicodemus' tender wind, the greatest transformation in our lives takes place.

Now let's see how this ancient sign of Jonah manifests itself in the story of Stephen in the New Testament, where we will also learn some additional concepts which we can apply to the stories of 1 Nephi.

- **Stephen's Patriarchal Defense**

Before the ancient apostle Stephen is stoned, he is allowed to first address the well-educated members of the Sanhedrin, at which time he courageously recounts the ancient histories of his patriarch fathers. Sadly, these typological witnesses of Christ, contained in stories which they knew well, fall on hardened (unfeeling) hearts. In chapter 6 of Acts we can read the events surrounding Stephen's trial:

13 And (they) set up false witnesses, which said, This man ceaseth not to speak blasphemous words against this holy place, and **the law**: 14 For we have heard him say, that this **Jesus of Nazareth shall destroy this place**, and shall **change** the customs which Moses delivered us. 15 And all that sat in the council, looking stedfastly on him, saw his face as it had been the face of an angel.

Stephen is talking about change; that the failing temple priesthood has been rejected, and that the lifeless customs of the law need to be transformed to heart felt love for God and others. Indeed, Stephen comes to the temple with the same message that Jonah delivered to Nineveh (and intriguingly in forty years [not days] the temple and unrepentant Jerusalem is destroyed). The heading in the LDS scriptures for Acts 6 reads; "Stephen transfigured before the Sanhedrin," and verse 15 tells us that Stephens face was like an angel's. We might therefore anticipate that Stephen's words, in such an inspired state, will be dazzling. Consider for a moment the place where Stephen stands. It is very near the exact spot that Christ stood before the Sanhedrin; it is also Mt. Moriah where father Abraham took Isaac his only son in similitude to be sacrificed, it is the threshing floor of Ornan where the pure wheat is separated from the chaff, the same floor that David bought for a price, insisting that "I will surely buy [it] of thee at a price: neither will I offer burnt offerings unto the LORD my God of that which doth cost me nothing" (1 Ch 21:24); and it is fittingly a symbolic foundation upon which all temple and Godly worship is built, a sacrificial place where Christ has promised to return and reign in glory. Surely the significance of that place and its sacred history (and future that will come full circle there) was not lost to Stephen. Filled with the power of the Holy Ghost, so much so that his very countenance changed (much as the Spirit filled Nephi "unto the consuming of his flesh", 1 Ne 17:48), Stephen is divinely guided as he testifies before the same men that had callously sacrificed the promised Messiah.

Stephen narrates the patterned lives of the patriarchs which testified of Christ and his atoning plan. Below is the first of Stephen's *three* chiastic stories (parenthesis mine):

Appendix 1

A 2 And he said, **Men, brethren**, and **fathers,** hearken;

    B The **God of glory** appeared unto our father **Abraham** (covenant)**,** when he was

        C **in Mesopotamia,** before he dwelt in Charran,

            D 3 **And said** unto him, **Get thee out of** thy country, and from thy kindred, and **come into** the land which I shall shew thee. 4 Then came he out of the land of the Chaldaeans,

                E and dwelt in **Charran**: and from thence, when his **father was dead,**

                    F he **removed him into** this land, wherein ye now dwell.

                        G 5 And **he gave him none inheritance in** it, no,

                            H **not [so much as] to set his foot** on:

                                I yet **he promised** that he would give it

                                  J to **him** for a **possession,**

                                  J' and to **his seed** after **him,**

                            H' when [as yet] **he had no child**.

                            I' 6 And **God spake** on this wise,

                        G' That **his seed should sojourn in** a strange land;

                    F' and that they should **bring them into** bondage, and entreat [them] evil four hundred years.

                E' 7 And the nation (**Egypt**) to whom they shall be in bondage **will I judge** (**death** of firstborns),

            D' **said God**: and after that shall **they come forth**, and serve me

        C' **in this place (Mt Sinai** and Mt Zion).

    B' 8 And **he (the God of glory)** gave him **(Moses)** the covenant of circumcision:

A' And so [Abraham] begat **Isaac**, and circumcised him the eighth day; and Isaac [begat] **Jacob**; and Jacob [begat] the **twelve patriarchs** (Fathers).

This chiasmus could be simplified and distilled to the following outline. It is a template for Stephen's next chiasmi, and will make it easier to compare them side by side:

    God's glory in Mesopotamia

        Charan – death of father

            No inheritance, no foot to stand on

                Promise of possession

            Sojourn in land (of inheritance)

        Egypt – death of firstborns

    God's glory on Sinai\Mt Zion

Notice that this first of three chiastic structures in Acts 7 covers the entire cycle of all the patriarchs, starting with Abraham through Moses, coming full circle to the current Sanhedrin! Stephen even parallels Abraham to Moses, both given a covenant by the "God of glory" (B,B'). To insure that they will have no doubts about his message, Stephen's next two chiasmi offer the individual stories of Joseph and Moses, which as we shall see, follow the same pattern. But first, there are several items to consider in this scintillating first chiasmus.

Stephen starts out in verse 2 boldly addressing his audience, the Sanhedrin, as "Men, brethren, and fathers." If we look across the chiasmus to its parallel verse 8, we see the fathers who the Sanhedrin should reflect, yet sadly seem to be the antithesis - Abraham, Isaac, Joseph, and their seed the twelve patriarchs. Stephen then speaks of how father Abraham set the example, leaving Mesopotamia, which in the Hebrew is *'Aram Naharayim*, which means *exalted place* of two rivers[137], and enters Charan a hot or parched place[138]. If we apply a figurative significance to these verses, leaving Mesopotamia is symbolic of leaving the exalted place of heaven, dying spiritually and entering mortality. Abraham's father dies in Charan as a figure of all mankind (E) who die spiritually as they enter mortality, where carnal man has no inheritance (G), or no foot to stand on until he receives the divine promise of seed and possession (I-J). After obtaining this promise, Israel, as a figure of mankind, must sojourn or walk by faith, even in bondage for 400 years (F')[139], at which time he and the world (Egypt) will be judged (E') and afterwards be brought forth and once again exalted, to serve God "in this place".

Stephen's phrase, "serve me in this place" (C') also deserves some extra attention. If we look at its parallel in verse 2 (C) we see that it corresponds to the Father's glory in the "exalted place" of Mesopotamia. It is widely understood that Stephen here is alluding to what God said to Moses in Exodus 3:12 while speaking with the burning bush on Mt Sinai: [140]

> 12 And he said, Certainly I will be with thee; and this [shall be] a token unto thee, that I have sent thee: When thou hast brought forth the people out of Egypt, **ye shall serve God upon this mountain.**

Stephen wonderfully conflates the two mountains – the earlier Sinai and the latter Mt. Zion.[141] During the time of Moses, Israel did stop at Mt. Sinai for instruction; and Mt. Zion, where Stephen stands to testify, is also a place of God's glory, a temple to serve the Lord and receive his instruction. For his audience, a group of learned Jews, Stephen's intended allusion would have been easily understood. The place of sacred history upon which they spent their days carried a hallowed and weighty heritage to which they woefully failed to cherish or live up to. (Stephen mentions the scene of Moses on Mt. Sinia a few verses later, Acts 7:30, which suggests that this passage of scripture [Ex 3:12] was likely on his mind.)

In addition, at the center of this first chiasmus there is also a direct allusion to the verses in Noah's story that we previously looked at! The unique phrase, "not so much as to set his foot on" is borrowed here by Stephen to describe Abraham's situation, which he cleverly compares to Noah's dove! Hoping to draw comparisons, Stephen evidently again conflates two stories, this time Abraham and Noah's. Below is a side by side assessment of the center of Abraham's story contrasted with Noah's dove, in chiastic format:

Noah's Dove (Gen 8:8-12)	Abraham's Promise (Acts7:5-6)
Returns to ark with nothing No rest for sole of foot	Abraham enters Canaan with No foot to stand on
Returns with Promise Olive Branch	Receives promise of Inheritance and seed
Does not return to ark Sojourns in the earth (fruitful)	Abraham sojourns in a new land Walks in faith (fruitful)

As we discussed earlier, the *three* stages of Noah's dove represent a process whereby fruitLESSness becomes fruitfulness, hinged on a divine promise of new life. Abraham's story, as Stephen's allusion indicates, communicates this same message of rebirth. Indeed, spiritual rebirth, in similitude of Christ's resurrection from death to life, is at the center of all the patriarch stories, not just Abraham's. Poignantly, the Sanhedrin could only be able to understand these promises of renewal if they were spiritually reborn through the Spirit (the dove) themselves. Using the sign that Christ instituted, Stephen's allusion provides extra special testimony to all who seek confirmation that Jesus is the Christ. Only by this sign, the dove that brings the promise of Christ, can they know the truth of Stephen's words.

Augustine, the early church leader, is noted for saying that the Old Testament *conceals* the New Testament and the New Testament *reveals* the Old Testament.[142] Noah's, Jonah's, and Abraham's ancient stories are examples of an Old Testament pattern which is a New Testament outline of the gospel plan of spiritual renewal.[143] And as we will continue to see, it is also a pattern repeated in the lives of the other patriarchs.

- **Second of Three Chiasmus- Descent into Egypt**

Let's look again at Acts 7: 9-16. This is the story that we already examined in chapter 3 (the story of Nephi and Laban). Stephen intentionally backs ups chronologically in order to present the account of the patriarch Joseph, with the same parallel features found in the last chiasmus (it starts in verse 9 and ends in 17). Remember, that Stephen's reason for telling these patriarchal stories is to convince the Sanhedrin that Christ was the Messiah, and therefore we should find many elements that prophecy of Christ (parenthesis mine):

A 9 And the **patriarchs**, moved with envy (near **Sychem**), **sold Joseph into Egypt**: (near **Sychem**)

    B but **God was with him**, 10 And **delivered him out of all his afflictions**, and

      gave him favour and wisdom in the sight of Pharaoh king of Egypt; and he

    made him governor over Egypt and all his house.

        C 11 Now there came a **dearth over all the land** of **Egypt** and Chanaan,

          D and great affliction: and **our fathers** found **no sustenance.**

          E 12 But when **Jacob** heard that there was corn (**seed**) in Egypt,

            F he **sent out our fathers** first.

              G 13 And at the second [time] Joseph was **made**

              known to his brethren;

             G' and **Joseph's kindred** was **made known unto**

             Pharaoh.

            F' 14 Then **sent Joseph, and called his father**

          E' **Jacob** to [him], and all his kindred (**seed**), threescore and fifteen souls.

        C' 15 So Jacob went down **into Egypt**, and **died, he,**

      D' **and our fathers**,

A' 16 And were **carried over into Sychem**, and laid in the sepulchre that Abraham **bought for a sum** of money of the sons of Emmor [the father] of **Sychem.**

    B' 17 But when the **time of the promise** drew nigh, which **God had sworn to**

      Abraham, the **people grew and multiplied in Egypt**,

These verses give the story of Jacob and Joseph's descent into Egypt, and Israel's return to Canaan. Below is a simplified chiasmus formed within these verses, with my comments included:

    Joseph (sold for a price) by "patriarchs" in land of Promise – near Sychem in Canaan

      Dearth over Egypt – Famine, Death – fathers found no Sustenance

        Brothers first sent for wheat (seed), meet but do not know Joseph

          Brothers sent second time; Joseph is made known, (their redeemer)

        All of the kindred (seed) sent for by Joseph, are fruitful in new land

      Jacob and fathers, all die in Egypt

    Joseph returned to Abraham's tomb (bought for a sum) – Sychem in Canaan

As you can see, Stephen has given us a near duplicate pattern of his first and historically broader chiasmus, again with a revelatory event in the middle. I should point out that there is some historical data that is helpful when identifying some of these parallel verses which Stephen's audience, the Sanhedrin, would have readily known, but we may not. Though Sychem is not specifically mentioned in verse 9, it is exactly parallel to verse 16 because Sychem is not only the place where Joseph is buried in a *purchased* sepulcher (vs

16), but it is also the place to where young Joseph was sent when he was initially *sold* into bondage (vs 9) by his brothers - Sychem in the Greek, or Shechem in the Old Testament (Gen 37:13). Shechem is also significant because it is the first place that Abraham stayed when he entered Canaan, and it was there that the Lord promised the land to his posterity (Gen 12:6-7). [144]

Jacob's family goes into Egypt to be saved as a nation, which interestingly becomes a two-edged sword; a blessing and a curse. Egypt paradoxically saves the covenant seed of Abraham, yet it also introduces a 400 year period of oppression and bondage. As his type, following this eternal covenant pattern, the road we travel in mortality is the same as the prophetic pattern that Stephen presents to the Sanhedrin. When we compare the center of this chiasmus about Joseph, to that of the first (Abraham and Noah's conflated dove), the names are different but the message discovered is the same – at its center there is a promise of salvation. If you recall, Joseph weeps and lovingly embraces his brothers when he reveals his identity – their brother who is able to save them (Gen 45:3). Such powerful emotion and comfort perhaps you have also felt, embraced by the Spirit as the promise of your Savior has been gently spoken to you. Like Joseph's brothers who sought sustenance, as we hold Him close, our welfare is also assured through a plan of provision; a storehouse of heavenly bread in the midst of a spiritually famished world. Joseph as a type of Christ is a theme which Nephi also investigates. In fact, Nephi alludes to this same story at the center of his own chiasmi in 1 Nephi, chapters 5 and 18.

- **Stephens Third Narration – Ascent out of Egypt**

Stephen's third narration is the life of Moses. Importantly, it repeats for a *third* time the same cycle as the first two narrations. Below is Acts 7: 17-37 (parenthesis mine):

Moses – 40,40,40

A 17 But when the time of the promise drew nigh, which God had sworn to Abraham, the people grew and **multiplied in Egypt,**

  B 18 Till another king arose, which knew not Joseph. 19 The same dealt subtilly with our kindred, and evil entreated our fathers, so that they **cast out their young children, to the end they might not live.**

    C 20 In which time **Moses** was born, and was exceeding fair, and **nourished up** in his father's house three months. 21 And when he was cast out, Pharaoh's daughter **took him up, and nourished him** for her own son.

      D 22 And **Moses** was learned in all the wisdom of the Egyptians, and was **mighty in words and in deeds** (signs and wonders).

        E 23 And when he **was full forty years old**, it came into his heart to visit his brethren the children of Israel.

          F 24 And seeing one of them suffer wrong, he defended him, and avenged him that was oppressed, and smote the Egyptian: 25 For he supposed his brethren would have understood **how that God by his hand would deliver them**: but they understood not.

            G 26 And the next day he shewed himself unto them as they strove, and would have set them at one again, saying, Sirs, ye are brethren; why do ye wrong one to another? (Moses acts as ruler)

              H 27 But he that did his neighbour wrong thrust him away, saying, **Who made thee a ruler and a judge over us?** 28 Wilt thou kill me, as thou diddest the Egyptian yesterday?

                I 29 Then **fled** Moses at this saying, and was a stranger **in the land of Madian,** where he begat two sons.

                  J 30 And when forty years were expired, there appeared to him in the wilderness **of mount Sina**

                    K an **angel of the Lord** in a flame of fire in a bush.

                  L 31 When **Moses** saw it, he **wondered** at the sight: and

                    M as he **drew near to behold** it,

                      N the **voice** of **the Lord** came unto him,

                      N 32 **Saying,** I am **the God** of thy fathers, the God of Abraham, and the God of Isaac, and the God of Jacob.

                  L Then **Moses trembled,**

                  M and **durst not behold.**

                K 33 Then said **the Lord** to him,

              J Put off thy shoes from thy feet: for the **place where thou standest** is **holy ground.** (mount Sina)

                I 34 I have seen, I have seen the affliction of my people which is in Egypt, and I have heard their groaning, and am come down to deliver them. And now **come**, I will **send** thee **into Egypt.**

              H 35 This Moses whom they refused, saying, **Who made thee a ruler and a judge?**

            G the same did God send to be a ruler

          F and a **deliverer by the hand of the angel** which appeared to him in the bush.

        D 36 He brought them out, after that he had shewed **wonders and signs** in the land of Egypt, and in the Red sea (mighty in words and deed),

        E and **in the wilderness forty years.**

    C 37 This is that **Moses**, which said unto the children of Israel, A prophet shall the **Lord your God raise up** unto you of your brethren, like unto me; him shall ye hear.

  B Missing Element – all the old die in wilderness ("to the end that they might not live")

A Missing Element - new generation enters Promised Land, people grow, are multiplied as God swore to Abraham

This third narration of Israel's ascent out of Egypt, verses 20-37, also forms the same simple and familiar chiastic pattern:

Multiply in Egypt (initially a land of promise)

  Death of babies in the land

    Moses accused of trying to rule, people confused, not known as deliverer – **40 years**

      In Midia (Madian), speaks with the Lord on Sinai – **40 years**

    Moses leads in the wilderness, sent by God to be deliverer - **40 years**

  All die in the wilderness

Enter land of promise - Canaan

Because Moses comes forth out of water (also the likely meaning of Moses' name[145]), we understand even his humble beginnings to be a foreshadowing of events to come, when later he will lead Israel through and out of the waters of the Red Sea, which is a symbol of rebirth (1 Cor 10:2). In his chiasmus Stephen compares such "wonders and signs" done by Moses in Egypt (C-D), to one "like unto Moses", who was also mighty in "word and deed" (C'-D'), who he suggests to the Sanhedrin is Christ. (Nephi also uses Deut 18:15, "one like unto to Moses", to prove Christ in his chiasmus in 1 Ne 22.) Intriguingly, Stephen doesn't actually include the last 2 patterned legs in his narration, though no doubt his Jewish audience easily fills in the necessary historical information, which is that all of old Israel dies before the newly born generation enters Canaan.

Stephen instead concludes speaking of Israel's disobedience in the wilderness, of their worshipping other Gods, and their misconception of the temple's purpose, which continued even at the time of the Savior. He reveals to the Sanhedrin the hinge upon which their unbelief swings:

51 Ye stiffnecked and uncircumcised in heart and ears, **ye do always resist the Holy Ghost: as your fathers [did], so [do] ye.**

52 Which of the prophets have not your fathers persecuted? and they have slain them which shewed before of the coming of the Just One; of whom ye have been now the betrayers and murderers:

53 Who have received the law by the disposition of angels, and have not kept [it].

Indeed, when they resist the Holy Ghost (Jonah), the Sanhedrin overlooks the only means by which they could recognize Jesus as the Messiah, whose soft voice forever affirms the Lord as the saving promise at the heart of these patriarchal stories. Just as their fathers had slain all those prophets that had spoken of "the coming of the Just One", Stephen accuses them of something even worse, murdering the promised Messiah who was the very focus of the patriarchal stories, the hope for which all of Abraham's seed, by the timeless prompting of the Holy Ghost, had waited.

As the Serpent held up in the wilderness upon which one need only look upon to live, Stephen's wonderful words before the council have *three* times expounded, through ancient patriarchal pattern, the plan of salvation fulfilled in Christ. Indeed, in this final chiasmus Stephen's main point to his listeners (at the center of this structure) is that the "Lord" who spoke to Moses is Jesus Christ (vs 32). In a poignant and poetic twist, Stephen will be the means by which his unfinished chiasmus is completed; for he will die, as the patriarchal story pattern says all must, slain outside the city walls in similitude of his beloved Savior of whom he fearlessly testified. By Luke's account in Acts 7:

> 54 When they heard these things they were cut to the heart, and they gnashed on him with their teeth.
>
> 55 But he, being **full of the Holy Ghost**, looked up stedfastly into heaven, and saw the glory of God, and Jesus standing on the right hand of God,
>
> 56 And said, Behold, I see the heavens opened, and the Son of man standing on the right hand of God.

His life imitating scripture, Stephen personally completes the last legs of the pattern, dying at the hands of intellectually knowing but spiritually unfeeling Jewish leaders, figures of the disobedient children of Israel in the wilderness of whom he spoke. With the Dove alight upon his shoulder (vs 55), filling his soul, Stephen crosses into the Land of Promise, the exalted Father and the Son both welcoming him; just as he illustrated in prophetic pattern to the Sanhedrin they would (vs 56)! Fittingly, Luke's account in Acts squarely unites Stephen with the honored patriarchs of old of whom he so boldly proclaimed, all of whom were purposed types of the Savior. (His dying words even reflect those of Jesus upon the cross, "lay not this sin to their charge." [vs 60])

- **One Eternal Round – Plan of Salvation**

If we take the descent into Egypt, and combine it with the ascent out of Egypt, a very interesting pattern emerges, which is perhaps a sense of what Nephi means in 1 Nephi 10:19, "as well in these times as in times of old, and as well in times of old as in times to come; wherefore, the **course of the Lord is one eternal round**." Connecting the beginning and the ending lines of a chiasmus, the result is a circular image.

Appendix 1

In fact, chiasmi have been called "a visual and acoustic image turning around its centre."[146] Below is diagram of this constantly revolving patriarchal pattern (starting at the top and moving counterclockwise):

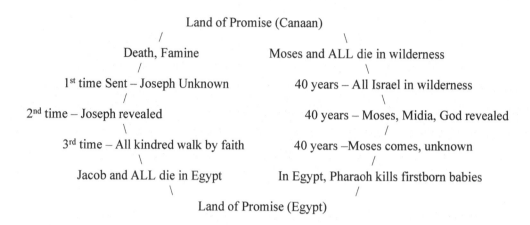

When we analyze Stephen's narration in this repeating pattern we observe that there are 7 items that repeat, as the days of the week. This structure could also be a model of mankind's history or a personal representation of the repeating pattern in all our mortal lives, as well as a pattern related to the 7 creative periods of Genesis, or the temporal 7 dispensations which ultimately result in redemption and a return to our heavenly promised land. As indicated earlier, preceding the entrance to the land of promise at either end of the cycle, is death. We spiritually die when leaving the Father's presence, and then we must physically die again before re-entering the Promised Land. Like life, death is an essential component (counterpart) of the cycle, or plan of salvation. However, perhaps most fascinating is that Stephen's patriarchal pattern, presented on the temple mount, is an exact blueprint of our modern temple endowment![147] (Go to the notes section, pg 286, for this outline.)

- **Jacob in Haran**

Stephen does not provide the Sanhedrin with a narration of the patriarch Jacob's life, though no doubt he could have easily done so using the same pattern. In fact, because Jacob is a patriarch, we might predict and expect his history to contain the same patterned elements. Jacob's story is also best saved for last so that it will be freshest on our memory as we consider the story of Nephi and Laban. As you will see, the Laban of Jacob's story has many similarities to the Laban of Nephi's story, and in fact is an important key to unlocking a greater understanding of Nephi's narrative. Below is the life of Jacob in chiastic form from Genesis 29-31:

232

With father Isaac in Canaan

    Goes to Haran (in Hebrew - parched place) pursued by Esau - death

        7 years- marries Leah

            7 years- marries beloved Rachel (Lamb in Hebrew)

        7 years- gathers flocks

    Leaves Haran with flocks – pursued by Laban - death

Returns to father's presence in Canaan

In the midst of Jacob's story are the same three periods that typify the lives of the other patriarchs. Below is a side-by-side comparison of the lives of three patriarchs.

Jacob	Joseph	Moses
7 Years – Marries Leah, not his beloved	Brothers don't know who Joseph is	40 years in Egypt - Moses serves Pharaoh, not God
7 Years – His beloved Rachel (means lamb) is known to Him	Joseph reveals his identity as savior to his brothers	40 years in Midia - God revealed to Moses on Sinai
7 Years – Jacob is fruitful in flocks, his seed multiplied, has 12 sons, spiritual Joseph is born	All of Abraham's seed move to Egypt, covenant preserved, multiplied	40 years in wilderness Moses and Abraham's seed are tested, refined, preserved, multiplied

- **We are his type – The Sign of Jonah is also our sign**

The patterns of Jacob, Joseph, or Moses are all identical examples of the covenant plan of salvation since before the world was created. Christ spends three days in the earth as a fulfillment of this three part pattern or rebirth, and like the patriarchs, our lives are a type of Christ's. Coming to earth we all descend below the heavens, are tried, are spiritually reborn and walk by faith, reflecting His redeeming love and bearing spiritual fruit in serving those around us. Anointed with the Holy Ghost's companionship, our impurities are removed as we prepare to inherit a promised heavenly kingdom.

Genesis 6:3 tells us that the life of man, like Moses', is 120 years, or 3 X 40. The three days we are on the earth is a symbolic time frame, slightly different, longer or shorter for everyone. The three 40 year periods of Moses are long, whereas Jacob's three seven year periods are much shorter, yet they are both a type of the same thing. With this blueprint in mind, consider the prophetic significance of some additional three period patterns:

Adam-Abraham	Abraham-Christ	Christ-Millennium
2000 years	2000 years	2000 years
40 Jubilee Years (40X50)	40 Jubilee Years	40 Jubilee Years
40 Years in Egypt	40 Years in Midia	40 years in Wilderness
Passover -1st Feast	Pentecost -2nd Feast	Tabernacles 3rd – Harvest
Noah's 1st Dove-nothing	Noah's 2nd –Olive Branch	Noah's 3rd – Dove sojourns
Faith Dormant - Unfruitful	Promise	Spiritual fruitfulness
Outer Courtyard of Temple	Holy Place	Holy of Holies
Telestial	Terrestrial	Celestial

Notice that these patterns also project where we are historically - see the second line of the chart above which indicates that we are at the end of 6,000 years, and on the cusp of the millennial age – the 7th and final period of 1,000 years.

* From the LDS Bible Dictionary we read how the jubilee year is symbolic of the Atonement - "A name given to every fiftieth year. It got its name from the fact that the beginning of the year was announced by the blowing of a trumpet on the Day of Atonement. In it, land that had changed hands reverted to the family to which it had belonged at the original settlement, and all bondmen of Israelitish birth were set free (Lev. 25:8–16, 23–55; 27:16–25)."[148]

Appendix 2

Agag – Laban

In the footnotes of the story of Nephi and Laban there is a cross reference to 1 Sam 15 and the story of Agag. Parts of this story will be familiar to some, though I dare say that only a few could render a version in their own words. Yet in so many ways it is a parallel story to the events of Nephi and Laban, and presents us with a very similar perplexing event. The most famous verse from this story is one that we all will recognize; 1 Samuel 15:12,

> 12 And Samuel said, Hath the LORD [as great] delight in burnt offerings and sacrifices, as in obeying the voice of the LORD? Behold, to obey [is] better than sacrifice, [and] to hearken than the fat of rams.

Speaking to Saul, Samuel clarifies that obedience is the highest form of sacrifice, offering one's self rather than an animal. What has Saul the King done wrong to deserve such correction from the prophet Samuel? It begins with Saul's anointing to be king, which also included a command (constraint) from the Lord to kill and "utterly destroy all" the Amalekites and their flocks. However, for prideful reasons Saul has half-heartedly complied with this command. In 1 Samuel we read:

> 1 Samuel also said unto Saul, The LORD sent me to anoint thee [to be] king over his people, over Israel: now therefore hearken thou unto the voice of the words of the LORD.
> 2 Thus saith the LORD of hosts, I remember [that] which Amalek did to Israel, how he laid [wait] for him in the way, when he came up from Egypt.
> 3 Now go and smite Amalek, and utterly destroy all that they have, and spare them not; but slay both man and woman, infant and suckling, ox and sheep, camel and ass.

Interestingly, Saul's anointing is connected to the charge to "hearken unto the voice of the words of the Lord", a stipulation which accompanies all divine anointing (of the Spirit). Saul does a fairly good job, but he fails to comply fully with the Lord's mandate:

> 7 And Saul smote the Amalekites from Havilah [until] thou comest to Shur, that [is] over against Egypt.

8 And he took Agag the king of the Amalekites alive, and utterly destroyed all the people with the edge of the sword.

9 But Saul and the people spared Agag, and the best of the sheep, and of the oxen, and of the fatlings, and the lambs, and all [that was] good, and would not utterly destroy them: but every thing [that was] vile and refuse, that they destroyed utterly.

Saul has spared the best sheep under the pretext that he might sacrifice them to the Lord, precipitating the verse that most recognize, that it is better to obey than sacrifice.

10 Then came the word of the LORD unto Samuel, saying,

11 It repenteth me that I have set up Saul [to be] king: for he is turned back from following me, and hath not performed my commandments. And it grieved Samuel; and he cried unto the LORD all night.

12 And when Samuel rose early to meet Saul in the morning, it was told Samuel, saying, Saul came to Carmel, and, behold, he set him up a place, and is gone about, and passed on, and gone down to Gilgal.

13 And Samuel came to Saul: and Saul said unto him, Blessed [be] thou of the LORD: I have performed the commandment of the LORD.

14 And Samuel said, **What [meaneth] then this bleating of the sheep in mine ears,** and the lowing of the oxen which I hear?

The meaning of the bleating sheep in Samuel's ear is easy to surmise, it is the sound of disobedience. Many high or "exalted" reasons could be listed for changing the command of the Lord, but Saul ultimately confesses one of the most common, that he "feared the people and obeyed their voice" (peer pressure). In Hebrew, Saul's name means "desire", and clearly, Saul "desires" to look good in the eyes of the people more than he cares about his obedience to the Lord. However, Samuel makes it clear that it is not man's place to modify God's command, especially a king which had been given "another heart" as was Saul (1 Sam 10:9). (If you think about it, there are comparisons in this story to Eden, where Eve, perhaps out of desire for the forbidden fruit, modifies [rationalizes] God's command, which causes Adam and Eve to lose their position as king and queen in Eden. Indeed, if self-rationalized desire had a hand in the fall, then righteous desires will determine man's re-admittance to Eden.)

And so, Samuel tells Saul that he is rejected by the Lord from being king because he has "rejected the word of the Lord".

19 And the LORD sent thee on a journey, and said, Go and utterly destroy the sinners the Amalekites, and fight against them until they be consumed.

20 And Saul said unto Samuel, Yea, I have obeyed the voice of the LORD, and have gone the way which the LORD sent me, and have brought Agag the king of Amalek, and have utterly destroyed the Amalekites.

21 But the people took of the spoil, sheep and oxen, the chief of the things which should have been utterly destroyed, to sacrifice unto the LORD thy God in Gilgal.

22 And Samuel said, Hath the LORD [as great] delight in burnt offerings and sacrifices, as in obeying the voice of the LORD? Behold, **to obey [is] better than sacrifice, [and] to hearken than the fat of rams.**

23 For rebellion [is as] the sin of witchcraft, and stubbornness [is as] iniquity and idolatry. **Because thou hast rejected the word of the LORD, he hath also rejected thee** from [being] king.

Recall that God's word is also the centerpiece in Nephi and Laban's story, and as indicated to Nephi by the constraint of the Spirit (1 Nephi 4:13), those who reject it "perish in unbelief". Samuel then does something akin to what Nephi does in 1 Nephi 4.

32 Then said Samuel, Bring ye hither to me Agag the king of the Amalekites. And Agag came unto him delicately. And Agag said, Surely the bitterness of death is past.

33 And Samuel said, As thy sword hath made women childless, so shall thy mother be childless among women. **And Samuel hewed Agag in pieces before the LORD in Gilgal.**

Though Saul is not the one to do it, the two stories apparently end the same when obedient Samuel, in order to preserve God's word (vs 23), slays Agag with a sword, even as Nephi slew Laban. Clearly the moral of the two stories is very similar, which is that God allows no quarter regarding sin; victory must be complete, and sin must be totally vanquished. Like the story of Nephi and Laban, we most easily come to terms with its seeming brutality when we approach it as a story of type, even as Nephi suggests in 2 Nephi 11:4, that "all is shadow and type." In addition, the manner in which Samuel slays Agag is reminiscent of how "atonement" is described in the story of Phinehas (Num 25), which we looked at earlier (pg 59).

Appendix 2

As already mentioned, Saul's name in Hebrew is "to ask for" or "desire", the essence of which Saul fatefully lives up to, questioning the Lord's desire, supplanting it with his own.[149] Saul's name ironically characterizes desire (good or misguided) on several levels of this story:

- Israel does not desire the Lord as their King, they want a mortal king
- Saul hides when presented as newly selected king, doesn't desire to be king
- Samuel, whose name means "God hears", desires for Israel to "hear" God; make God King
- God consents to Israel's desire, but desires for them to drive the Amalekites from the land
- Saul at first performs according to Gods desires, his heart is turned to God
- Saul follows his own desires, fails to perform as constrained by God's command
- Samuel slays Agag in accordance with God's desire

Like Saul, Nephi is also embroiled in a story line of multiple desires:

- The Lord desires to secure Brass Plates, to preserve nation (seed)
- Laman and Lemuel desire differently
- Nephi desires as his Father Lehi, and like Saul initially, has God's heart
- Laban desires to slay Nephi and brothers
- At first Nephi's shrinks to do the desires of the Spirit to slay Laban
- Nephi hearkens to Spirit's desire (constraint), slays Laban
- Nephi personifies what Saul should have been, one who hearkens to the desire (word) of God

Curiously, Saul, who refused to slay Agag, ultimately suffers the same demise as Laban; he is also beheaded and his armor is stripped off him.

1 Sam 28:31 And they **cut off his head, and stripped off his armour**, and sent into the land of the Philistines round about, to publish [it in] the house of their idols, and among the people.

Saul is also told that the Israel would perish because of his failure to obey the voice of the Lord.:

1 Sam 28:18-19 **Because thou obeyedst not the voice of the LORD, nor executedst his fierce wrath upon Amalek,** therefore hath **the LORD done this thing unto thee** this day.

238

Moreover the LORD will also deliver Israel with thee into the hand of the Philistines: and to morrow [shalt] thou and thy sons [be] with me: **the LORD also shall deliver the host of Israel into the hand of the Philistines.**

We can probably see parallels to our lives in the story of Saul; conflicted by desires, holding onto pride, and failing to obey God's voice. With so many similarities to the story of Nephi and Laban, we might wonder if Laban had been allowed to live, would he have later caught up to and beheaded Nephi, even as Saul was ultimately beheaded because he did not hew Agag (1 Sam 28:31)? Spiritually speaking, surely that would have been the case! Thus, Laban and Agag, as personifications of death and sin cannot be partially defeated. If not destroyed, they will slay us. It is a simple either/or proposition, with no "partial-ity". Our hope, the Atonement, mirrors this all-consuming struggle.

- **Hebrew meaning of Amalek and Agag and their significance**

Agag's name in the Hebrew means "I will overtop"[150], likely from the root verb *ga'ah*,[151] meaning:

> גָּאָה fut. יִגְאָה a poetical word.
> (1) TO LIFT ONESELF UP, TO INCREASE, used of water rising up, Eze. 47:5; of a plant growing, Job 8:11.—Job 10:16, וְיִגְאָה כַּשַּׁחַל תְּצוּדֵנִי "and (if) it (my head) raise itself up, as a lion thou wouldest hurt me."
> (2) Metaph. *to be exalted, magnificent,* of God, Ex. 15:1, 21. In the derivatives it is applied—
> (3) to *honour* (see גָּאוֹן No. 1), and—
> (4) to *pride and arrogance,* see גַּאֲוָה and גָּאוֹן No. 3. (Syr. Pael ܓܐ to decorate, to make magnificent. Ethpael, to boast oneself; ܓܐ, ܓܐ adorned, magnificent.) In the signification of pride, it accords with the Gr. γαίω.
> Derivatives follow, except גֵּא, גֵּוָה No. II.

Definition (4) immediately stands out, suggesting that Agag is a symbol of pride and arrogance. (Along these lines, in the book of Esther, the wicked Haman, whose name means "magnificent" [similar to the meaning of Agag's name] is an Agagite, and also a symbol of pride who ultimately shares the same fate as Agag.) Certainly by this definition we can understand Samuel's insistence that Agag be destroyed. And, if I might offer a play on an old saying — pride in the form of Agag, literally goeth before the fall of Saul. Also, by examining the Hebrew meaning of "Amalekite" we can learn even more about Agag's figurative meaning. Amalekite comes from the root *amal*:

עָמָל m. (once f. Ecc. 10:15)—(1) *heavy, wearisome labour*, Ecc. 1:3; 2:11; used figuratively of the mind, Ps. 73:16.

(2) *the produce of labour*, Ps. 105:44; Ecc. 2:19.

(3) *weariness, trouble, vexation*, Gr. κάματος, πόνος, Genesis 41:51; Deu. 26:7; Job 3:10; 16:2, מְנַחֲמֵי עָמָל "troublesome comforters." Isa. 53:11, מֵעֲמַל נַפְשׁוֹ " of the sorrow (or anguish) of his soul." It is rendered by some, *sin, wickedness* (i. q. אָוֶן), Nu. 23:21; Isa. 10:1; but the signification of vexation is not unsuitable in both places.

(4) [*Amal*], pr. n. m. 1 Ch. 7:35.

The Amalekites, therefore, also have a figurative significance that is very consistent with our assessment of this story. They represent the Laban or Ishmael character of this story, an embodiment of sorrow, sin, and death, which is overcome and defeated by the promised Messiah. In fact, notice the reference to Isaiah 53:11 and how this word *amal* is used prophetically to describe how the Savior was "weighed down with sorrow" in Gethsemane and on the cross:

> 53:11 He shall see of the travail (*amal*) of his soul, [and] shall be satisfied: by his knowledge shall my righteous servant justify many; for he shall bear their iniquities. 12 Therefore will I divide him [a portion] with the great, and he shall divide the spoil with the strong; because he hath poured out his soul unto death: and he was numbered with the transgressors; and he bare the sin of many, and made intercession for the transgressors.

Christ's atonement is pre-figured in the events of Exodus 17, where we read that Israel in battle defeated the Amalekites while Moses stood with his hands extended, in an image of the cross.[152] After driving off the Amalekites we are told that Moses built an altar of sacrifice and then received a promise from the Lord concerning these same Amalekites:

Ex 17:14 And the Lord said unto Moses, Write this for a memorial in a book, and rehearse it in the ears of Joshua: for **I will utterly put out the remembrance** of Amalek from under heaven.

Once we understand the symbolic significance of Amalek as a figure of carnal strife and death, we understand that this is quite a promise indeed – that Amalek will be utterly removed from under heaven! Certainly this promise was finally fulfilled by Christ's saving work, done in Gethsemane and upon the cross. Samuel's insistence that Saul do likewise (destroy the Amalekites "utterly") was in keeping with the Lord's earlier promise given to Moses.

- **Amalekites and Lamanites**

Thus we see that Saul's task represents our task, just as it was Nephi's task, and so it was Christ's messianic mission, which is to "utterly put out of remembrance" the labor of sin and death, and in so doing reunite us with God. Paul uses words in Romans 8 which aptly describe Saul's and our mortal conflict:

13 For if ye live after the flesh, ye shall die: but **if ye through the Spirit do mortify the deeds of the body**, ye shall live.
14 For as many as are led by the Spirit of God, they are the sons of God.

Verse 13 is a short chiasmus, with "through the Spirit" as the key. Starting in the center and going either way the message is the same. Paul places "the spirit" as the centerpiece of this chiasmus, which was also the emphasis of so many of Nephi's chiasmi, illustrating the primary way in which God reveals himself to us;

If ye **live**

After the **flesh**

Ye shall **die**

But if ye **through the Spirit**

Do **mortify**

The deeds of **the body**

Ye shall **live**

Saul chose his "desires" (the flesh) over the voice of the Lord (the Spirit), and as promised, he perished. Had he acted as Paul suggests, which was to "mortify" Agag, then he would have spiritually lived, and remained King (a son of God). Agag and the Amalekites are figures of the "deeds of the body" as Paul puts it, or its counterpart, "the flesh". In the Greek the word used for "deeds" is praxis which means mode of acting, doings, or practices (even sounds like praxis). In other words, we are talking about our patterned behavior driven by carnal/flesh desires. In the Greek, the word used for "mortify", is *thanatao*,[153] which means; to put to death, to make to die, to destroy, render extinct. All of which sounds exactly like what Nephi and Saul were asked to do to Laban and Agag respectively, and of course it is required of all those who follow Christ (Luke 9:22-24).

You may recall that in the Book of Mormon there are also Amalekites who join with the Lamanites (Alma 43:6). In the book of Alma as tensions grow, we know that the Lamanites, like the Amalekites of the Old Testament, could only be dealt with by the harshest of measures. A young Moroni becomes the "leader of the Nephites" and takes command of all the armies of the Nephites (Alma 43). A large man, like Saul or Nephi, he is described as a man who was "firm in the faith of Christ", and who had sworn an oath to defend his people, rights, country, and religion, "even to the loss of his blood", and gloried in "keeping the commandments of God, yea, and even resisting evil" (Alma 48). In highest praise, Helaman (a later keeper of the record) says of Moroni in verse 17:

17 Yea, verily, verily I say unto you, if all men had been, and were, and ever would be, like unto Moroni, behold, **the very powers of hell would have been shaken forever**; yea, the devil would never have power over the hearts of the children of men.
18 Behold, he was a man like unto Ammon, the son of Mosiah, yea, and even the other sons of Mosiah, yea, and also Alma and his sons, for they were all men of God.

Samuel of the Old Testament would have been very pleased if this had described Saul. Just as Moroni is compared in these verses to Alma, Ammon, and Mosiah, who were men of God, so King Amalickiah might be compared to men of wickedness, such as King Noah, or Laban who sought Nephi's life. And just as Moroni had sworn a blood oath to defend his people, rights, and religion (Alma 48:13), so his rival Amalickiah takes a counter oath of blood:

Alma 49:27 Yea, he was exceedingly wroth, and he did curse God, and also Moroni, swearing with an oath that he would **drink** his **blood**; and this because Moroni had kept the commandments of God in preparing for the safety of his people.

Notice that Amalickiah is also built from the Hebrew word *amal* (meaning travail, sin, and death), which certainly seems to characterize his nature. In fact, the spiritual chasm between Moroni and Amalickiah could not be wider, or deeper in blood. Allusive to the story of Saul, Samuel, and Agag, Moroni personally singles out wicked Amalickiah to be "put to death" (Alma 46:30), or mortified as Paul might say. Of course in figurative terms, that is how all "Lamanite" tendencies should be handled. To the extent that we find them alive and well within our souls, they still battle with an oath to drink our blood. As the Book of Mormon demonstrates, in the end there can be only one "seed" that prevails; Lamanite or Nephite, sin or righteousness, death or life.

- **How do we mortify the sinful nature (our unrighteous desires)?**

The quickest answer to this question is to simply stop (by use of our agency) doing the thing that separates us from God. If we are waiting for God to miraculously stop us, we are living another gospel, for that is not a promise he has given. Rather the pattern is plainly set forth in the story of Nephi and Laban, the Spirit constrains, we remember, and in faith obey. Each Laban or Agag in our lives should be dispatched in the same manner. Of course, the problem is our "desire" to let the unrepentant king, the best of the Amalekites, live. "He's really not so bad," we might say. We can spend a lifetime in this kind of denial, but the outcome we have already seen in the story of King Saul. Unrighteous desire, allowed to become ongoing sin, will take our head, drink our blood, and our nation will perish (all of Saul's sons were slain with him). In his discourse on the resurrection, Alma explains how our "desires" are restored to us (determine our inheritance):

> Alma 41: 3 And it is requisite with the justice of God that men should be judged according to their works; and if their works were good in this life, and **the desires of their hearts** were good, that they should also, at the last day, be restored unto that which is good.
>
> 4 And if their works are evil they shall be restored unto them for evil. Therefore, all things shall be restored to their proper order, every thing to its natural frame—mortality raised to immortality, corruption to incorruption—raised to endless happiness to inherit the kingdom of God, or to endless misery to inherit the kingdom of the devil, the one on one hand, the other on the other—
>
> 5 The one raised to happiness according **to his desires of happiness**, or good according to **his desires of good**; and the other to evil **according to his desires of evil**; for as **he has**

desired to do evil all the day long even so shall he have his reward of evil when the night cometh.

Since our desires precede our actions, we might ask, can they (our desires) be fundamentally changed? Let's talk for a moment about the role that faith and obedience play in changing the nature of our desires. First, faith necessarily implies a step into the dark, which the natural man in us resists, preferring the familiarity of sin to the unseen realm of faith. Like Laman and Lemuel, we want to see the Promised Land immediately, and when we don't, before long we yearn (desire) for the comfort of Jerusalem and its worldly pleasures. This tug between the natural world and the divine was characterized in Lehi's vision by the iron rod (word) and the surrounding mist of darkness. Symbolically, those who let go of the rod (word) represent those who lose their faith. They wander from the path of righteousness and are lost in a condition of faithlessness, while those who hold to the rod in darkness represent those with faith. ("For we walk by faith, not by sight", 2 Cor 2:15).[154] In addition, faith is a "principle of action or power", which requires us to do, not merely believe.[155] Consequently, where we find faith we also find obedience (doing). And, because faith is a gift of the Spirit (Gal 5:22), exercising it (in obedience to God's word) over time also changes the nature of our desires. This is so because whenever we encounter a gift of the Spirit (such as faith), we also find the Spirit, who transforms and sanctifies our hearts and minds. (This is something that we cannot do by simply working harder or developing greater discipline.[156]) Out of a sanctified heart come righteous desires. Thus, the faithful who steadfastly hold to the rod are necessarily in the process of having the desires of their hearts changed by the power of the Holy Ghost. And as a further consequence, if the Holy Ghost is working in us, then invariably it will prompt us to mortify sin and its desire.

Because all the principles of the gospel are interwoven and interrelated, when we speak of one (such as faith) we end up discussing many. Indeed, when we hold to the iron rod there is more going on than perhaps initially meets the eye.

- **Mortifying Sin a Sanctifying and Revelatory Experience**

In order to defeat sin/carnal desires we must remember our blood oath (like Moroni's) to mortify it, which is done by **faithfully** exercising our will. Hence, if you are rude to your wife or spouse – stop it, replace it with kindness. Slay your desire to be "right"! Too much TV – turn off the TV, find a good book, get involved with the family, follow the Spirit's promptings for service. Mortify the comfortable inclination/desire to just sit! Inappropriate music – instead listen to uplifting music. Mortify worldly influences that separate you from God by listening to messages that invite the Spirit. Foul mouth – quit swearing. Stop it. If the urge arises out of anger, or for fun – kill the natural man within you that would profane! If you gossip – don't do it! When it starts – slay the natural man in you that enjoys gossip. Lying – when the temptation stirs, mortify it. Don't let a thought to lie become a sin. Kill it as dead as Nephi killed Laban. ("For out of the abundance of the heart the **mouth** speaketh" [Mat 12:34], and "Not that which goeth into the **mouth** defileth a man; but that which cometh out of the **mouth**, this defileth a man" [Mat 15:11]).

Mortification of carnal desire is done "through the Spirit" (Rom 8:13), or "constrained by the Spirit", as outlined by Nephi's mortifying Laban. King Benjamin also confirms the Holy Ghost's involvement in this process in Mosiah 3:18, "For the natural man is an enemy to God, and has been from the fall of Adam, and will be forever, unless he yields to the enticings of the Holy Spirit, and putteth off (mortifieth) the natural man." Aligning our will with the promptings of the Spirit is a sanctifying experience. The preceding list of carnal desires is brief, and each of us, if honest, can construct a much longer personal list. And finally, as we speak of overcoming (Rev 2:7), the rub is this – that mortification is an un-ending process. Complete victory doesn't "arrive" for anyone while in mortality, but rather we face the onslaught daily. John Owen, a 19th century Puritan, writes of mortification and sin's unchanging nature:

> Mortification abates [sin's] force, but doth not change its nature. Grace changeth the nature of man, but nothing can change the nature of sin. . . . Destroyed it may be, it shall be, but cured it cannot be. . . . If it be not overcome and destroyed, it will overcome and destroy the soul. And herein lies no small part of its power. . . . It is never quiet, [whether it is] conquering [or] conquered. Do you mortify; do you make it your daily work; be always at it whilst you live; cease not a day from this work; **be killing sin or it will be killing you**. [157]

The Atonement doesn't alleviate the attack of the enemy, but it does provide us the way to overcome, which is through the blood of the Lamb as we yield to the Spirit's promptings. Just as the sacramental wine is symbolic of Christ's blood, so our daily "taking up the cross" and "losing our life" reflects why that blood was freely spilt. As we obediently mortify the sinful natural man within us, we express love to our God in the same manner in which Christ expressed his love to us. This symbolic daily sacrificial process is where the Spirit will lead, and those that follow the "constraint" will be the sons of God.

Appendix 3

"Better that one man should perish" – Nephi and Caiaphas

The words of the Spirit spoken to Nephi at the apex of his struggle in Jerusalem are curiously the same words of the high priest Caiaphas, 600 years later, who also said that it is better that one man (referring to Christ) should die than the Jewish nation (Jn 11:50). It is a bit unexpected to find that the words given to Nephi in the midst of his struggle are the very ones which Caiaphas uttered to the to the Sanhedrin as it plotted "from that time forward to take away his (Christ's) life" How can it be that the Spirit would use the adversary's crucial argument, even the very same words? Or, is it that the adversary usurped and modified an otherwise divine idea? Regardless, we know that there was "one" who needed to perish if all men were to prosper. Undeniably, in both instances there is more to consider than what appears on the surface, and if we look deeper, both direct our focus to the heart of a great paradoxical battle between good and evil, life and death, and love and hate. For answers, let's briefly examine John's gospel (my observations are in italics):

Jn 11:47 Then gathered the chief priests and the Pharisees a council, and said, What do we? for this man doeth many miracles.

The priests appear to care little that the source of these miracles might in fact be divine. Divine or not, they seem to be a nuisance.

48 If we let him thus alone, all [men] will believe on him: and the Romans shall come and take away both our place and nation.

Morally bankrupt, they seek opportunity to solidify their political power. The nation's interest is secondary, only their "place" of prominence truly concerns them.

49 And one of them, [named] Caiaphas, being the high priest that same year, said unto them, Ye know nothing at all,

By his slight – "ye know nothing at all", Caiaphas asserts his evil leadership, taking the Sanhedrin's wicked scheming to another level. Reminding us of Judas, who had it "put into his heart" to betray Christ, it is not hard to imagine that Caiaphas is also Satan's pawn. Caiaphas means rock in the Aramaic, thus adding to the irony. Christ, as the true Rock and great high priest, is juxtaposed to Caiaphas, the false rock (more like quicksand) and wicked high priest.

50 Nor consider that it is expedient for us, that one man should die for the people, and that the whole nation perish not.

These are also the words of the Spirit to Nephi. The source of Caiaphas' thinking, however, is not the Spirit. The references to "us", "the whole nation", and "the people" are pretexts for his personal selfish desires. Misguided and unrighteous, Caiaphas would gladly sacrifice any lamb, including the Holy Lamb of God, in order to do what is expedient for "him." We might even hear Satan's refrain from the pre-existence, "the honor (glory) be mine." (Moses 4:1)

51 And this spake he not of himself: but being high priest that year, he prophesied that Jesus should die for that nation;

Ironically, Caiaphas' remarks are correct. Though he is oblivious to the truth of his words, indeed Christ must die if his nation is to be saved! The phrase, "this spake he not of himself" is interesting because it suggests that perhaps Caiaphas' was previously talking about himself as "the one man" who should die. (Remember that the "one man" is also ambiguous in Nephi's story.) However, it is now clear that that was never the case. Whereas John said I must decrease so that He might increase, Caiaphas envisions quite the opposite - he is a taker, not a giver, and will hold on to his self importance and false authority at any cost.

52 And not for that nation only, but that also he should gather together in one the children of God that were scattered abroad.

John leads us from the temporal, to the spiritual and prophetic meaning of these words. Like Laman and Lemuel, Caiaphas has been confusing what is life and what is death, prizing temporal success over what is spiritually expedient. The "gathering together" that John speaks of is the spiritual gathering of God's elect, which is only possible because of Christ's death and Atonement. Ironically, the consequences and covenant fulfillment of Caiaphas' proposal was much bigger than he ever imagined.

53 Then from that day forth they took counsel together for to put him to death.

Caiaphas put the idea of murder into the hearts of the high priests, just as Satan put the idea of murder into the heart of Cain to kill his righteous brother Abel.

Upon analysis, the words of Caiaphas have two very distinct meanings and two very different prophetic outcomes. On the one hand there is his harsh and intended meaning, a justification for murdering Christ. Prophetically this meaning fails miserably, for we know that Jerusalem would soon be destroyed in spite of Christ's death, and her inhabitants scattered. On the other hand, this prophecy had a deeply spiritual meaning, the eternal impact of which Caiaphas hadn't a clue, for indeed, Christ died that He should "gather together in one" all the spiritual children of God which were scattered. In this regard the prophecy of Caiaphas was precise.

We might also consider that while Nephi is struggling in the Spirit to make his decision, Caiaphas was not. Rather, Caiaphas speaks out of his own second nature, or carnal man, concerned with his own self interest and how it might best be served. We shouldn't imagine that Caiaphas' words, though ironically prophetic, come via the constraint of the Spirit of God. They absolutely came from the opposite source; from Satan, the false rock upon whom Caiaphas relied. Whereas Nephi is constrained by these words ("better that one man perish") to obey God, Caiaphas uses them to tempt the Sanhedrin to destroy God! (We might even be reminded of the garden and the serpent that varies the intent of God's words to tempt the heart of Eve.) In Nephi's story, Laban is a symbol of the same dark power, for he seeks to slay Nephi, even as Caiaphas sought the Savior's life. In poetic reversal, the words used to urge the slaying of an innocent Christ are used in Nephi's story to slay the cunning usurper of those words. Indeed, like the two-edged sword of Laban, the phrase "better that one should perish" cuts both ways (which makes Nephi's use of Laban's personal sword to slay him all the more poignant).

If we trace the source of these words to their earliest utterance we might find ourselves in the pre-mortal council in heaven (Moses 4:1), Christ once again offering himself as willing sacrifice for the nation, and Satan instead proposing to sacrifice the nation's collective will. While Satan's proposal, that "one soul shall not be lost" would have denied us agency, more importantly it would have denied us using that agency to personally sacrifice for others. Obedient sacrifice in similitude of Christ's greatest sacrifice is the reason for agency. Indeed, the Father's plan is that "every soul shall be lost" in loving service to others; and herein are life's great lessons learned. Truly, the "gathering in one" that John speaks of is the collective heart, mind, and self-will that all who belong to God's nation freely give, which cannot by forcibly taken.

The idea that "it is better that one man should perish" is only true when its source is from God, otherwise its meaning can easily be twisted for self-serving reasons. Satan has always thought to *preserve* his "place" or position first; at all cost to others. However, as we know, man's agency to count himself last (least) is the key and foremost consideration in order for God's plan to work (Mar 10:44). When Nephi allows his will to perish, in order to be at-one with the heart mind, and will of God, then his actions are truly expedient, a type of Christ's actions, and in line with the great plan of salvation. Below is a side by side list of ironic differences between Christ and Caiaphas:

Council to murder	Pre-mortal Council - life
Caiaphas means rock (false rock)	Christ is the Rock (True and Living)
Caiphas was a high priest	Christ is the Great High Priest (Heb 4)
Caiaphas was appointed by corrupt Roman governor, guided by Satan	Christ was appointed and guided by the governor of the universe – his Father.
Caiaphas would perform a meaningless atonement in the temple that year	Christ would perform the great Atoning sacrifice in the garden and cross for all time
Caiaphas' falsely judges Christ	Christ will righteously judge all men
Caiaphas spoke NOT of himself	Christ spoke OF himself, and savored the opportunity to perish for all (Mk 8:33)
Selfish	Selfless
Saved no one, not even self	Saved all by losing self

Appendix 4

Alma 36 – Chiasmus of Rebirth, a Tree of Life [158]

a) My son give ear to my words (v 1)

  b) Keep the commandments and ye shall prosper in the land (v 1)

   c) Do as I have done (v 2)

    d) Remember the captivity of our fathers (v 2)

     e) They were in bondage (v 2)

      f) He surely did deliver them (v 2)

       g) Trust in God (v 3)

        h) Supported in trials, troubles and afflictions (v 3)

         i) I know this not of myself but of God (v 4)

         j) Born of God (v 5)

          k) I sought to destroy the church (v 6-9)

           l) My limbs were paralyzed (v 10)

            m) Fear of the presence of God (v 14-15)

            n) Pains of a damned soul (v 16)

             o) Harrowed up by memory of sins (v 17)

              p) I remembered Jesus Christ, a son of God (v 17)

              p) I cried, Jesus, son of God (v 18)

             o) Harrowed up by memory of sins no more (v 19)

            n) Joy as exceeding as was the pain (v 20)

            m) Long to be in the presence of God (v 22)

           l) My limbs received strength again (v 23)

          k) I labored to bring souls to repentance (v 24)

         j) Born of God (v 26)

        i) Therefore my knowledge is of God (26)

        h) Supported under trials and troubles and afflictions (v 27)

       g) Trust in him (v 27)

      f) He will deliver me (v 27)

     e) As God brought our fathers out of bondage and captivity (v 28-29)

    d) Retain in remembrance their captivity (v 28-29)

   c) Know as I do know (v 30)

  b) Keep the commandments and ye shall prosper in the land (v 30)

a) This according to his word (v 30)

Like Lehi and Nephi, Alma also partakes of the tree of life. In Alma 36:24 he says, "Yea, and from that time even until now, I have labored without ceasing, that I might bring souls unto repentance; that I might bring them to **taste of the exceeding joy of which I did taste**; that they might also be **born of God, and be filled with the Holy Ghost**." Notice that Christ, who is the tree of life, is also at the center of Alma's chiasmus. Alma equates the joy of tasting the fruit to being "born again," which Nephi described as "the love of God shed abroad in the hearts of the children of men" (1 Ne 11:22).

Appendix 5

Tree of Life – Fountain of Living Water – River of Life – Jesus Christ

Lest we fail to recognize or remember how scripture's symbols are connected, the fountain of living water begins at the Tree of Life, flows out into the world, is referenced thereafter in many scriptures, and returns to the the Tree of Life from whence it began - who is Jesus Christ. 1 Ne 11:25 helps us to understand that the tree of life and the fountain of living waters are the same thing – the Love of God. Notice the beginning and end (Genesis and Revelation) are connected by the Tree of Life as the Axis Mundi. [159]

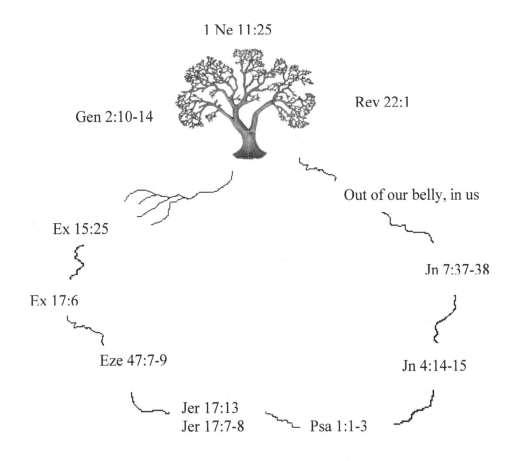

1 Ne 11:25

Gen 2:10-14

Rev 22:1

Out of our belly, in us

Ex 15:25

Jn 7:37-38

Ex 17:6

Eze 47:7-9

Jn 4:14-15

Jer 17:13
Jer 17:7-8   Psa 1:1-3

1 Ne 11:25 And it came to pass that I beheld that the rod of iron, which my father had seen, was the word of God, which led to the fountain of living waters, or to the tree of life; which waters are a representation of the love of God; and I beheld that the tree of life was a representation of the love of God.

Gen 2:10 And a river went out of Eden to water the garden; and from thence it was parted, and became into four heads. (The Pison, Gihon, Hiddekel, and Euphrates. The meaning in Hebrew for all of these conveys a springing forth or fruitfulness.)

Ex 15:25 And he cried unto the LORD; and the LORD shewed him a tree, [which] when he had cast into the waters, the waters were made sweet: there he made for them a statute and an ordinance, and there he proved them.

Ex 17:6 Behold, I will stand before thee there upon the rock in Horeb; and thou shalt smite the rock, and there shall come water out of it, that the people may drink. And Moses did so in the sight of the elders of Israel.

Eze 47:7 Now when I had returned, behold, at the bank of the river [were] very many trees on the one side and on the other. 8 Then said he unto me, These waters issue out toward the east country, and go down into the desert, and go into the sea: [which being] brought forth into the sea, the waters shall be healed. 9 And it shall come to pass, [that] every thing that liveth, which moveth, whithersoever the rivers shall come, shall live: and there shall be a very great multitude of fish, because these waters shall come thither: for they shall be healed; and every thing shall live whither the river cometh.

Jeremiah 17:7-8 Blessed is the man that trusteth in the Lord, and whose hope the Lord is. For **he shall be as a tree planted by the waters**, and that spreadeth out her roots by the river, and shall not see when heat cometh, but her leaf shall be green; and shall not be careful in the year of drought, neither shall cease from yielding fruit. 13 O LORD, the hope of Israel, all that forsake thee shall be ashamed, [and] they that depart from me shall be written in the earth, because they have forsaken **the LORD, the fountain of living waters**.

Psa 1:1-3 Blessed is the man that walketh not in the counsel of the ungodly, nor standeth in the way of sinners, nor sitteth in the seat of the scornful. But his delight is in the law of the Lord; and in His law doth he meditate day and night. And he shall be like a **tree planted by the rivers of water**, that bringeth forth his fruit in his season; his leaf also shall not wither; and whatsoever he doeth shall prosper.

Jn 4:14 Jesus answered and said unto her, Whosoever drinketh of this water shall thirst again: 15 But whosoever drinketh of the water that I shall give him shall never thirst; but the water that I shall give him **shall be in him** a well of water springing up into everlasting life.

Jn 7:37 If any man thirst, let him come unto me, and drink. 38 **He that believeth** on me, as the scripture hath said, **out of his belly** shall flow rivers of living water.

Rev 22:1 And he shewed me a **pure river of water of life**, clear as crystal, proceeding out of the throne of God and of the Lamb. 2 In the midst of the street of it, and on either side of the river, [was there] **the tree of life**, which bare twelve [manner of] fruits, [and] yielded her fruit every month: and the leaves of the tree [were] for the healing of the nations.

* In addition, consider the barren waters of Jericho which Elisha heals with salt (2 Ki 2:21). According to Matthew 5:13-14, salt is parallel to light (salt without savor = hidden light). In a manner, when Elisha re-savors the water, he energizes it with the light of Christ. This is also a parallel story to Ex 15:25 when Moses places a tree (of Life) in the water to make it drinkable. Thus we can perhaps metaphorically correlate, across these verses from Matthew, Exodus, and 2 Kings, that the tree = salt = light = Jesus Christ!

Appendix 6

Walk in the Darkness to Come into the Light

At the center of Nephi's first book, the angel and Nephi try to express in words what they feel as they experience God's love at the tree of life. Nephi describes it as "the most desirable above all things", and the angel describes what he feels as "the most joyous to the soul". Even though we can't actually see the tree with our physical eyes, we can experience it as they did – in our hearts as we exercise faith in Nephi's words written upon the page. We might want to reflect for a moment on the importance "the word" (written or spoken), and its relationship to faith. Because we cannot see God physically, we must use our hearts to "feel" him spiritually. Initially we learn of him by the descriptions and "words" of others who have spoken with him, seen him, or had visions such as Nephi's. Their Spirit filled words are recorded in scripture, and when we read them or hear them, our hearts and minds fill with warmth and love. Thus we begin to know God; to establish relationship with Him; comprehend how his word nourishes and renews our minds (Rom 12:1); over time even transforming who we are.

- **Alma understood how the seed (word) becomes fruit of the tree of life.**

To amplify our understanding, let's reexamine how a later prophet, Alma, uses the tree of life to explain to the Zoramites (means seed) how faith begins and continues to develop. I have emboldened all of the references to seed, which Alma uses to represent "the "word" (as Nephi often did). Alma 32: 28, 30-33, 36, 39-42:

28 Now, we will compare the **word** unto a **seed**. Now, if ye give place, that a **seed** may be planted in your heart, behold, if it be a true **seed**, or a good **seed**, if ye do not cast it out by your unbelief, that ye will resist the Spirit of the Lord, behold, it will begin to swell within your breasts; and when you feel these swelling motions, ye will begin to say within yourselves—It must needs be that this is a good **seed**, or that the **word** is good, for it beginneth to enlarge my soul; yea, it beginneth to enlighten my understanding, yea, it beginneth to be delicious to me.

----

30 But behold, as the **seed** swelleth, and sprouteth, and beginneth to grow, then you must needs say that the **seed** is good; for behold it swelleth, and sprouteth, and beginneth to grow. And now, behold, will not this strengthen your faith? Yea, it will strengthen your faith: for ye will say I know that this is a good **seed**; for behold it sprouteth and beginneth to grow.

31 And now, behold, are ye sure that this is a good **seed**? I say unto you, Yea; for every **seed** bringeth forth unto its own likeness.

32 Therefore, if a **seed** groweth it is good, but if it groweth not, behold it is not good, therefore it is cast away. 33 And now, behold, because ye have tried the experiment, and planted the **seed**, and it swelleth and sprouteth, and beginneth to grow, ye must needs know that the **seed** is good.

36 Behold I say unto you, Nay; neither must ye lay aside your faith, for ye have only exercised your faith to plant the **seed** that ye might try the experiment to know if the **seed** was good.

----

39 Now, this is not because the **seed** was not good, neither is it because the fruit thereof would not be desirable; but it is because your ground is barren, and ye will not nourish the tree, therefore ye cannot have the fruit thereof.

41 But if ye will **nourish the word, yea, nourish the tree** as it beginneth to grow, by your faith with great diligence, and with patience, looking forward to the fruit thereof, it shall take root; and **behold it shall be a tree springing up unto everlasting life.**

42 And because of your diligence and your faith and your patience with the **word** in nourishing it, that it may take root in you, behold, by and by ye shall pluck the fruit thereof, which is most precious, which is sweet above all that is sweet, and which is white above all that is white, yea, and pure above all that is pure; and ye shall feast upon this fruit even until ye are filled, that ye hunger not, neither shall ye thirst.

Isn't it interesting that we can only partake of the fruit of the tree of life if we personally grow it (something Nephi never told us)! Also, Alma tells us in verse 36 that we "exercise faith to plant the word (seed)", but in verse 30 that the word "will strengthen your faith", begging the question, which comes first, the word or faith? Regardless, they appear to have a symbiotic relationship – each necessary to the other, each helping the other to grow. Verse 42 provides us with this same summation – that if we nourish the word with diligence, faith, and patience, its fruit in turn nourishes us.

Indeed, to feast upon the word is akin to feasting upon the tree of life (who is Christ, in whom we place our faith). Alma repeats these concepts in Alma 33, once again explaining that the tree of life is grown within us, as well as explaining what\who the seed of the word represents!

22 If so, wo shall come upon you; but if not so, then cast about your eyes and begin to believe in **the Son of God**, that he will come **to redeem** his people, and that **he shall suffer and die to atone for their sins**; and that he **shall rise again** from the dead, which shall **bring to pass the resurrection**, that all men shall stand before him, to be judged at the last and judgment day, according to their works.

23 And now, my brethren, **I desire that ye shall plant this word in your hearts,** and as it beginneth to swell even so nourish it by your faith. And behold, **it will become a tree, springing up in you unto everlasting life.** And then **may God grant unto you that your burdens may be light, through the joy of his Son.** And even all this can ye do if ye will. Amen.

More concisely, the "word" that Alma wants us to plant in faith is the promise of the Son of God; his death, Atonement, and resurrection. And according to Alma, this promise of Christ, nourished in faith, becomes a joyous tree of everlasting life! Such imagery is reminiscent of Galatians 4:19 where Paul speaks of travailing in birth until "Christ be formed in you". Perhaps with so much figurative language we might wonder if there was an actual (physical) tree in Eden, or will there be in heaven. Because Alma tells us, "and ye will not nourish the tree, therefore ye cannot have the fruit thereof," for us the spiritually formed tree is what really matters, and will eventually exist in any eternal realm only if we have spiritually planted it and nurtured it in faith.

- **Strong roots of faith**

In the physical world, most seeds require three things in order to germinate or sprout; correct amount of light or darkness, proper moisture, and proper warmth.[160] Though this varies slightly from seed to seed, it is a reliable formula for predicting a seed's ability to grow. Likewise, Alma also prescribes the moisture or nourishment required for the seed of the word to germinate and continue growing. In 32:28 he says that, "if ye do not cast it out by your unbelief, that ye will resist *the Spirit of the Lord*, it will begin to swell." The Spirit of the Lord then, along with a desire to believe, is the moisture and warmth which brings the seed to life. However, Alma also warns that even though the seed has "sprouted up" and enlightens the understanding, we must not neglect to continually nourish the root system by our faith (vs 42). Like all trees, it seems that Alma's tree of life must take root downward in order to grow upwards (Isa 37:31).

In Nephi's vision of the tree of life, a person can only come to the tree by **holding to the word** of God in the **mists of darkness**, whereas Alma's allegory of the tree of life describes how **nourishing the word** with **faith** allows one access to the tree of life. Obviously, "holding to the word" and "nourishing the word" are similar ideas, which surprisingly makes faith and darkness parallels as well. If we put this into an equation we have:

<u>Nephi's requirement</u>   <u>Alma's requirement</u>

Holding to the iron rod (word)   =   nourishing the word
      in darkness   in faith

In Nephi's and Lehi's vision of the tree of life the word faith is not mentioned, yet we know that the tree of life cannot be reached without it (Alma makes this clear). Instead of using the word faith outright, its operation is illustrated in Lehi's vision by walking in darkness (which is often the way that it was presented anciently, as we shall discuss). Obviously, faith is something practiced when our temporal eyes have difficulty seeing, and as Paul tells us, "we walk by faith, not by sight". Darkness is the condition in which faith can work; if we could "see" we wouldn't need faith.

Glance at the picture above and notice how the root system of a large tree, which you don't see, is almost as large as the part of the tree that we see in the natural light above ground. Clearly, the survival of our tree of life depends on the activities which occur in the darkness below. The same moisture which first caused the sprouting also provides the continued nourishment of the growing tree, which moisture ultimately flows to (and is even found in) the delicious fruit. Though seemingly far removed from one another, the fruit plucked from the limb of the tree of life owes much to the root, which shares the nourishment it acquires in the darkness. In fact, Alma tells us that when the living tree is in the light, it is in danger of being scorched, which is even more reason to nourish the roots (vs 38).

Therefore, as we imagine the beautiful exterior of what such a tree of life might look like, we may also want to consider the magnificent root system that has evolved over time in the soil below, watered with the continual moisture and warmth of the Spirit of the Lord, "given place" by our faith. Though unseen, Christ promises that his presence can be found even in our darkest storms. We become the Sons of light above as we come to know and trust him in the depths below. It is there he whispers, "learn of me, for I am lowly and meek in heart: and ye shall find rest unto your souls." God's covenant plan cannot move forward, nor long exist, without faith.

- **More to consider about darkness**

Alma's allegory of the word (and faith) is consequently best understood when we contemplate not just the white and brilliant fruit that is plucked from the branches of the tree of life, but also when we consider that it would be non-existent without the necessary roots which are nourished only in the darkness. We might even be led to contemplate that perfect faith perhaps requires absolute darkness. Surprisingly, the Bible has a lot to say about this. Let's start by taking a look at the Holy of Holies in the ancient temple. Remarkably, the holiest part of the ancient temple, where the Lord dwelt, was in thick darkness. 1 Kings 8 tells us:

> 10 And it came to pass, when the priests were come out of the holy [place], that the cloud filled the house of the LORD,
> 11 So that the priests could not stand to minister because of the cloud: for the glory of the LORD had filled the house of the LORD.
> 12 Then spake Solomon, **The LORD said that he would dwell in the thick darkness**.
> 13 I have surely built thee an house to dwell in, a settled place for thee to abide in for ever.

Whereas in modern temples light symbolically increases as one progresses further into the endowment, in the Bible the opposite is true, or rather, the ancient symbolism is reversed. Exodus 20 tells us more:

> 21 And the people stood afar off, and Moses drew near unto **the thick darkness where God [was].**

In the scriptures, darkness can be a metaphor for several different things; evil, death, despair, or the unknown,[161] and sometimes it might mean a combination of these possibilities. Often, however, darkness in scripture highlights the inability to use ones eyes, which signifies that one's spiritual eyes must be relied upon. God wants us to know and be one with his heart, which cannot be understood by trusting only our physical senses. The 3rd stage of the patriarchal pattern described by Stephen (see chapter 1) is symbolic of the 3rd part of the ancient temple, both symbolic places of deep darkness where faith is practiced (e.g. Nephi walked in darkness into Jerusalem to face Laban, who could slay 10,000).

- **Hebrews 11 – Faith and a "cloud of witnesses"**

An excellent example of how faith is nurtured in darkness is found the book of Hebrews. In chapter 11 Paul describes the attribute of faith as "the substance of things hoped for, the evidence of **things not** seen", after which he reviews a long list of heroes that anciently exhibited great faith. Several names at the end of the list have puzzled bible scholars for centuries. For instance, Hebrews 11:31-33 tells us,

> 31 And what shall I more say? for the time would fail me to tell of Gedeon, and [of] Barak, and [of] Samson, and [of] Jephthae; [of] David also, and Samuel, and [of] the prophets:, 32 Who through faith subdued kingdoms, wrought righteousness, obtained promises, stopped the mouths of lions, 33 Quenched the violence of fire, escaped the edge of the sword, out of weakness were made strong, waxed valiant in fight, turned to flight the armies of the aliens.

David and Samuel we can certainly understand, but what of Gideon, Barak, Samson, and Jephthae. As elders that lived during the time of the judges, their faith has long been considered flawed by comparison to other biblical figures. Upon examination, however, there is an intriguing common denominator that unites this group in faith. Below are verses from Heb 11. In the left column is the faithful servant, and to the right is an explanation of how their faith operated without "seeing". (In verses 1-19 Paul provides the explanation or precedent, however, after that the reader is expected to know the biblical events which repeat the pattern of exercising faith in darkness. I provide that for you from verses 20 – 32):

1. Now faith is	the evidence of things **not seen**. For by it (not seeing) the elders obtained a good report
11:3 Through it the worlds were framed by the word of God	3 "so that things which are seen were **not made of things which do appear**" (unseen)
11:4 Abel offered unto God a more excellent sacrifice, by which he obtained a witness that he was righteous	"and by it he being dead yet speaketh" (we **can't see** him, only hear him)
5 Enoch translated	5 "did **not see** death"
7 Noah warned of God	7 "of things **not seen** as yet"
8 By faith Abraham, when he was called to go out into a place which he should after receive for an inheritance, obeyed	8 "he went out **not knowing** (seeing in Greek) wither"
11 Through faith also Sara herself conceived seed, and was delivered of a child when she was past age	11 "because she **judged** him faithful who had promised." (promises are future – not yet seen**)**
13 These all died in faith, not having received the promises	13 "but **having seen them afar off**, and were persuaded of [them]" (too far away to see clearly)

17 By faith Abraham, when he was tried,
offered up Isaac: and he that had received the
promises offered up his only begotten [son],

19 "Accounting that God was able to raise him up, even
from the dead; from whence also he received him as
as **a figure**" (a type of something to come, but **not presently
seen**. Abraham's sacrifice of Isaac was a similitude of the
sacrificial Lamb that would be seen in the flesh. Abraham
and Isaac left for Moriah **in the night** [darkness]).

20 By faith Isaac blessed Jacob and Esau
concerning things to come.

"And it came to pass, that when Isaac was
old, and his eyes were dim, so that **he could not see**." (Gen
27:1) Isaac tastes the savory meat, feels the hairy arms,
smells the scent of the field, however, he hears the voice of
Jacob. Confused by 5 senses, he must rely on Spirit and faith.
In darkness he blesses Jacob and gives him the promise.

21 By faith Jacob, when he was a dying,
blessed both the sons of Joseph; and worshipped,
[leaning] upon the top of his staff.

"Now the eyes of Israel were dim for age, [so that]
he could not see. And he brought them near unto him; and he
kissed them, and embraced them." (Gen 48:10) Jacob
(Israel) in darkness "wittingly" places right hand on the
younger Ephraim. Joseph tries to correct him, but is
reassured by blind Jacob.

22 By faith Joseph, when he died, made mention
of the departing of the children of Israel; and
gave commandment concerning his bones.

Still a long ways off, Joseph **will not** live **to see** the
fulfillment of this promise – the salvation of Israel.

23 By faith Moses, when he was born, was
hid three months of his parents, because they
saw [he was] a proper child; and they were not
afraid of the king's commandment.

27 "By faith he forsook Egypt, not
fearing the wrath of the king: for he
endured, as **seeing him who is invisible**"

28 Through faith he kept the Passover, and the
sprinkling of blood, lest he that destroyed the
firstborn should touch them.

Passover is kept in the **darkness** at
midnight. (Ex 12:29)

29 By faith they passed through the Red sea
as by dry [land]: which the Egyptians assaying
to do were drowned.

"And Moses stretched out his hand over
the sea; and the LORD caused the sea
to go [back] by a strong east wind
all that night, (in darkness) and made the sea dry
[land], and the waters were divided." (Ex 14:21)

31 By faith the harlot Rahab perished not with
them that believed not, when she had received
the spies with peace.

"And the woman took the two men,
and **hid** them, and said thus, There came
men unto me, but I wist not whence they
[were]." (Jos 2:6) Rahab **hides** the spies
in the night (darkness), saving them.

32 And what shall I more say? for the time
would fail me to tell of Gedeon,

Gideon's famous battle with the vastly
superior Midianite army is fought entirely
at night. His chosen 300 break their vessels
in **the darkness**, shining the light within,
ultimately confusing and destroying the enemy. (Jdg 6-7)

32 Barak	Barak's name means "lightning". God won the victory for Israel over Sisera and the Canaanites by sending the **darkness** of a rainstorm. In her song Deborah recalled a time when God did the same thing for Israel in the days of the Exodus (also done in darkness of night).
32 Samson	Samson's name means "the sun". "But the Philistines took him, and **put out his eyes,** and brought him down to Gaza, and bound him with fetters of brass; and he did grind in the prison house" (Jdg 16:21). Samson, **in darkness,** cries to the Lord and is given strength to destroy the Philistines, giving his own life.
32 Jephthae	Jephthae's name in Hebrew means "he opens". Rejected by his brethren, Jephthah is asked to return and captain the Israelite army against the Ammonites. With the Spirit of the Lord upon him he vows that **the first to be seen** leaving his house upon his return will be sacrificed. After saving Israel in battle, **not knowing** who he **will see** first, it is his beloved only begotten child, who willingly, like Isaac and our Savior, agrees to perform the demands of Jephthah's vow. In the third month (sign of Jonah) she is sacrificed. (Jdg 11)
32 David	David's life is full of examples of great faith. In the spirit of this book, and the story of Nephi and Laban, we will cite his defeat of Goliath. All of the army **sees** a giant and fears. David response is to remember that, "The Lord delivered me out of the paw of the lion, and out of the paw of the bear, he will deliver me out of the hand of this Philistine." (1 Sa 17:37) Obviously, David trusts the Lord **more than what he sees**, be it lion, bear, or giant.
32 Samuel	"And the word of the LORD was precious in those days; [there was] **no open vision**" (1 Sam 3:1) **It is night** and Samuel **is in the darkness** of the temple when the voice of the Lord calls to him, three times (sign of Jonah). He informs Eli and returns in the night to be instructed by the Lord concerning Israel's future (things not seen).

Whenever conditions of darkness exist, be it a storm, or night, or blindness, or the unknown, there is opportunity for faith to grow. In the case of the Gideon, Barak, Samson, and Jephthah, under conditions of darkness they each defeat a superior foe or nation that the Lord had commanded Israel to eradicate (mortify) in order to posses their promised land; the Midianites, Canaanites, Philistines, and Ammonites. We might pause to consider that these victories, while historical, are as importantly spiritual and typifying. In the darkness of night the Lord walks between the sacrificial animals confirming his covenant with Abraham (Gen 15). Nephi as a type, suffering to save his family, is bound and praises God while in the darkness of the storm. If you recall, Helaman and his stripling warriors of renowned faith, perform many of their military maneuvers at night, or concealed and out of sight. Christ, who is sleeping on the ship, is wakened by his alarmed apostles in the midst of a dreadful storm. In the darkness of the raging tempest he asks, "Where is your faith?" He also walks to the apostles on the water in the darkness of the storm, demonstrating the power of faith. In the darkness of his last night this same caliber of faith will be tested to the full in Gethsemane. Jesus is falsely accused and tried in the middle of the night before the Sanhedrin at Gabbatha. And, as the darkness of the storm rages on Golgatha, blackening the afternoon sky, Christ dies on the cross and descends into the darkness of the tomb to overcome death, fulfilling the promises to all those who have believed, hoped, and faithed throughout the ages.

Metaphorically and literally, faith is tempered/strengthened and even flourishes by the varied elements of darkness. As another example, Jacob also ascends the ladder to heaven during the darkness of night. Of that event Marion G. Romney comments, "Jacob realized that the covenants he made with the Lord there were the rungs on the ladder that he himself would have to climb in order to obtain the promised blessings—blessings that would entitle him to enter heaven and associate with the Lord. Because he had met the Lord and entered into covenants with him there, Jacob considered the site so sacred that he named the place Bethel, a contraction of Beth-Elohim, which means literally "the House of the Lord." He said of it: "… this is none other but the house of God, and this is the gate of heaven." [162] Jacob noticeably enters into these temple covenants (symbolized by the rungs) in the darkness of night; ascending higher into the unfamiliar; needing ever greater faith until the perfect light is received. This is also reminiscent of Nephi's iron rod which leads through darkness until the brilliant whiteness of the tree of life is reached. Unavoidably, our covenants require that we also walk through the darkness so that our faith can be magnified; before we are allowed into the fullest revelation of light.

Our temples at night, and how brightly they appear, are also wonderful examples of the bright hope and promise of God, intensified against the surrounding darkness. In the natural light of day, temples often fade into the surrounding scenery, but at night, contrasted by its opposite, the lighted temples are unmistakably defined. "One night Harold B. Lee sat with the president of the Manti temple looking up towards the floodlighted skies. A dark storm raged around them. The temple president said, "You know Brother Lee, the temple is never more beautiful than during a storm.""[163] Indeed, the temple is a great symbol of Christ, inviting all to walk in darkness into the light. In her Poem "At the Gate of the Year" Louise Haskins reflects on this perspective:

> I said to the man who stood at the gate of the year
> "Give me a light that I may tread safely into the unknown."
> And he replied, "Go into the darkness and put your hand into the hand of God
> That shall be to you better than light and safer than a known way!"

Appendix 7

Abinadi's Beautiful Chiasmus

Like 1Nephi, all of Mosiah can be expressed chiastically with Mosiah 15 as its epicenter:

A King Benjamin exhorts his sons (1:1-8)
 B Mosiah chosen to succeed his father (1:10)
  C Mosiah receives the records (1:16)
   D Benjamin's speech and the words of the angel (2:9-5:15)
    E People enter into a covenant (6:1)
     F Priests consecrated (6:13)
      G Ammon leaves Zarahemla for the land of Lehi-Nephi (7:1-6)
       H People in bondage, Ammon put in prison (7:15)
        I The 24 gold plates (8:9)
         J The record of Zeniff begins as he leaves Zarahemla (9:1)
          K Defense against the Lamanites (9:14-10:20)
           L Noah and his priests (11:1-15)
            M Abinadi persecuted and thrown in prison (11-12)
             N Abinadi reads the old law and old Messianic prophecies to the priests that are about Christ (13-14)
              O How beautiful upon the mountains (15)
             N'Abinadi makes new prophecies about Jesus Christ (16)
            M' Abinadi persecuted and killed (17:5-20)
           L' Noah and his priests (18:32-20:5)
          K' Lamanites threaten the people of Limhi (20:6-6-26)
         J' Record of Zeniff ends as he leaves the land of Lehi-Nephi
        I' The 24 gold plates (21:27, 22:14)
       H' People of Alma in bondage (23)
      G' Alma leaves the land of Lehi-Nephi for Zarahemla (24)
     F' The Church organized by Alma (25:14-24)
    E' Unbelievers refuse to enter covenant (26: 1-4)
   D' The words of Alma and the words of the angel of the Lord (26-27)
  C' Alma the Younger receives the records (28:20)
 B' Judges chosen instead of a king (29:5-32)
A' Mosiah exhorts his people (29:5-32)   164

In 1 Nephi the centermost thought was the tree of life and God's love. Perhaps we can find something similar at the apex of Mosiah, maybe even another tree of life. As we will see, Mosiah's center, which is Abinadi's discourse, is about "His seed", those who have heard the word or declared the "desirable" and "joyous" tidings of God's word. Just as the tree of life is beautiful, all those who publish this message are described as beautiful

In Mosiah 12, when Noah's priests try to ensnare Abinadi in his words, one of them (perhaps Alma) asks him the meaning of Isaiah 52:7, "How beautiful upon the mountains are the feet of him that bringeth good tidings, that publisheth peace; that bringeth good tidings of good, that publisheth salvation; that saith unto Zion, Thy God reigneth!" Though Abinadi's explanation falls mostly on deaf ears, one man will be changed forever – Alma, who believes Abinadi's words concerning Christ and who preserves for us a tribute to Abinadi; the very words which softened his heart and changed his life:

AA 1 **God himself shall come down**, 2 **dwell in the flesh**, being **the Father and the Son**, 3 The Father because he was conceived by power of God, the Son because of the flesh, 4 They are one God, 5 Suffers temptation, mocked scourged, but yields not.

BB 6 After working mighty miracles, he shall be led, yea, even **as Isaiah said**, as a sheep before the shearer is dumb, so he opened not his mouth. **(Isaiah 53:7)**

C vs 7-9

He breaketh bands of death
Power to intercede
For children of men
Mercy and Compassion
Towards children of men
Betwixt them and justice
Broken the bands of death

D vs 10-18

10 Who shall be his seed?
11 They shall be his seed
12 Are they not his seed?
13 Holy prophets are his seed
They have published **Salvation (Jesus),**
And said unto Zion: **Thy God reigneth**
15 How beautiful were there feet
16 How beautiful are their feet
17 How beautiful will be their feet
18 How beautiful are His feet

D' vs 24-28

20 Bands of death broken, Son has power over death
21 Commeth a resurrection
21 Those **who** have been, **who** are, **who** shall be
21 **Christ (Messiah)** – so **he** shall be called
22 **All** the prophets, **all** believers, **all** obedient
22 Shall come forth in resurrection
23 Bands of death broken, though Christ they have eternal life

C' vs 24-28

They that died not having salvation declared
Have part in resurrection
Being redeemed of the Lord,
Ought to fear and tremble
None redeemed that rebel against God
Ought ye not to tremble?
Neither can the Lord redeem such and deny justice
They have no part in resurrection
Salvation to be declared to all people

BB '28-30 Yea Lord, thy watchmen shall **lift their voice, shall they sing**, they shall see eye to eye when the Lord shall bring forth Zion. Break forth into joy, **sing** together; for the Lord had comforted his people. **(Isa 52:9)**

AA' 31 The Lord has made **bare his holy arm in the eyes of all** the nations; and **all shall see the salvation** (Yeshua – Jesus) **of our God.** (Isaiah 52:10)

Here we can easily identify four fully developed chiasmi. Further, the two middle chiasmi (D,D') are parallel, as are the outer chiasmi (C,C') – creating beauty and symmetry. Notice that the outside two chiasmi are principles which intersect in Christ, the first (C) centering on the Son's mercy and compassion, and the second (C') telling of His justice, that it lays claim on those who willfully rebel. The two inner chiasmi share a common focus intended to reveal the two names of the Son of God who shall dwell in the flesh – "Salvation" which is the meaning of Jesus' name (D), and "Christ – so he shall be called" (D'), which means Messiah (anointed one).

Also, in the D-D' parallels the four uses of "his seed" in verses 10,11,12,13 match the four uses of "beautiful upon the mountain" in verses 15,16,17, and 18! The parallel verses 10 and 18 are particularly interesting. In fact they are reminiscent of a parallel in Nephi's vision of the tree of life; the beautiful and precious tree parallel to the cross upon which the Son of God was "lifted up for the sins of the world". Here in Mosiah we have the similar parallel, "**his** soul has been made as offering for sin" (vs 10), which reflects "how beautiful upon the mountain are the feet of **Him**" (vs 18).

The two center chiasmi (D, D") also share a unique series of past, present, and future statements. In the first we find the "beautiful feet" of those that were, are, and shall hereafter publish peace. In the second center chiasmus this distinct parallel sequence is repeated, that those who *have been*, who *are*, and *who shall* believe and keep the commandments, will come forth in the first resurrection. In other words, those with beautiful feet (D) are those who will come forth in the first resurrection (D'), i.e. the same group – both spiritually begotten of Christ.

- **Two Condescensions – Like the Tree of Life**

Mosiah 15's entire structure is marvelously buttressed at both end with quotes from Isaiah 53 and 52. When we look at these book-end Isaiah passages we find that they present a very fascinating antithetical. The first (BB), in verse 6, is from Isaiah 53:7 – "he shall be led, yea, even as Isaiah said, as a sheep before the shearer is **dumb,** so he opened not his mouth." It's parallel (BB'), verses 29-30, comes from Isaiah 52:9 – "with the **voice together shall they sing**; for they shall see eye to eye, when the Lord shall bring again Zion. Break forth into joy, **sing together**; for he the Lord hath comforted his people, he hath redeemed Jerusalem." Silently shorn as a sheep (symbol of shame, loss of covering) Jesus Christ brings our comfort and redemption, for which all nations break forth into joy, given a voice to sing! Whether these were actually the ordered words of inspired Abinadi, or whether we can attribute their artistic arrangement to Alma, these interwoven antitheticals are truly "beautiful", stirring and lifting our minds and hearts.

Finally, also notice that the first five verses of Mosiah 15 are about God's condescension (AA), "God himself will come down among the children of men" in the form of the Son. The parallel to this, verse 31 (AA') is fascinating – Isa 52:10, "The LORD hath made bare his holy arm in the eyes of all the nations; and all the ends of the earth shall see the salvation of our God."

Appendix 8

Jonah – Ingenious Book and Sign.

In this book we have looked for and discussed the sign of Jonah in the stories of the Bible and Book of Mormon. And while there are many aspects of Jonah's story which foreshadow Christ (see pg 219), there are other dimensions of his story that do not. This aspect is part of what makes the story of Jonah so fascinating. For instance, if you were asked, would you rather be Jonah or a Ninevite, what would be your reply? Though some might answer Jonah, I think that the better response would be a Ninevite, because they experience a mighty change of heart, and it is unclear if Jonah ever does. None the less, we can still learn a great deal from Jonah's story, good and bad.

Jonah is a man who seems to lack the Spirit, even though his name (the dove) is a symbol of the Holy Ghost. His performance as a prophet of God is noticeably half-hearted. He is Christ-like one moment, but indifferent and unkind the next - God says go this way, and he goes the other. He is miraculously saved from the depths of the sea, and then declares he wants to die. Though God forgives Jonah's shortcomings, Jonah is unforgiving of others. He serves without love - mourning the passing of the gourd that provided his comfortable shade more than the destruction of a city. Much of the time he is a picture of hypocrisy, rather than a role model.

Indeed, who is in need of the Spirit more than Jonah? Going through the motions, Jonah rarely seems to follow the Spirit's promptings. Nineveh, on the other hand, is miraculously moved by the Spirit, and repents. In the end, the enormous whale apparently fails to change Jonah's attitude, whereas the small dove (Jonah's spiritual namesake) "overthrows" and saves gigantic city of Nineveh (120,000 souls). Things are opposite of how we suppose they should be; the heathens are saved and the mighty prophet is not. We might think of Christ's teaching to his disciples, that the least is the greatest, and the master is servant. Counterintuitive to the natural mind, this is also how we are saved, a sign that Jonah is working quietly in our lives. Jonah's story teaches that even a prophet can't fake spirituality.

Did Jonah ever change? What we do know is that only by the power of Holy Ghost (what his name represents) he could have. The fact that his brief prophecy to Nineveh ("yet forty days and Nineveh shall be overthrown") produced the miracle it did makes it as great a wonder as a divinely sent whale – for only by the Spirit, and in spite of Jonah the man, did these many people feel God's love and turn their hearts to the Lord.

Finally, I am left to wonder how Jonah's short, small, and understated message of destruction or salvation has allusions to other stories in scripture. For instance, Jonah's few words are not like the earthquake or the storm, but perhaps more like 1 Kings 19:2 and the "still small" voice that Elijah heard. His minimal message also reminds us of Naaman who listens to an insignificant servant girl and consequently undertook a distant journey only to be told, "wash and be clean" (1 Kings 5:13). Like the citizens of Nineveh, in that story Naaman is changed (his skin of leprosy is transformed to that of a newborn [he is reborn]) as he yields to a short, true, and faithful message. If we learn anything from Jonah's story it is that the power of God's word is truth, light, and Spirit, even the Spirit of Christ (D&C 84:45).

May it also softly alight upon us as the dove, and fill our hearts with His love and mercy, just as it did it long ago for Nineveh, Elijah, and Naaman.

Appendix 9

1 Nephi 2 parallel to 1 Nephi 19-21
Thou Shalt be Made a Teacher over thy Brethren - I did Teach my Brethren

In writing this book I was perplexed by the Isaiah verses – chapters 20 and 21 – which seemed to be outside of Nephi's symmetric chiastic structure. As large chunks of scripture I wasn't sure how they could be parallel to first Nephi chapter 2, its apparent spatial and sequential partner. However, upon examination there are several relationships between 1 Nephi 2 and 1 Nephi 20-21. For example, Nephi is promised by the Lord in chapter 2:22 that he will be a teacher unto his brethren, and in chapter 19:22 we read that Nephi consequently "did teach my brethren" – followed by the scriptures which he uses to instruct his brothers, Isaiah 48 and 49!

2:22 And inasmuch as thou shalt keep my commandments, thou shalt be a ruler and **a teacher over thy brethren.**

19:22 And now it came to pass that I Nephi, did **teach my brethren these things;** and it came to pass that I did read many things to them, which were engraven upon the plates of brass.

Curiously, the words "teach" and "teacher" are highly specialized words in 1 Nephi. For instance, **teach** is used just one time in first Nephi. And, the word "**teacher**" is also very unique, found only twice in Nephi's chiastic first book. Below is a diagram of this book-wide relationship:

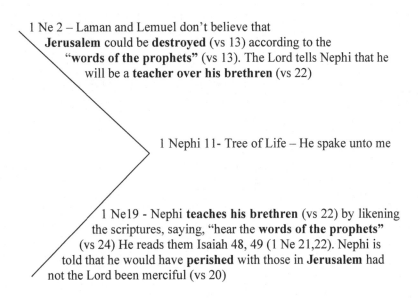

1 Ne 2 – Laman and Lemuel don't believe that **Jerusalem** could be **destroyed** (vs 13) according to the "**words of the prophets**" (vs 13). The Lord tells Nephi that he will be a **teacher over his brethren** (vs 22)

1 Nephi 11- Tree of Life – He spake unto me

1 Ne19 - Nephi **teaches his brethren** (vs 22) by likening the scriptures, saying, "hear the **words of the prophets**" (vs 24) He reads them Isaiah 48, 49 (1 Ne 21,22). Nephi is told that he would have **perished** with those in **Jerusalem** had not the Lord been merciful (vs 20)

Before looking at some of the other highly distinctive phrases which consentrate in these two sections, it might be valuable to read about Nephi's teaching method. In the last 2 verses of chapter 19, Nephi uses the phrase "liken" twice, suggesting to his brethren that Isaiah 48 and 49 will be for their profit and learning; that along with all the scattered house of Israel they might also have hope in a Redeemer:

> 19:23 And I did read many things unto them which were written in the books of Moses; **but that I might more fully persuade them to believe in the Lord their Redeemer** I did read unto them that which was written by the prophet Isaiah; for I did **liken** all scriptures unto us, that it might be **for our profit and learning.** 24 Wherefore I spake unto them, saying: Hear ye the words of the prophet, ye who are a remnant of the house of Israel, a branch who have been broken off; hear ye the words of the prophet, which were written unto all the house of Israel, and **liken** them unto yourselves, **that ye may have hope** as well as your brethren from whom ye have been broken off; for after this manner has the prophet written.

This explanation is significant, because Nephi then actually utilizes the concept of "likening scriptures" to form his parallels. For instance, in Isaiah 48:4 (1 Nephi 20:4) the Lord tells Israel, "And I knew that thou art obstinate, and thy **neck is an iron sinew**, and thy brow brass", which is likened to his brother's similar condition in 1 Nephi 2:11, "Now he spake because of the **stiffneckedness** of Laman and Lemuel." In addition, the term "stiffneckedness" is used only once in 1 Nephi, as is its parallel "neck is an iron sinew", which makes their corresponding and symmetric usage highly unique. Below is a list of some other distinctive parallels.

Highly Distinctive Parallels Phrases/Ideas

1 Ne 2:21	1 Ne 20:9
"And inasmuch as thy brethren will rebel against thee, they shall be **cut off** from the presence of the Lord"	"Nevertheless, for my name's sake will I defer mine anger, and for my praise will I refrain from thee, that I **cut thee not off.**"
The phrase "cut off" is first used in 1 Nephi 2, and not again until its parallel, 1 Ne 20!	*This is the promise and hope that Nephi wants his brothers to learn by reading and likening Isaiah.*

1 Nephi 2:12

"And they did murmur because **they knew not the dealings of that God** who had **created** them."

This is the only use of "dealings" in first Nephi.

1 Ne 19:22

I did read many things unto them which were engraven upon the plates of brass that they **might know concerning the doings of the Lord** in other lands.

*The word "doings" is a unique word, used only twice in 1 Nephi. Further, Nephi also likens his brother's murmuring to Israel's in Isaiah 48:7 (1 Ne 20:7) – Yea, and thou heardest me not; **yea thou knewest not**, yea, from that time thine ear was not opened; for I knew that thou wouldst **deal** very treacherously, and wast called a transgressor from the womb. They are **created** now, and not from the beginning, even before the day when thou heardest them not they were declared unto thee, lest thou shouldst say – Behold I knew them." Like "dealings," the* word "deal" is used only once in 1 Nephi.)

1 Ne 2:13

"And they (Laman and Lemuel) were like unto the Jews **who were at Jerusalem**, who sought to take away the life of my father"

The phrase "who were (are) at Jerusalem" is very distinctive. Though there are many references to Jerusalem, or the "land of Jerusalem", this exact form is not used again until chapter 19!

1 Ne 19:20

"For behold, I have workings in the spirit, which doth weary me even that all my joints are weak, for those **who are at Jerusalem**; for had not the Lord been merciful, to show unto me concerning them, even as he had prophets of old, I should have perished also."

*In this verse Nephi compares himself to the prophets of old, having been divinely shown the destruction of those "who are **at** Jerusalem."*

1 Nephi 2:9

"He spake unto Laman, saying: **O that thou** mightest **be like unto this river**, **continually** running into the fountain of all **righteousness!**
And he also spake unto Lemuel: O that thou mightest be like unto this valley, firm and **steadfast** (constant, continual), and immovable in keeping **the commandments** of the Lord!

I have often wondered if Lehi's blessing was scripturally based. Was the source "taught" to his sons, and did it become part of Nephi's chiastic structure?

1 Ne 20:18

"**O that thou hadst** hearkened to **my commandments** – then had thy peace been **as a river**, and thy **righteousness** as the waves of the sea." (constant, **continual**)

The phrase "O that thou" is found only in 1 Ne 2 and 1 Ne 20! Lehi appears to extract his blessing from these Isaiah 48 verses using the elements of - constancy in keeping the commandment; righteousness; and a river.

1 Ne 2:20

"And inasmuch as ye shall keep my commandments, **ye shall prosper**, and shall be led to a land of promise"

1 Ne 20:15

"Also saith the Lord; I the Lord, yea, I have spoken; yea, I have called him to declare, I have brought him, and he **shall make his way prosperous**."

Appendix 10

1 Nephi 1:1-3 – A Prelude to God's Throne

Before telling us about his father's vision of God's heavenly throne, Nephi begins his writing with a brief description of his own life. His first few verses also preface upcoming personal life-changing and visionary experiences (e.g. angelic visitations and heavenly promises [1 Ne 2, 3]; the tree of life [1 Ne 11]; divine instruction on the mount [1 Ne 16,17]).

Others have written that these beginning verses focus on the "learning of the Jews" as the pivotal phrase.[165] However, I believe that putting emphasis there probably misses the primary nexus of Nephi's opening colophon.[166] Below is a proposed parallelistic pattern which covers the entirety of Nephi's first three verses (parenthesis and bold print mine):

A. a. I *Nephi,*
    having been born (created, begat, made) of
a'. *goodly* parents,

  B. therefore I was taught somewhat in **all the learning of**

    C. **of my father**;

      D. and having seen many afflictions **in the course of my days,**

        E. nevertheless, **having been highly favored** of the
          Lord in all my days;

        E. yea, **having had a great knowledge** of the goodness and
          mysteries of **God,**

      D'. therefore I make a record of **the proceedings of my days.**"
      Yea, I make a record in the language

    C'. **of my father,**

  B'. which consists **of the learning of** the Jews and the language of the Egyptians.

A'. a. And *I know* that the record that I make is true;
    and I make it (create, begat) with mine hand;
  a'. and I make it according to my *knowledge.*

The preceding outline is appealing because it accommodates Nephi's first verses as an integral structure.[167] While the learning of the Jews is undeniably a key to understanding the Book of Mormon, the spiritual turning-point of Nephi's first 3 verses is that he has been highly favored of the Lord with divine knowledge, superceding all secular learning. There is also no more exciting hinge our hope for our lives.

A – A'

These book-ends are fascinating parallels because they both relate to creation; first Nephi's physical creation or genesis (A), and then its parallel, the spiritual record to which he will give birth (A'). Nephi suggests that just as he was created in the image of his goodly parents (A), he will now create (*make*) a record born of true knowledge (A'). Nephi is co-creator with God; inspired by the Holy Ghost to write the words which will touch the hearts of future readers – leading to spiritual birth in their lives.

Also, in order to extract the fullest meaning of Nephi's first small chiasmus (A), we might want to utilize some "learning of the Jews" which occurs often in the Hebrew scripture – a play on words. As one author suggests, there is "a possible wordplay in the first verse of the Book of Mormon that provides internal textual evidence that the name *Nephi* derives from the Egyptian word *nfr*. While *nfr* denotes "good, fine, goodly" of quality, it also signifies "beautiful, fair" of appearance."[168]

It is possible that Nephi is mirroring his goodly (beautiful) appearance to his goodly parents, a seed begotten after its own kind. In the 1828 Webster's Dictionary (a lexicon of Joseph Smith's day) the primary definition of "goodly" is given as, "being of a handsome form; **beautiful**"[169] Supporting this idea, the Nephites were called fair and delightsome, after the name of their founder (1 Ne 13:15, 4 Ne 1:10). As well, in the KJV "goodly" often means beautiful, fair, or comely (e.g. Ex 2:2, Ex 39:28, 1 Sa 16:12). It may also be more than coincidence that Lehi's name in the Hebrew Lexicon is defined as, "the cheek, so called as being the **seat of beauty**."[170]

In Genesis, God looks at his creation and calls it "good." In these verses the Hebrew word for good is *tov*, which can also mean "beautiful"[171] (which in many ways makes more sense). If Nephi was making a clever reference to beauty to begin his literary creation it therefore would not be surprising. As well, the theme of creation perfectly harmonizes with the temple panorama which Nephi will immediately narrate.

B – B'

When Nephi mentions "all the learning of my father" (B) he subsequently parallels it to what it *consists of*, which is "the learning of the Jews and the language of the Egyptians" (B'); a fairly straightforward explanation. Hence, the "learning of the Jews," likely encompassed ancient teaching on a broad range of secular and religious subjects.[172] Though much of this learning was surely practical in nature, like, for instance, how to properly set up a tent in the desert, undoubtedly there was also a lot of instruction which directly influenced his family's spiritual lives, including lessons on the Abrahamic covenant and the patterned lives of the patriarchs to whom Lehi and Nephi often allude. With respect to the language of the Egyptians, it appears to be a skill that Lehi acquired and taught his sons, but whose purpose was mostly for record keeping.[173] Whether he learned it solely for this purpose (to keep records), or whether he learned it because he was a merchant who conducted commerce with the Egyptians, the Lord clearly foreknew its importance and utilized it as a primary means of preserving his word and his remnant.

E – E'

At the apex of his chiasmus Nephi equates his *high* favor from the Lord (E) to his *great* knowledge of the goodness and mysteries of God (E'). How Nephi merited such favor is explained to us in Mosiah 10:13, ". . . Nephi was more faithful in keeping the commandments of the Lord—therefore he was *favored* of the Lord . . ."[174] Also, Nephi use of the "knowledge of the goodness and mysteries" is pivotal. For context there are many verses in the Book of Mormon from which we gain insight. For example, before Nephi sees in vision the tree of life and learns its mystery he tells us how he will obtain this knowledge:

> 1 Nephi 10:19 For he that diligently seeketh shall find; and the mysteries of God shall be **unfolded** unto them, **by the power of the Holy Ghost** . . .

Surprisingly, in his vision Nephi is never actually told the meaning of the tree of life; but rather he spontaneously announces its meaning as he personally experiences the love of God shed abroad in his heart by the power of the Holy Ghost.[175] And though he never says that he is partaking of its fruit, he nonetheless describes its taste as "most desirable above all things" and the "most joyous to the soul." Nephi's brilliantly recorded experience is an eloquent blueprint of how the mysteries and goodness of God are truly known – in our hearts and souls by the power of the Spirit. And poignantly, when we read Nephi's vision and ponder his words, we become participants with him; we also come to the tree of life (whose beauty exceeds all beauty [1 Ne 11:8]); we are created anew; and the mystery and goodness of God's love is shed abroad in our hearts![176]

- **Book-Wide Considerations**

Since 1 Nephi is chiastically written there is parallel information in 1 Nephi 22 which enhances our overall understanding of chapter 1. If we do some analysis of Nephi's final verses we find several elements which parallel his beginning phrases:

1 Nephi 1	1 Nephi 22
Jerusalem must **repent** or be destroyed – vs 4	All nations, kindreds, tongues, and people shall dwell safely in Holy One of Israel if they **repent** – vs 28
I Nephi, having been **born** – vs 1	**I Nephi**, make an **end** – vs 29
Record which I make is **true** – vs 3	Plates of Brass are **true** – vs 30
I was **taught** somewhat in all the learning of my **father** - vs 1	I and my **father** not the only ones to have testified and **taught** them - vs 31 [177]
having seen (endured) many **afflictions**, - vs 1	if ye shall be obedient to the commandments, and **endure** (afflictions) to the end, ye shall be saved – vs 31
highly favored with a knowledge of the goodness and **mysteries of God** - vs 1	a man must be obedient to the **commandments of God** - vs 30

Most of these proposed parallels are self-apparent; however, the last one on this list deserves closer examination. If you recall we just looked at Mosiah 10:13 where Alma tells us why Nephi was favored with great knowledge of God's mysteries; because he "was more faithful in keeping the commandments of the Lord." Seemingly, this is also reflected in Nephi's book-wide beginning and ending thought. Elucidating this point, in a recent conference talk President Thomas Monson said; "*A knowledge of truth* and the answers to our greatest questions (mysteries) come to us as we are obedient to the commandments of God." [178] This relationship is symbiotic in that we need revelatory knowledge in order to know whom and how to obey, and we gain greater spiritual knowledge as we obey. The greatest knowledge of truth is therefore acquired as we *endure* the inner struggle to obey; i.e put off (offer up) the natural man and yield to the enticings of the Spirit (Mosiah 3:19).

Finally, we spoke earlier about Nephi's beginning as an allusion to the beauty of creation. We might also ponder how this aesthetic relates to obeying the commandments. Consider, for example, the modern temple. In the temple endowment there is first a presentation of how the earth was created, which is a process of being clothed in beauty, progressing from "without form and void" to abundant with life (bringing forth fruit). Upon completion it is pronounced beautiful (*tov*). Immediately afterwards is a second creation process - man's spiritual creation and adornment. In this parallel presentation, like the six creative periods, we are gradually clothed (endowed in Greek) with beautiful robes symbolizing righteousness (Eph 4:24, Rev 19:8, Ex 28:40). As important, each change of clothing is accompanied by covenants and laws (commandments) which require our obedience and sacrifice (the hallmark of covenants). "Learning" to obey transforms and refines (beautifies) our nature, and we experience the sanctifying process of *becoming* what our robes symbolize – kings of righteousness (*melchizedek*).

In the last chapter of Revelation, at the throne of God, John sees the beautiful tree of life and confirms Nephi's parallels, "Blessed are they that do his commandments, that they may have right to the tree of life" (Rev 22:14). Christ is the King of righteousness and glory, and because of his perfect obedience we can *know* God's love\goodness. He is the tree of eternal life which Nephi tells us is "exceeding of all beauty" (1 Ne 11:8). As we "learn of him," (instructed by the Spirit), we "shall be like him." After all, he created us *to be* in his image – beautiful.[179]

Notes

[1] Bruce R. McConkie, "A New Commandment: Save Thyself and Thy Kindred!" *Ensign,* Aug. 1976, 11.

[2] Jeffrey Holland, "I Have a Question" Ensign, Sept. 1976.

[3] John W. Welch, "Legal Perspectives on the Slaying of Laban," *JBMS* 1/1 (1992): 119–41.

[4] Jeffrey R. Holland and Patricia T. Holland, On Earth As It Is in Heaven, p. 139.

[5] Gerhard Kittel and Gerhard Friedrich, Theological Dictionary of the New Testament, Volume 4, Pg 802

[6] Elder Dallin H. Oaks, "The Historicity of the Book of Mormon", Foundation for Ancient Research and Mormon Studies, Annual Dinner, Provo, Utah, October 29, 1993

[7] Joseph Henry Thayer, A Greek-English Lexicon of the New Testament, 1889

[8] John Breck, Scripture in Tradition: The Bible and Its Interpretation in the Orthodox Church

[9] Undoing Forgetfulness: Chiasmus of Poetical Mind – a Cultural Paradigm of Archetypal Imagination, Nicoletta Isar, http://www.ejop.org/archives/2005/08/undoing_forgetf_1.html, June 2, 2009

[10] http://www.worsleyschool.net/socialarts/allusion/page, Apr 15 2010

[11] John W. Welch, "Chiasmus in the Book of Mormon," *New Era*, Feb 1972, 6

[12] Welch, BYU Studies, Vol. 10, No. 1, p.82

[13] The Amazing Structure of the Gospel of John, Kym Smith, Sherwood Publications 2005, 328 pages. ISBN 0-646- 37447-8

[14] Neal A. Maxwell, "'Endure It Well'," *Ensign*, May 1990, 33

[15] We should perhaps note that all three members of the Godhead are now present, a very rare event. Of course Jesus' baptism comes to mind as another such occasion.

[16] "Sea of Glass - answering to the molten sea or great brazen laver before the mercy seat of the earthly temple, for the purification of the priests; typifying the baptism of water and the Spirit of all who are made kings and priests unto God. Mingled with fire and answering to the baptism on earth with fire, that is, fiery trial, as well as with the Holy Ghost, which Christ's people undergo to purify them, as gold is purified of its dross in the furnace." James, Fausett, Brown, Commentary Critical and Explanatory on the Whole Bible, http://www.searchgodsword.org/com/jfb/view.cgi?book=re&chapter=015, 12 Nov 2011

[17] The Feast of St. Gregory the Great; Why sing the Mass, Michael E. Lawrence, http://www.newliturgicalmovement.org/2007/03/feast-of-st-gregory-great-why-sing-mass.html, Jan 10 2010

[18] We all come from the throne of God singing this song, adoring and loving our Father for his merciful plan. The veil of mortality takes its awareness from us, but when the word of the gospel falls upon our ears, faith plants its seed and we begin to walk back to the presence of God's throne, armed with a comprehension of the same plan over which we once rejoiced, the sweetness of which endures, and perhaps is even greater, revealed by the Holy Spirit to our hearts.

[19] In the LDS Bible dictionary, page 608, under the heading angels, we read that "there are two classes of beings who minister for the Lord; those who are spirits, and those who have bodies of flesh and bone. Ordinarily the word *angel* means those ministering persons who have a body of flesh and bone, being either resurrected from the dead, or else translated, as were Enoch, Elijah, etc (D&C 129)." Thus, the angels that Lehi hears "singing and praising their God" could also be the resurrected redeemed who John sees and hears in Rev 15:3.

[20] Consider how the word *pele* is suggestive of the grandest of wonders in Psa 119:129-130, "Thy testimonies [are] wonderful (*pele*): therefore doth my soul keep them. The entrance of thy words giveth light; it giveth understanding unto the simple." We might contemplate that the wonders which delivered Egypt are not any grander than the wonder of His word unto deliverance!

[21] Below is an expanded form of the center 3 verses from 1 Nephi 1, which has some additional parallels in verses 15 and 17:

J 15 And **after** this manner was the **language of my father**

    a. in the *praising* of his God;

    a. for his soul did *rejoice*,

      X. and **his whole heart** was filled,

    c. because of the things which *he had seen*,

    c. yea, which the Lord *had shown unto him.*

      K 16 And now I, Nephi, **do not make a full account**

        L of the things **which my father hath written,**

          M for he hath **written many things** which he saw in

            N **visions** and in

            N' **dreams**; and

          M' he also hath **written many things**

        L' **which he prophesied and spake** unto his children,

      K' of which I **shall not make a full account.**

    a. 17 But I shall make *an account of my* proceedings in *my days.*

      b. Behold, I make an *abridgment*

        c. of the *record of my father,*

          X. upon plates which I have made with **mine own hands**;

      b. wherefore, after I have *abridged*

        c. the *record of my father* then will I

    a. make *an account of mine* own *life.*

    J' **After** I have abridged the **record of my father** then will I make an account of mine own life

Notice that J' participates simultaneously in two parallels, that is, it serves as a parallel to J (vs 15), and it also doubles as the last leg of the small chiasmus in verse 17. One verse that is shared by two contiguous chiasmi also occurs in 1 Nephi 13 (see pg 111 for another example of one verse which ends and also begins a second chiasmus).

[22] Because Nephi's words are uttered some 200 years before the time of Malachi, how do we explain the similarity of language? Elder Bruce R. McConkie has explained: "Our understanding of the prophetic word

will be greatly expanded if we know how one prophet quotes another, usually without acknowledging his source. Either Isaiah or Micah copied the prophetic words of the other relative to the mountain of the Lord's house being established in the last days with all nations flowing thereto. Their ministries overlapped, but we assume that the lesser Micah copied from the greater Isaiah and then appended some words of his own about the Millennial Era. Some unnamed Old Testament prophet, who obviously was Zenos, as the Book of Mormon testifies, spoke of the day when the wicked would be destroyed as stubble; when the righteous would be "led up as calves of the stall"; when Christ should "rise from the dead, with healing in his wings"; and when the Holy One of Israel would then reign on earth. Malachi, who lived more than two hundred years after Nephi, uses these very expressions in his prophetic writings. *Can we do other than conclude that both Nephi and Malachi had before them the writings of Zenos*? . . . Once the Lord has revealed his doctrine in precise language to a chosen prophet, there is no reason why he should inspire another prophet to choose the same words in presenting the same doctrine on a subsequent occasion. It is much easier and simpler to quote that which has already been given in perfection. We are all commanded—including the prophets among us—to search the scriptures and thereby learn what other prophets have presented." Doctrinal Restoration 17–18, Bruce R. McConkie; see also *New Witness* 402, 563

[23] Bruce R. McConkie, "Promises Made to the Fathers," in Genesis to 2 Samuel, vol. 3 of Studies in Scripture, ed. Kent P. Jackson and Robert L. Millet (Salt Lake City: Deseret Book, 1989), 3:51–52.

[24] *M. Catherine Thomas,* Alma the Younger Covenants with the Fathers (Part 1), Maxwell Institute, http://www.farms.byu.edu/publications/transcripts/?id=43#19, 28 Oct 2008

[25] Ancient Schooling - We might imagine that the following verse from Proverbs 4:1 is a picture of Lehi teaching his sons: "Hear, ye children, the instruction of a father, and attend to know understanding. 2 For I give you good doctrine, forsake ye not my law (torah). 3 For I was my father's son, tender and only [beloved] in the sight of my mother. 4 He taught me also, and said unto me, Let thine heart retain my words: keep my commandments, and live." Outside of perhaps the King's household, there was no formal schooling in Lehi's ancient Israel which proliferated the learning that Nephi speaks of. Rather, teaching was done, as commanded in Duet. 4:9, by the father of the family, and the textbook would have been the books of the Old Testament up until that that time, or largely what was found in the brass plates. To get a better understanding of ancient education and Nephi's learning, consider Psalms 78, which speaks of the mysteries (dark sayings) as curriculum:

> 1 Give ear, O my people, [to] my **law (*torah*)**: incline your ears to the words of my mouth.
>
> 2 I will open my **mouth in a parable**: I will utter dark sayings of old:
>
> 3 Which we have heard and known, and our fathers have told us.
>
> 4 We will not hide [them] from their children, shewing to the generation to come the praises of the LORD, and his strength, and his wonderful works that he hath done.
>
> 5 For he established a testimony in Jacob, and **appointed a law in Israel, which he commanded our fathers, that they should make them known to their children**:
>
> 6 That the generation to come might know [them, even] the children [which] should be born; [who] **should arise and declare [them] to their children**:
>
> 7 That they might set their hope in God, and not forget the works of God, but keep his

commandments:

8 And might not be as their fathers, a stubborn and rebellious generation; a generation [that] set not their heart aright, and whose spirit was not stedfast with God.

[26] From the LDS Bible Dictionary we read, "There are many instances in scripture of the use of lots for the purpose of making a choice." In Leviticus 16:8-9 Aaron is given instructions by the Lord to select the sacrificial goat and the scapegoat by casting lots, and Jonah is correctly determined to be the cause of the tempest, also by casting lots (Jon 1:7) In today's world we think of casting dice as a game of chance, but apparently God has used this method in the past to guide and direct his people. Certainly we can see the similitude of the lot falling to Christ to be the sacrifice for Atonement, appointed by God, just as the priests of the temple chose the sacrifice on the day of Yom Kippur (atonement) by that same method. Smith's Bible Dictionary, http://www.bible-history.com/smiths/L/Lot+%282%29/, May 19 2009

[27] There are perhaps echoes of the Old Testament story of Jacob's purchasing the blessing from Esau in this story. Laban, like Esau, appears to be unappreciative of the birthright "genealogy" of Abraham's seed. As a matter of fact if you look at the chiasmus of Jacob's life you will see that Nephi's Laban is also a type of Jacob's Laban who also reflected Esau's character. Similarly, Esau and Laban both pursued Jacob to destroy him, Esau first for taking his blessing out of Canaan, and Laban second for taking his inheritance (flocks) out of Haran.

[28] Extra Parallel – How Laban is "destroyed" commemorates the manner in which God made ancient covenant. God's covenant with Abraham was made by dividing the sacrifice and then walking between the parts. Moses' dividing the Red Sea was also a miraculous similitude of Abraham's covenant. Nephi's dividing Laban, head from body, hints at this pattern.

[29] Gospel Symbolism, Joseph Fielding McConkie, 1985, p 173

[30] Blue Letter Bible. "Dictionary and Word Search for *Yowceph (Strong's 3130)*". Blue Letter Bible. 1996-2009. 20 May 2009 < http:// www.blueletterbible.org/lang/lexicon/lexicon.cfm?Strongs=H3130&t=KJV >

[31] Blue Letter Bible. "Dictionary and Word Search for *Laban (Strong's 03837)*". Blue Letter Bible. 1996-2008. 8 Sep 2008

[32] "The name Laban comes from the unused root לבן (*lbn* 1074), and is identical to the word לבן (*laban* 1074a), white, a word which is often used to indicate leprosy." Abarim Publications Biblical Name Vault, http://www.abarim-publications.com/Meaning/Laban.html, 9 Sep 2008

[33] Alonzo L Gaskill, The Lost Language of Symbolism, p 126. "Lepers were symbols of those who are spiritually unclean, spiritually dying because of their sins, just as a leper is one who is physically dying because of disease."

[34] LDS Bible Dictionary, 724. "The disease was regarded as a living death"

[35] http://ldsces.org/inst_manuals/ot-in-1/ot-in1-05-lev.htm#15-6 9 Sep 2008

[36] "When Moses came to Egypt to deliver the sons of Israel, you will recall that Pharaoh made them make the same amount of bricks, but they had to start gathering their own straw as well. It is quite interesting that they were in fact using this straw to make "labans." The word here for "brick" is "laban." So, the affliction of the sons of Israel in their bondage was that they had to make "labans," along with gathering straw. And this is not the only place where these "labans," or bricks, were made. We find that the tower of Babel was equally

made of "labans" burned by fire, with tar used for mortar. Thus we see that the tower of Babel that reached into heaven was fired "laban," united with tar." The Rod, Its Representation and the Right to Bear it, http://www.remnantbride.com/ The_Rod/The_Rod.1.htm 9 Sep 2008

[37] In the Gospel of Thomas we find an interesting allusion to those that have partaken of the wine of the tree of knowledge of good and evil: (28) Jesus said, "I took my place in the midst of the world, and I appeared to them in flesh. I found all of them intoxicated; I found none of them thirsty. And my soul became afflicted for the sons of men, because they are blind in their heart and do not have sight; for empty they came into the world, and empty too they seek to leave the world. But for the moment they are intoxicated. When they shake off their wine, then they will repent." Gospel of Thomas, http://www.gnosis.org/naghamm/gthlamb.html, 1 Jan 2012

[38] "O Ye Fair Ones": An Additional Note on the Meaning of the Name Nephi, Matthew L. Bowen, Insights Volume 23, Issue-6, Provo, Utah:Maxwell Institute

[39] http://www.webster1828.com/websters1828/definition.aspx?word=Goodly, 1 May 2011

[40] Blue Letter Bible. "Dictionary and Word Search for *Lechiy (Strong's 3896)*". Blue Letter Bible. 1996-2011. 31 May 2011

[41] "O Ye Fair Ones": An Additional Note on the Meaning of the Name Nephi, Matthew L. Bowen, Insights Volume 23, Issue-6, Provo, Utah:Maxwell Institute

[42] Similarly, in terms of what is literal or figurative, when we hear the words, "Greater love hath no man than this, that a man **lay down his life** for his friends" (Jn 15:13), we understand that though the meaning can be literal, primarily the meaning of these words is spiritual. In fact, John later builds on Christ's admonishment with these instructions: "Hereby perceive we the love [of God], because he laid down his life for us: and we ought to lay down [our] lives for the brethren. But whoso hath this world's good, and seeth his brother have need, and **shutteth up his bowels** [of compassion] from him, how dwelleth the love of God in him?" (1 Jn 3:16). Obviously these verses cause us to think of our Savior's selfless sacrifice, which he encourages us to emulate. However, John also tells us why this is hard for us to do, which is because we "shutteth up" our bowels of compassion. If Christ had failed in Gethsemane and on the cross, it would have been for the same reason; that he chose to put himself before God and others. When we lay down our lives for others, we intersect with Gethsemane's great pattern - obedience and love's triumph over selfishness and pride (the carnal man).

[43] Is it possible that Nephi had an experience like Orson Whitney who dreamed that he was with the Savior in the garden on the night of the Atonement? Jeffrey R. Holland, "The Atonement of Jesus Christ," *Ensign*, Mar 2008, 32–38

[44] Jeffrey R. Holland and Patricia T. Holland, *On Earth As It Is in Heaven*, p. 139.

[45] Targ. Yer. to Num. xxii. 5; compare Gen. R. lvii., end; and Sanh. 105*a*, where Laban is identified with Beor, the father of Balaam, http://www.jewishencyclopedia.com/view.jsp?letter=B&artid=161#551#ixzz0mRqdNiPW, 2 May 2011

[46] Blue Letter Bible. "Dictionary and Word Search for *Kozbiy (Strong's 3579)*". Blue Letter Bible. 1996-2011. 21 Aug 2011.

[47] Blue Letter Bible. "Dictionary and Word Search for *Piynĕchac (Strong's 6372)*". Blue Letter Bible. 1996-2012. 1 Jan 2012

280

[48] The meaning of Phinehas' name is rich with possibilities. Another interpretation of the Hebrew is conceivably – peh mouth or edge, and nachash steel (brass as a feminine noun is also rendered as steel), which together would be mouth or edge of steel. Phrases similar to this in scripture are "the sword of my mouth", or "the rod of my mouth", both of which are used as metaphorical instruments of God's judgment. In Phinehas story, he personifies God's sword, executing divine judgment, much as the sword used to cut of Laban or Goliath's head. Another very real possibility is that Phinehas could be interpreted as "commandment of the Serpent", or "word of brass". Because words come from the mouth, Peh is also translated over 40 times in the Old Testament as "commandment" or "word". Thus, rendering Phinehas as "command or word of the Serpent" makes very good poetical sense in light of the Jehovah's command to slay the worshippers of Baal, which command Phinehas literally performs. Remember that Jehovah in Numbers 21 was just represented as the Brass Serpent and ergo the Serpent is symbolically the one who has given the command to slay the Baal worshippers in Numbers 25. Quite wonderfully, subtle variations of the Hebrew root *nachash* (brass\serpent\diviner) are diffused in multiple nuances throughout the storyline of Numbers 21-25. Moses, as author, masterfully involves his reader's sense of imagination and mental acuity on several levels.

[49] Alonzo L. Gaskill, The Lost Language of Symbolism, pg 123

[50] http://www.hebrew4christians.com/Holidays/Fall_Holidays/Yom_Kippur/yom_kippur.html, 9 Sep 2008

[51] Mosiah 3:18-19 is chiastic. Notice how the fall is reversed by yielding to the Spirit.

(a)   They *humble* themselves
   (b)   and become as little *children*
      (c)   believing that salvation is in the *atoning blood of Christ;*
         (d)   for the *natural man*
            (e)   is an enemy to God
               (f)   and *has been* from the fall of Adam
               (f)   and *will be* forever and ever
            (e)   unless he yieldeth to the *Holy Spirit*
         (d)   and putteth off the *natural man*
      (c)   and becometh a saint through the *atonement of Christ*
   (b)   and becometh as a *child*
(a)   submissive, meek and *humble* (Mos 3:18–19)

Chiasmus in the Book of Mormon, John W. Welch, http://maxwellinstitute.byu.edu/publications/books/?bookid=111&chapid=1292, 21 Jan 2011

[52] Neal A. Maxwell, "'Deny Yourselves of All Ungodliness'," *Ensign*, May 1995, 66

[53] William D. Ramey, Christian Publishers' Bookhouse, InTheBeginning.org 10 Oct 2010

[54] Blue Letter Bible. "Dictionary and Word Search for *haphak (Strong's 2015)*". Blue Letter Bible. 1996-2011. 23 Aug 2011.

[55] "For both David and Nephi, the swords of Goliath and Laban were symbols of obedience and divine authority, for it was by faith and obedience that they were able to slay their antagonist. The swords became not only a symbol of divine authority to the people, but also of kingship, for whoever possessed the swords possessed God's favor and retained the right to rule and administer." Brett L. Holbrook, The Sword of Laban as a Symbol of Divine Authority and Kingship, Journal of Book of Mormon Studies, Volume2, Issue 1, p 39-72

[56] Evidences for the Book of Mormon, http://james.jlcarroll.net/LDS/evidence/bom/hebr.html 9 Sp 2008

[57] Blue Letter Bible. "Dictionary and Word Search for *zara`* (*Strong's 02232*)". Blue Letter Bible. 1996-2008. 5 Sep 2008

[58] Hugh Nibley, Teachings of the Book of Mormon, sememster 2, lecture 55, p 3.

[59] "Names also mattered to the sages of Israel. They reflected on the one hand that, "It is the custom of the righteous to name their children from some event which has occurred" (Exodus Rabbah on Exodus 2:22). On the other hand they said, "The ancients, because they could avail themselves of the Holy Spirit, named themselves in reference to forthcoming events…" (Genesis Rabbah on Genesis 10:25). Naming a person with reference to a future event is in accord with how God Himself engages in granting names. The names which God has bestowed tell much about the destiny of their bearers and of the Jewish people as a whole. "Y'shua …Why That Name," Stuart Dauermann, http://www.jewsforjesus.org/publications/issues/3_10/whythatname, 12 Sep 2010

[60] Killing Laban: The Birth of Sovereignty in the Nephite Constitutional Order, Val Larsen, Journal of Book of Mormon Studies: Volume - 16, Issue - 1, Provo, Utah: Maxwell Institute, 2007

[61] Killing Laban: The Birth of Sovereignty in the Nephite Constitutional Order, Val Larsen, Journal of Book of Mormon Studies: Volume - 16, Issue - 1, Provo, Utah: Maxwell Institute, 2007

[62] Richard Leonard, http://theresurgence.com/richard_leonard_1993-04_worship_of_christ_and_the _biblical_covenant, 12 Sep 2008

[63] When we examine Nephi's two great parallel feats, there is also a possible interesting Hebrew play-on-words. The plates contain the "word of the Lord", and in the Old Testament this is written as "dabar Adonai." Curiously its parallel, the phrase "promised land" is never used in the Old Testament, but rather it is found several times as "the land which He promised." In the Hebrew this is written "eretz asher diber" (*dabar* conjugated in third person singular is *diber*). Importantly, both phrases use the word dabar, one in noun form (**word** of the Lord), and the other as a verb (land of which he **spake** or promised).

[64] Blue Letter Bible. "Dictionary and Word Search for *yachas* (*Strong's 3188*)". Blue Letter Bible. 1996-2011. 9 Oct 2011

[65] James L. Farrell, The Hidden Christ, p. 78-79

[66] Constructing the parallels of this chiasmus are not so much precise as they are intuitive, based on the precedents set in previous models or patterns. One could make the accusation that there is a bias or predisposition to find yet again the same pattern, which is a somewhat valid argument, though easily countered by the abundance of previous and later occurrences, themselves more concrete.

[67] Blue Letter Bible. "Dictionary and Word Search for *Yishma`e'l* (*Strong's 3458*)". Blue Letter Bible. 1996-2009. 28 May 2009

[68] Psalm 52:8 - "But I [am] like a green olive tree in the house of God: I trust in the mercy of God for ever and ever." If we consider that the mercy of God is comparable to the love of God found in Nephi's vision, then perhaps the green olive tree is comparable to the tree of life, also in Nephi's vision. Also notice that the green olive tree is found in the temple (the house of God), where the tree of life is also found.

[69] Christ crucified on the Tree of Life. Giovanni da Modena; from a fresco in the church of San Petronio, Bologna, Italy.

[70] Mircea Eliade, *The Myth of the Eternal Return*, http://rjohnhowe.wordpress.com/2010/06/06/the-tree-of-

life-design-by-christine-brown-part-1/, Jan 9, 2010

[71] Mary Douglas, Thinking in Circles: An Essay on Ring Composition, p. 10

[72] In Lehi's vision there are several other prominent images besides the tree of life, one of which is the opposite of the tree of life - the spacious building. It definitely has an appeal for it sits exalted in the air, and the people within wear fine clothes and act arrogantly towards those at the tree. We learn in 1 Nephi 11:36 that it is a symbol of the pride of the world, and that one day it will fall. In the mean time it remains with us today. Paradoxically it is located exalted and above while those at the tree remain below in a seemingly lesser or subordinate position. Obviously Satan is sowing his tares (seed) in the hearts of many even as they arrive at the tree, and the confusion created is the same as it was for Eve, the first to have experienced Satan's tares. Even as they taste the sweet, their eyes wander elsewhere, looking beyond the mark (Jacob 4:14). In the Hebrew, the concept of spacious comes from the Hebrew *yasha* which means:

> יְשַׁע unused in Kal, Arab. وسع TO BE SPACIOUS, AMPLE, BROAD, figuratively *to be opulent*, kindred to שׁוּע. See Jeuhari in A. Schultens, Origg. Heb. tom. i. p. 20. The signification of *ample space* is in Hebrew applied to liberty, deliverance from dangers and distresses (compare רָחַב, רְוַח), as on the other hand narrowness of space is frequently used of distresses and dangers (comp. צוּר, צָרָה).

This word *yasha,* which is used dozens of times in the Old Testament, is almost always rendered as "save" and sometimes as "savior". Isaiah's name in the Hebrew is Yeshayah, which means "the salvation of Jehovah", or "Jehovah has saved." Obviously, in the Hebrew sense of this word there is irony, for the "spacious" building does not provide salvation and freedom, but rather it is really death. Notice in the lexicon entry above (last two lines) that we are also given a Hebrew meaning for "narrowness", which is the opposite of spacious, "used of distresses and dangers." Ironic as well is that the iron rod, or word of God seems narrow and constricting to many, but like the spacious building, it really is just the opposite of distress, danger, and death, and in fact is "life" (John 6:62). Christ plays on this paradox when he says in Mat 7: 14 Because strait [is] the gate, and narrow [is] the way, which leadeth unto life, and few there be that find it.

Lehi's vision, which also plays on these images, is not without precedent. Remember that Egypt once saved and preserved life (*yasha*) during the famine for Jacob the patriarch's family. However, Egypt in Hebrew is *Mitsrayim,* which antithetically means "limits" or "boundaries" a narrow place of distress. In fact in its adjective form it means "double straits". It seems to us paradoxical that Jacob descends into a land of extreme "narrowness" (*mitsayim*) in order to save (*yasha-spacious*) his seed, which however is just as Christ said it should be, because it "leadeth to life"! A good example of this is the temple. Before we enter the celestial room which is spacious, we first must learn in a smaller narrower place, and can only enter the spacious room if we have first spent required time in the other. Though Satan would have us believe otherwise, the lesson is that things are not what they seem. Death of self-pride is life, the first will be last, the servant is the master, and narrowness in Christ is celestial spaciousness! A yoke, if His, is easy; it's a matter of spiritual perspective.

[73] "The New Testament also alludes to the cross of Jesus as a tree. (See Acts 5:30; Gal. 3:13; 1 Pet. 2:24.) Some have noticed that the Greek word used in these passages is the same as that used for the tree of life in the Septuagint, different from the usual New Testament word for *tree*. According to a number of sources, some early Christians thought of the cross as a tree of life. Later sources likewise relate the cross to the tree of life, as in some hymns attributed to St. Ephraem the Syrian: "The tree of life is the cross which gave a radiant life to our race. On the top of Golgotha Christ distributed life to men. And henceforth he further promised us the pledge of eternal life.'Our Savior typified his body in the tree, the one from which Adam did not taste because he sinned." Even a spare sampling of writings from the early Church Fathers shows their awareness of the power of the symbol of the tree of life in ancient Christianity. The *Instructions of Commodianus,* for example, states in chapter 35 that 'by this tree of death we are born to the life to come; … therefore, pluck believingly the fruits of life.'" C. Wilfred Griggs, "The Tree of Life in Ancient Cultures," *Ensign,* June 1988, 27

[74] Jeffrey R. Holland, *Christ and the New Covenant* [1997], 160, 162

[75] In interesting takeaway from Paul's words in Rom 5:5, which so closely mirror those of Nephi in his vision, is that Paul has undoubtedly come to the tree himself and partaken of its fruit!

[76] Jn 2:3-5 is also chiastic:

And **hereby we do know that we know him**, if we keep his commandments.
> He that saith, I know him,
>> and **keepeth not his commandments**,
>>> is **a liar**,
>> and the **truth is not in him**.
> But whoso **keepeth his word**,
in him verily is the love of God perfected:
hereby know we that we are in him.

Notice the two parallels – "He that saith I know him", which is parallel to "in him verily is the love of God perfected." Again we have the definition of eternal life, which is to know God, which again is defined as perfect love.

[77] Maxwell Institute, Forms of Repetition, Hugh W. Pinnock, http://maxwellinstitute.byu.edu/publications/books/?bookid=39&chapid=133, 3 Apr 2011

[78] If you look at the center of the of Nephi's apex in 13:34 you will see that the angel of the Lord is parallel to the Lamb of God. Could it be that the identity of the angel is revealed by its parallel to be the Lamb of God. There are many occasions in the Old Testament where the angel of the Lord is identified as the Lord. "Because it is difficult to distinguish between "the angel of the Lord" and Jehovah in Genesis 16:7–11, Exodus 3:2, and Judges 2:1–4, Nephites who recorded seeing "the angel of the Lord" might have been indirectly writing about the Lord himself. It is therefore possible that prophets such as Alma also saw the Savior and conversed with him (see Mosiah 27:25, "And the Lord said unto me")."

http://byustudies.byu.edu/januarybomcharts/charts/41.pdf, 31 Mar 2011

[79] Blue Letter Bible. "Dictionary and Word Search for *doxazō (Strong's 1392)*". Blue Letter Bible. 1996-2012. 3 Jan 2012.

[80] Guzik, David. "Study Guide for Revelation 22." Enduring Word. Blue Letter Bible. 7 Jul 2006. 2010. 21 Sep 2010.

[81] Isaac and Ishmael, Charles Lee Feinberg, Th.D., Ph.D., http://www.christianactionforisrael.org /judeochr/isaac_ishmael.html

[82] Many have recognized this act to be a similitude of the scapegoat, which on the Day of Atonement was placed the carnal sin of Israel and sent to die in the wilderness. The sacrificial goat was then slain on the altar and its blood sprinkled eastward on the mercy seat for purification and cleansing (Lev 16). Isaac would be a type of second goat, even as Christ was the second Adam.

[83] 1 Corinthians 15:46 – "Howbeit that [was] not first which is spiritual, but that which is natural; and afterward that which is spiritual."

[84] http://www1.davidson.edu/academic/music/news/stasack_premiere.htm, 15 Sep 2008

[85] Alonzo L. Gaskill, The Lost Language of Symbolism, p 323

[86] Number in Scripture: Its Supernatural Design and Spiritual Significance, E. W. Bullinger (1837-1913), http://philologos.org/__eb-nis/four.htm

[87] The Four Gospels, D. Kelly Ogden and Andrew C. Skinner, 452

[88] "South in Hebrew is associated with the covenant or covenant making because when we face east, south is at our right hand. In Greek south is associated with that which is from heaven, such as heaven sent refreshment or revelation." Alzonzo L. Gaskill, The Lost Language of Symbolism, p 318

[89] "Traditionally associated with the presence of God or his influence. To face east was to face God. To move eastward was to move toward him. An attack from the east symbolized receipt of the wrath of God." Ibid., p 318

[90] Hugh Nibley, Lehi in the Desert [Salt Lake City, Utah: Bookcraft, 1952], p 90

[91] Joseph F. McConkie, Gospel Symbolism, p 274

[92] Blue Letter Bible. "Dictionary and Word Search for *'Eylim (Strong's 362)*". Blue Letter Bible. 1996-2011. 7 Nov 2011

[93] Blue Letter Bible. "Dictionary and Word Search for *Nacham (Strong's 05163)*". Blue Letter Bible. 1996-2008. 16 Sep 2008

[94] http://www.biblestudy.org/bibleref/meaning-of-numbers-in-bible/8.html, 16 Dec 2011

[95] Blue Letter Bible. "Dictionary and Word Search for *machashabah (Strong's 4284)*". Blue Letter Bible. 1996-2013. 11 Jan 2013

[96] Blue Letter Bible. "Dictionary and Word Search for *Choreb (Strong's 2722)*". Blue Letter Bible. 1996-2011. 12 Apr 2011

[97] L. H. Read, "The Ark of the Covenant: Symbol of Triumph," *Ensign*, Jun 1980, 20

[98] ibid

[99] "What I've Become" by Doug Walker, from the album *What Heaven Sees in You*, ©2010 House of Light Music. Used by permission.

[100] Isn't it interesting that in 1 Ne 4 (the parallel to 1 Ne 18) there is also an ambiguous use of a term which

plays a prominent role in the story, and which also seems intentional. Remember the use of "better that one should perish", which also allows for interpretation of who the "one" is. I cannot think of any other such ambiguous usages in all of 1 Nephi. That they should appear where they do, in parallel, adds credence to our belief that Nephi designed a grand macrostructure.

[101] "The binding of Jesus is a central symbol in all of the Gospels—most dramatically in Mark, when the Jews, after the trial before the high priest, "bound Jesus" and sent him to Pilate (Mark 15:1; see also Matthew 27:2). But in the Gospel of John, Jesus was bound when He was arrested. The binding of Jesus reminds us of the binding of Isaac in the *Akedah*—from the Hebrew word *'aqad*, "to bind," that only appears in the Bible in Genesis 22:9, but in postbiblical Hebrew the word means "to bind the legs of an animal for sacrifice." In the case of animals, the binding was to keep them from struggling at the moment of slaughter. In the case of Abraham and Isaac, commentators have noted that the binding of the youthful Isaac by his elderly father serves as a symbol of the willingness of Isaac to submit himself to the will of his father."
David Rolph Seely and Joann H. Seely, "Behold the Lamb of God" in *"Behold the Lamb of God": An Easter Celebration,* ed. Richard Neitzel Holzapfel, Frank F. Judd Jr., and Thomas A Wayment (Provo, UT: Religious Studies Center, Brigham Young University, 2008) 17–47.
http://byueasterconference.com/seely.php

[102] http://en.wikisource.org/wiki/Ante-Nicene_Fathers/Volume_VIII/Remains_of_the_Second_and_Third _Centuries/Melito%2C_the_Philosopher/Chapter_12, Apr 7 2009

[103] This verse in Mosiah 15 is part of a wonderful chiasmus:

A 7 Yea, even so he shall he be led crucified and slain, the flesh becoming subject even unto death, the will of the Son being swallowed up in the will of the Father.

    B 8 And thus God **breaketh the bands of death;**
        C 8 giving the Son power to make **intercession**
            D 8 For the **children of men**
                E 9 Having ascended into heaven having the **bowels of mercy;**
                E' 9 being filled with **compassion**
            D' 9 towards the **children of men;**
        C' 9 **betwixt** them and justice;
    B' 9 having **broken the bands of death,**

A' 9 taken upon himself their iniquity and their transgressions, having redeemed them and satisfied the demands of justice

Notice that the bookends, A and A', each have three parallel aspects of the Atonement. Being swallowed up in the "will of the Father" is parallel to "taken upon himself their iniquity and transgressions."

[104] Power through Repetition: The Dynamics of Book of Mormon Parallelism from Book of Mormon Authorship Revisited: The Evidence for Ancient Origins pp. 295–309

[105] Blue Letter Bible. "Dictionary and Word Search for `arab (Strong's 6148)". Blue Letter Bible. 1996-2009. 1 Apr 2009

[106] Blue Letter Bible. "Dictionary and Word Search for *chata' (Strong's 2398)"*. Blue Letter Bible. 1996-2009. 1 Apr 2009

[107] "When a Jew heard a phrase in scripture that was also repeated in a different part of the Bible, he knew

that those scriptures were tied together and had application for both texts. A single word could link dozens of ideas together and give the listener much material to ponder. Every scripture could have dual meanings – personal and collective." Donna B. Nelson, Beloved Bridegroom, pg 95-96

108 Blue Letter Bible. "Dictionary and Word Search for *yadah (Strong's 3034)*". Blue Letter Bible. 1996-2009. 1 Apr 2009

109 Henry, Matthew. "Commentary on Genesis 49." . Blue Letter Bible. 1 Mar 1996. 2010. 26 Sep 2010.

110 There is, however, one last parallel in Jacob's blessing to consider. Notice that the second line of Judah's blessing (Gen 49:8) states that "thy *hand* [shall be] in the neck of thine enemies". This is likely another play on the etymology of Judah's name, which is rooted in *yad*, hand. With reference to Christ - sin, misery, and death are the enemies that He came to vanquish. You might think for a moment of the typifying story which parallels this prophecy, found in chapter 4. Isn't Laban an enemy and type for death, upon whose neck Nephi, as a type of Christ, places his hand, smiting off Laban's head.

111 "Entry for 'Hoary'". "King James Dictionary". http://www.studylight.org/dic/kjd/view.cgi?number=T2910, 11 Sept 2011

112 Blue Letter Bible. "Dictionary and Word Search for *shuwb (Strong's 7725)*". Blue Letter Bible. 1996-2008. 9 Dec 2008

113 Blue Letter Bible. "Dictionary and Word Search for *nadab (Strong's 5068)*". Blue Letter Bible. 1996-2008. 9 Dec 2008

114 Similarly, Jonadab in the Old Testament, whose name also comes from *nadab*, is also a story in which the outcome is reflected by the meaning of his name. In 2 Kings 10 we read how King Jehu is cleansing the land of Baal worship and is going to Samaria in his chariot. Along the way he meets Jonadab and asks, "Is thine heart right, as my heart [is] with thy heart? And Jonadab answered, It is. If it be, give [me] thine hand. And he gave [him] his hand; and he took him up to him into the chariot." In figurative language, the King, whose name means "Jehovah is he", allows only those whose hearts are "right", which is willing (*nadab*), to be taken up into his chariot, which is a symbol of the throne of God (the throne of God is represented in the Old Testament as a chariot of fire, 2 Ki 2:22). This Jonadab becomes the patriarch of a group called the Rechabites, which in Hebrew means to have a broken or contrite heart (Jer 35:18). In similar fashion, in the next chapter of Helaman, Helaman 6, we are told that the Nephites dwindle in unbelief because of the hardness of their hearts, while the converted Lamanites have the Spirit of the Lord "poured out" on them because of their easiness and "willingness (*nadab*) to believe in his words" (Hel 6:36).

115 Joseph R. McConkie, *Gospel Symbolism* [Salt Lake City: Bookcraft, 1999], p 37-39

116 Library of Congress, Religion and the New Republic, http://www.loc.gov/exhibits/religion/rel07.html, 14 Sept 2011

117 http://biblicalchiasmus.wordpress.com/category/people/lundbom-jack-r/, 16 Dec 2011

118 http://www.sfheart.com/beauty_quotes.html, 10 Oct 2011

119 http://www.quotesby.net/John-Muir, 10 Oct 2011

120 "Lifted up" is uniquely used in the second half of Nephi vision, chapters 12-14, where it describes how the Gentiles will be collectively and symbolically resurrected upon the land of promise (vs 30). A later parallel usage refers to individual Gentiles participating in the Restoration, who will be resurrected "at the last day" (vs 37). Below is a diagram of this relationship in 1 Nephi 12-14 (for the entire chiasmus, see pg 110-111):

13:30 Nevertheless, thou beholdest that the Gentiles who have gone forth out of captivity, and have been **lifted up** by **the power of God** above all other nations, upon the face of the **land which is choice above all other lands**, which is the land that the Lord God hath covenanted with thy father that his seed should have for the land of their inheritance; wherefore, thou seest that the Lord God will **not suffer that the Gentiles will utterly destroy** the mixture of thy seed, which are among thy brethren.

33 Lamb of God will be **merciful** unto Gentiles

The angel spake unto me

34 Lamb of God will be **merciful** unto Gentiles

13:37 And blessed are they (Gentiles) who shall seek to bring forth my Zion at that day, for they shall have the gift and the **power of the Holy Ghost**; and if they endure unto the end they shall be **lifted up** at the last day, and shall be saved in the **everlasting kingdom** of the Lamb; and whoso shall publish peace, yea, tidings of great joy, **how beautiful upon the mountains shall they be**.

Besides the parallel use of "lifted up" in these verses, you might notice that Nephi also seems to be comparing the "land choice above all lands" (America) in verse 30 to the "everlasting kingdom of the Lamb" in verse 37. Nephi also wonderfully adds a caveat to verse 37, "how beautiful upon the mountain shall they be." If you think about it, this is a repeated comparison that those "lifted up" are beautiful, which is exactly what Nephi intimates concerning the cross that is lifted up in the first half of this vision, chapter 11!

In addition, if you look at the center, vs 33 and 34, notice how the two statements of "merciful" are parallel to one another. Because this center is parallel to the center of chapter 11 and the tree of life, we can also easily recognize that God's mercy to the Gentiles is a reference to the tree of life, which is the "love of God shed abroad" in their heart! In order to explore a few more ideas, below is an outline of the corresponding parallels from chapter 11 (tree of life):

11:7 And behold this thing shall be given unto thee for a sign, that after thou hast beheld the tree which bore the fruit which thy father tasted, thou shalt also **behold a man descending out of heaven**, and him shall ye witness; and after ye have witnessed him ye **shall bear record** that it is **the Son of God.** 8 And it came to pass that the Spirit said unto me: Look! And **I looked and beheld a tree** (*ets*); and it was like unto the tree which my father had seen; and the beauty thereof was far beyond, yea, exceeding of all beauty; and the whiteness thereof did exceed the **whiteness** of the driven snow.

22 Tree of life represents - **love of God** shed abroad in hearts of men

Most desirous, and he spake unto me saying: and the most joyous to the soul

24 Tree of life represents **love of God** - Son of God goes forth among men

11:32 And it came to pass that the angel spake unto me again, saying: Look! And I looked and **beheld the Lamb of God**, that he was taken by the people; yea, **the Son of the everlasting God** was judged of the world; and I saw **and bear record**. 33 **And I, Nephi, saw** that **he was lifted up upon the cross** (*ets*) and slain for the **sins** of the world.

The word "love" is used at the center of chapter 11 (above), whereas "merciful" is the term used in the center of chapters 12-14 (previous page). Also, notice that Nephi is told in verse 7 that he will see and bear witness of the Son of God, and in verse 32 he both sees and bears that witness! And, as mentioned before, the tree which exceeds the whiteness of the snow in 11:8, is apposite the cross with the dark sins of the world in verse 23. This contrast might remind us of Isaiah 1:16 wherein the scarlet of sin and death is promised to be transformed into the whiteness of snow (the very description of the tree).

[121] Marion G. Romney, Conference Report, Oct 1963, 23.

[122] Watchman Nee, "A Life of Feeling or Faith", http://www3.telus.net/trbrooks/lifeoffaith, 2 Jan 2011

[123] Blue Letter Bible. "Dictionary and Word Search for *checed (Strong's 2617)*". Blue Letter Bible. 1996-2011. 16 Dec 2011

[124] Chacyid is also rendered as "godly" in Psa 4:3, and "Holy One" (name of Christ) in Psa 16:6.

[125] John Paul II, Dives in Misericordia, http://www.vatican.va/holy_father/john_paul_ii/encyclicals/documents/hf_jp-ii_enc_30111980_dives-in-misericordia_en.html, 22 Oct 2013

[126] In the first Psalm there is instruction which sounds very similar to Nephi's exhortation to feast upon the words of Christ:

> 1 Blessed [is] the man that walketh not in the counsel of the ungodly, nor standeth in the way of sinners, nor sitteth in the seat of the scornful.
> *The psalmist, like Nephi, admonishes that a correct path needs to be followed, like the path which leads to the tree of life. Also notice that the psalmist identifies a group that sits and scorns, which is what those in Lehi's spacious building do.*

> 2 But his delight [is] in the law of the LORD; and **in his law doth he meditate day and   night.**
> *Meditating on the word day and night, is also what Nephi encourages – feasting upon the word. As in the tree of life and the doctrine of Christ, the word leads to eternal life (the fruit of the tree).*

> 3 And he shall be like a tree planted by the rivers of water, that bringeth forth his fruit in his season; his leaf also shall not wither; and whatsoever he doeth shall prosper.
> *Like Lehi's vision (and John's in revelation) there is a river or fountain of water which runs by the tree of life. How do we know that the Psalmist is also describing the tree of life? – because he tells us that the leaves never wither, or in other words, it lives eternally. Notice that like Alma, who tells us that we grow the tree of life (Alma 32), the Psalmist also says that we become the eternal tree.*

In the footnotes for verse 2 it tells us that "his law" means, "teaching, direction, doctrine", which is another way of saying, "his word." What Nephi tell us the Psalmist recapitulates, which is that as we endure in hope, feasting upon the word (or meditating day and night), we become as He is, a tree (of life) - a "representation "of God's love! Or according to Nephi's parallel, "having a love of God, and love of all mankind", which is parallel to "have eternal life"! (2 Ne 31:20).

[127] Bruce R. McConkie, "Promises Made to the Fathers," in Genesis to 2 Samuel, vol. 3 of Studies in Scripture, ed. Kent P. Jackson and Robert L. Millet (Salt Lake City: Deseret Book, 1989), 3:51–52.

[128] Immediately, right from "the beginning" we find parallel poetry in scripture. Genesis 1:1-5 can easily be arranged in a chiasmus:

a In **the beginning**
> b God created (bara-divided)
>> c the heaven
>>> d and the earth.
>>>> e And the earth was without form, and **void**;
>>>>> f and **darkness** [was] upon the face of the deep.
>>>>>> g And the **Spirit** of God moved upon the face of the waters.
>>>>>> g And God said, Let there be **light**: and there was light.
>>>>> f And God saw the **light**,
>>>> e that [it was] **good**:
> b and God divided
>> c the light
>>> d from the darkness.

a And God called the light Day, and the darkness he called Night.
And the evening and the morning were **the first day**.

Notice how the Hebrew for "created" is bara, which is reflected perfectly by "divided", and that heaven is parallel to light and earth is parallel to darkness. Of course, the center is a comparison of the Spirit to light, both of which are the hinge for the first day. The earth is void until the Spirit moves and light appears. Notice that f and f' are antithetical (darkness, light), as are e and e', (void and good).

[129] Blue Letter Bible. "Dictionary and Word Search for *rachaph (Strong's 7363)*". Blue Letter Bible. 1996-2011. 30 Oct 2011

[130] Blue Letter Bible. "Dictionary and Word Search for *Gethsēmani (Strong's 1068)*". Blue Letter Bible. 1996-2008. 7 Sep 2008

[131] "From Talmudic references it would appear that reading from the prophetic books had become a well-established custom long before the destruction of the Second Temple. There are also early Christian allusions to the "reading of the Law and the Prophets" (Luke 4:17; Acts 13:15)." Encyclopedia of Judaism, http://www.answers.com /topic/haftarah

[132] Encyclopedia Judaica Jr.

[133] Joseph Smith, History of the Church, 5:260-261

[134] "The human body contains from 55% to 78% water, depending on body size. To function properly, the body requires between one and seven liters of water per day to avoid dehydration; the precise amount depends on the level of activity, temperature, humidity, and other factors." What percentage of the human body is composed of water? Jeffrey Utz, M.D., The MadSci Network. http://en.wikipedia.org/wiki/ Water#cite_note-45, 16 Dec 2011

[135] Blue Letter Bible. "Dictionary and Word Search for *pneuma (Strong's 4151)*". Blue Letter Bible. 1996-2011. 27 Sep 2011.

[136] "God's Love," Children's Songbook of The Church of Jesus Christ of Latter-day Saints, 97

[137] Blue Letter Bible. "Dictionary and Word Search for *'Aram Naharayim (Strong's 0763)*". Blue Letter Bible. 1996-2008. 7 Sep 2008

[138] Blue Letter Bible. "Dictionary and Word Search for *Charan (Strong's 2771)*". Blue Letter Bible. 1996-2011. 23 May 2011

[139] The account in Genesis 15 also tells us that Abraham's seed will be in Egypt for four generations. Four is

commonly thought of to be a symbol of the earth or created world; i.e. the four winds. The Lost Language of Symbolism, Alonzo L Gaskill, 2003, p 119

[140] According to The Believer's Study Bible: "Stephen apparently conflates or "telescopes" two separate texts (later in v. 16, he will telescope or conflate two separate incidents). This was a popular method of recounting history in Stephen's day. The statement is true as we recognize that in one breath Stephen alludes to two different texts. Further, the fact is that they did worship God both in "this place" (Canaan, Gen. 15:13–15) and on Mt. Horeb (Ex. 3:12)." http://www.tektonics.org/tk-lk.html, 7 Sept 2008

[141] ibid

[142] "What is concealed in [the Old Testament] under the veil of earthly promises is clearly revealed in the preaching of the New Testament. Our Lord Himself briefly demonstrated and defined the use of the Old Testament writings, when He said that it was necessary that what had been written concerning Himself in the Law, and the Prophets, and the Psalms, should be fulfilled, and that this was that Christ must suffer, and rise from the dead the third day, and that repentance and remission of sins should be preached in His name among all nations, beginning at Jerusalem." Augustine, On the Merits and Forgiveness of Sins, and on the Baptism of Infants," Book 1, Chapter 53, "The Utility of the Books of the Old Testament"

[144] Later, Jacob builds an altar in Shechem when he first returns to Canaan. Also, as a scriptural crossroads, 500 years after that Joshua is instructed to renew Israel's covenant there upon returning from Egypt. During his ministry, Christ will come to the well in Shechem to offer the Samaritan woman living water. In the Hebrew Shechem means shoulder portion, which signifies strength.

[145] Blue Letter Bible. "Dictionary and Word Search for *Mosheh (Strong's 4872)*". Blue Letter Bible. 1996-2010. 27 Dec 2010

[146] Nicoletta Isar, Undoing Forgetfulness: Chiasmus of Poetical Mind – a Cultural Paradigm of Archetypal Imagination, Europe's Journal of Psychology, http://www.ejop.org/archives/2005/08/undoing_forgetf_1.html, Aug 25, 2008

[147] Let's apply Stephen's instruction to our modern temple endowment. Below is a diagram of how his patterned plan of salvation is remarkably evidenced in the modern temple endowment:

Garden of Eden – with Father

The garment – Gen 3:15

Telestial World

Terrestrial World

Celestial World

The veil - Hebrew 10:19

Celestial Room – with Father

Certainly we understand that the fall of Adam and Eve represents the spiritual death that we all experience, and that the veil represents our return into the Father's presence when we physically die. Moreover, each of these parallel deaths also directs us to Christ's great atoning sacrifice.

The garment is a symbol of Christ and his atoning sacrifice – In Gen 3:5 we read that the blood of an animal was shed to provide coats for Adam and Eve, to cover their nakedness (a symbol of their shame). This death foreshadows and is a symbol of Christ's atoning sacrifice for all of fallen man.

The veil is also a symbol of Christ and his atoning sacrifice - In Heb 10:19-20 we read (parenthesis mine): "Having therefore, brethren, boldness to enter into the holiest by the blood (sacrifice) of Jesus, By a new and living way, which he hath consecrated for us, through the veil, that is to say, his flesh (sacrifice)." Rightly so, our only access into God's holy presence is because of and "through" the blood of His sacrifice.

This parallel of the garment and the veil suggests that we enter mortality with the promise of His atoning sacrifice (garment), and that by the fulfillment of that same atoning sacrifice (veil) we are able to return spotless back into our Father's presence. Adding to the significance, a new name is given when Adam and Eve receive their garments, just as a new name is learned at the veil. As our mortal test is bracketed by (covered by) His great sacrificial offering, so the Hebrew word for Atonement is *kaphar*, which means to cover. Connected to this idea, consider the words of Paul in Romans 13:11-13, "let us therefore cast off the works of darkness, and let us **put on** (*enduo*) the armour of light. Let us walk honestly, as in the day; not in rioting and drunkenness, not in chambering and wantonness, not in strife and envying. But **put ye on** (*enduo*) the Lord Jesus Christ, and make not provision for the flesh, to [fulfil] the lusts [thereof]." The highlighted word in these verses is the original Greek word which means to endow, or to clothe! Certainly, the garment is an "endowment" of light which symbolizes putting on Christ, and "casting off" (putting to death) the natural man (Mosiah 3:19).

In the temple endowment the seven days of creation (how the earth is clothed with beauty) precede the seven steps of man's spiritual creation. And though temporal creation is important, it is only a reflective prelude to the purpose of all creation – man's spiritual creation. In Ephesians 4 Paul speaks of this in terms of the endowment (*enduo*), and relates that through it (putting on the new man) we are spiritually created and beautified: "22 That ye put off concerning the former conversation the old man, which is corrupt according to the deceitful lusts; 23 And be renewed in the spirit of your mind; 24 And that ye **put on** (*enduo*) the new man, which after God **is created** in righteousness and true holiness." Paul's conclusions that the endowment's creative goal is righteousness and holiness is supported by John's description of the splendid clothing worn by those who enter God's presence: "Let us be glad and rejoice, and give honour to him: for the marriage of the Lamb is come, and his wife hath made herself ready. And to her was granted that she should be arrayed in fine linen, clean and white: for the fine linen is the righteousness of saints." (Rev 19:7-8) As it relates to us, "putting on the new man" is how "holiness to the Lord", the inscription on every temple, is "honoured". It is also the "new and living way" (yielding to the enticings of the Spirit) whereby we have access to "the holiest", the presence of God. We cannot be true and faithful to the covenants we make there in any other way.

[148] LDS Bible Dictionary, Pg 718

[149] Blue Letter Bible. "Dictionary and Word Search for *Sha'uwl (Strong's 07586)*". Blue Letter Bible. 1996-2008. 7 Aug 2008

[150] Blue Letter Bible. "Dictionary and Word Search for *'Agag (Strong's 090)*". Blue Letter Bible. 1996-2008.

5 Aug 2008

[151] Blue Letter Bible. "Dictionary and Word Search for *ga'ah (Strong's 01342)*". Blue Letter Bible. 1996-2008. 7 Aug 2008

[152] It is Joshua (which translated is Jesus) whom we are told in Ex 17:13, "discomfited Amalek and his people with the edge of the sword." Jesus Christ also came with a sword of truth (Hebrew 4:11-12), to defeat and overcome sin and death, which perhaps also reminds us of Nephi's use of Laban's sword.

[153] Blue Letter Bible. "Dictionary and Word Search for *thanatoō (Strong's 2289)*". Blue Letter Bible. 1996-2008. 14 Aug 2008

[154] Similarly, the sword used by the cherubim guard the tree of life is also a symbol of the word. By it (the sword of the word), the faith of all those who wish to partake of the tree is tested.

[155] Kevin M Pearson, "Faith in the Lord Jesus Christ," Ensign, April 2009,

[156] "This mighty change is not simply the result of working harder or developing greater individual discipline. Rather, it is the consequence of a fundamental change in our desires, our motives, and our natures made possible through the Atonement of Christ the Lord. Our spiritual purpose is to overcome **both sin and the desire to sin**, both the taint and the tyranny of sin." David A. Bednar, "Clean Hands and a Pure Heart," Ensign, Nov 2007, pg 80–83

[157] John Owen, *The Works of John Owen* (16 vols., 1967 reprint; Edinburgh: Banner of Truth, 1853) 6:177, 6:9.

[158] John W. Welch, Chiasmus in the Book of Mormon, *New Era*, Feb 1972, pg 6

[159] "The Romanian historian of religion, Mircea Eliade, talks of the "symbolism of the Centre," and mankind's intense desire to grasp the essential reality of the world, especially the origins of things. The center is where the supernatural beings of myth, or the gods or God of religion, first created humankind and the world. In the symbolic language of myth and religion, the center is imagined as a vertical axis, the cosmic axis, or Axis Mundi, or the Tree of Life. The tree of life image is often used to express the ancient mythological idea of a threefold structure of the cosmos. Roger Cook: "The Tree of Life or Cosmic Tree, penetrates the three zones of heaven, earth, and underworld, its branches penetrating the celestial world, and its roots descending into the abyss."" The "Tree of Life" Design by Christine Brown, Part 1, http://rjohnhowe.wordpress.com/2010/06/06/the-tree-of-life-design-by-christine-brown-part-1/, Oct 20 2011

[160] http://www.bestgardening.com/bgc/howto/propseeds02.htm 10 Sep 2008

[161] "dark." *The American Heritage Dictionary of the English Language, Fourth Edition.* Houghton Mifflin Company, 2004. 23 Sep. 2008. Dictionary.com http://dictionary.reference.com/browse/dark.

[162] Marion G. Romney, "Temples—The Gates to Heaven," *Ensign*, Mar 1971, 12

[163] ibid.

[164] Chiasmus in the Book of Mormon, John W. Welch, BYU Studies, Autumn 1969 (I have modified the center, adding a singular apex, "how beautiful upon the mountains.")

[165] Donald W. Parry, *The Book of Mormon Text Reformatted according to Parallelistic Patterns* (Provo, Utah: FARMS, 1992), p. 1

    A. having had a great knowledge of the goodness and the mysteries of God,
       B. therefore I make a record of my proceedings in my days.
        C. Yea, I make a record in the language of my father,

       D. which consists of the learning of the Jews
     C'. and the language of the Egyptians
    B'. And I know that the record which I make is true; and I make it with my own hand;
 A'. and I make it according to my knowledge.

[166] Hugh Nibley identifies 1 Nephi 1:1-3 as a colophon, which is a structured passage used at the beginning or end of many ancient documents. Hugh Nibley, *Since Cumorah*, pp. 170-171.

[167] Notice how the center of this proposed structure (D – E) contains the symmetrically repeated thought - "course of my days", "all my days", and "proceedings in my days." This poetic repetition is explained by Donald Parry: "The inspired authors had a purpose in employing the repetition of the same word. Such frequent usage tends to join the several expressions of the paragraph into a unified body, the various parts connected by the repeated word." In this case, repetition perhaps emphasizes the center of Nephi's chiastic thought. Donald W. Parry, *The Book of Mormon Text Reformatted According to Parallelistic Patterns*, p. 56

[168] "O Ye Fair Ones": An Additional Note on the Meaning of the Name Nephi, Matthew L. Bowen, Insights Volume 23, Issue-6, Provo, Utah:Maxwell Institute

[169] http://www.webster1828.com/websters1828/definition.aspx?word=Goodly, 1 Oct 2013

[170] Blue Letter Bible. "Dictionary and Word Search for *Lechiy (Strong's 3896)*". Blue Letter Bible. 1996-2011. 18 Nov 2013
[171] The Creator, like a divine poet, composed his "Symphony in Six Days," the *Hexameron*. After each one of his creative acts, he "saw that it was *beautiful*." The Greek text of the biblical story uses the word *kalon*– beautiful–and not *agathon*–good; the Hebrew word carries both meanings at the same time. Paul Evdokimov, The Art of the Icon: a Theology of Beauty, p. 2

[172] John L. Sorenson takes the "learning of the Jews" to mean the cultural contexts, which would include the language itself. John L Sorenson, 1985, An Ancient American Setting for the Book of Mormon, p. 74

[173] "And now, behold, we have written this record according to our knowledge, in the characters which are called among us the reformed Egyptian, being handed down and altered by us, according to our manner of speech. And if our plates had been sufficiently large we should have written in Hebrew; but the Hebrew hath been altered by us also; and if we could have written in Hebrew, behold, ye would have had no imperfection in our record." Mormon 9:32-33

[174] Favor in the KJV comes from the Hebrew word *chen,* meaning grace (see Gen 18:3, Num 11:11). www.blueletterbible.org/lang/lexicon/lexicon.cfm?Strongs=H2580&t=KJV, 22 Nov 2013

[175] Romans 5:5 And hope maketh not ashamed; because the love of God is shed abroad in our hearts **by the Holy Ghost** which is given unto us.

[176] Lehi and Nephi are the first of many in the pages of the Book of Mormon who come to possess a knowledge of God's goodness and mysteries. Another excellent example of how one gains this knowledge is found in Mosiah 19:6, "Now, this was what Ammon desired, for he knew that king Lamoni was under the power of God; he knew that the dark veil of unbelief was being cast away from his mind, and the light which did light up his mind, which was the light of the glory of God, which was a marvelous **light of his goodness**—yea, this light had infused such joy into his soul, the cloud of darkness having been dispelled, and

that the light of everlasting life was lit up in his soul, yea, he knew that this had overcome his natural frame, and he was carried away in God"

[177] The past tense of teach (taught) is highly unusual in 1 Nephi, and is used in only two instances; in 1 Ne 1 and 1 Ne 22.

[178] Thomas S. Monson, "Obedience Brings Blessings," Ensign, May 2013, p. 89

[179] Matthew 111:29, 1 John 3:1-3, Genesis 1:27

Made in the USA
Columbia, SC
28 March 2018